american economic life

yesterday and today

roger leroy miller

UNIVERSITY OF WASHINGTON

canfield press ⌀ san francisco
a department of harper & row, publishers, inc.
new york   evanston   london

ACKNOWLEDGMENTS

A NUMBER OF people helped me throughout this project. I am deeply grateful to the editorial associate on this project, Professor Robert Higgs, who very conveniently has his office next to mine. I was also aided by seven key reviewers who made sure that as objective a view of American economic life as possible was presented. They also pointed out pedagogical areas they felt needed improvement and different interpretations of historical facts. To the following kind but sometimes cutting reviewers I extend my thanks:

Maryanna Boynton, California State University, Fullerton
Claudia Goldin, University of Wisconsin at Madison
Chalmers A. Monteith, Kent State University
Allan E. Neils, Eastern Washington State College
M.K. Ohlson, Metropolitan College, Denver
William R. Purrington, American River College
Baldwin Ranson, Western State College of Colorado

As always, I am sincerely thankful for the unfailing (and unending) typing services of Ms. Georgiana Schuder.

AMERICAN ECONOMIC LIFE: YESTERDAY AND TODAY

International Standard Book Number: 0-06-385456-2

Library of Congress Catalog Card Number: 73-19936

74 75 76   10 9 8 7 6 5 4 3 2 1

Library of Congress Cataloging in Publication Data

Miller, Roger LeRoy.
    American economic life.

    Bibliography: p.
        1.   United States—Economic conditions.
2.   Economics. I. Title.
HC103.M55   330.9'73   73-19936
ISBN 0-06-385456-2

CONTENTS

ECONOMICS is more alive today than ever before. We are all faced with continuing economic crises, problems, and proposals for solutions. We are bombarded with economic statements through all the media—newspapers, TV, radio, magazines, books—from economists, cabinet members and advisors, Congressmen, labor leaders. Now more than ever before students can appreciate the importance of having at least a minimum, fundamental understanding of the economic world in which we live. The question remains, then, how best to teach this basic understanding. I have always advocated an issues approach to interesting students in economics and to presenting them with a method by which they can painlessly (or at least not too painfully) acquire some basic skills.

Numerous instructors desire to impart to students not only some sense of the current economic issues but also a sense of history, of a continuity of economic problems and solutions throughout the history of the world and, more specifically, of the United States. This book is meant to satisfy the need for a historical issues development of basic economic principles. Every chapter is accompanied by an issue, and eleven chapters are accompanied by a biography. The issues take up some particular problem or controversy that was treated in the foregoing chapter and isolate it from that larger context to allow the student a closer, undistracted scrutiny of it. Issues range from "Can Economics Explain Everything?" to such historical questions as "Did the Second World War Pull Us Out of the Depression?" The biographies portray such diverse figures as Benjamin Franklin, Jay Gould, John L. Lewis, and Henry Ford II to personify both the roles that men play in economic life and the roles that economics can play in men's lives.

The book begins with a general introduction to the science of economics and to some of the key tools that will be used over and over again in the book, such as the laws of supply and demand. After a chapter and issue on medieval societies and population problems, the development of American economic life is studied. For the most part, the chapters follow chronologically with, of course, overlapping sections where needed to illustrate the continuity of an economic problem or a solution. In order to demonstrate the problems facing the government in financing its economic activity, wartime periods are given a certain amount of stress. For those who wish to introduce students to alternative economic systems and to problems of underdevelopment, two chapters and accompanying issues are included. Finally, there is a brief discussion of current crises and recommended solutions.

Economic jargon has been kept to a minimum. Economic terms that it was deemed necessary to include occur the first time in bold type, which means that the student will find a further definition at the end of the chapter or issue. Students will also find point by point summaries of the chapters and general questions for thought and discussion for chapters and issues. The questions can be discussed in class or among the students themselves without the aid of an instructor. In addition, at the back of the book will be found selected references for further reading by the student. (Further readings for the instructor are listed throughout the instructor's manual.) Because another helpful pedagogical device is repetition of economic concepts in different contexts, references to the laws of demand and supply and references to such issues as the government's budget constraint recur throughout the text.

This text is not intended to be all-encompassing, either historically or theoretically; its goal is to get students interested in economics so that they can be better informed citizens. The historical issues approach should be useful and effective either as an accompaniment to a regular principles course or, more generally, as a main text for a one-term introduction to economic thinking from a more or less historical point of view. Also, with appropriate additions during class discussions and lectures, and perhaps accompanying historical materials, this text is suitable for a nonrigorous introduction to American economic history—"nonrigorous" because not all of the institutional or historical facts have been included that a more rigorous course would require. Instructors of social science survey courses should find this book especially appealing for the weeks spent on economics.

For instructors who wish supplementary materials and ideas about how to use this book, I have prepared a fairly extensive instructor's manual. There you will find analytic graphic material if you wish to use it. However, the graphic material is not necessary for the effective use of this book, for many instructors have expressed a desire for a book that can be used without the standard graphical tools that economists have become so fond of using. That does not mean that there are no graphics in the text, as a quick glance through it will demonstrate. Many, many figures presenting unemployment rates, prices, and other historical data are included to give the student a sense of continuity in the economic events discussed, and also to give him or her visual relief through a more graphic presentation of ideas.

Student response to this text in manuscript form was extremely encouraging. It is my sincere hope that potential adopters will share in some of this enthusiasm. I look forward to any and all comments and criticisms on the book and I promise to answer all correspondence concerning this text (or any other that I have written, for that matter). My continuing dialogue with professors throughout the United States is, I hope, helping me to present economics in a manner that will keep today's students as interested in the topic as we, the professional economists, would like them to be.

ROGER LeROY MILLER

Seattle, Washington
December, 1973

Economic Life, Yesterday and Today

Where are we today? Well, we're rich, but at the same time millions of Americans are suffering from malnutrition, inadequate housing, insufficient education and training—the list goes on and on and on. We're certainly not experiencing a great depression these days, but at the same time millions of workers can't find jobs, and many who do find them barely earn poverty-level wages. We don't have to live with the specter of prices rising 100 percent a day, as they did in Germany after World War I, but nonetheless we find that every year our dollar buys a little less, for **inflation** seems to have become a more or less permanent feature in our gyrating economy.

The fact is that for a number of years now, many Americans have started to question the basic underpinnings of the economic system within which we live. Economics hasn't yet become a dirty word, but among certain circles, anything that smacks of economics is considered tainted. Stubbornly proclaiming dislike for the crasser material problems in life, however, will not allow us to understand the problems around us, or solutions which might ameliorate the situation in the future.

We cannot easily ignore economic life, for a day does not go by that a newspaper, a news weekly, or a news program does not spend time dealing with a current economic problem, be it inflation, unemployment, consumer safety, monopolistic practices by businessmen, or the myriad economic statements and pontifications emanating from various and sundry government officials.

WHY ECONOMICS?

Even if you don't have a clear understanding of what economics is all about and what the study of it involves, you must admit that economic problems constitute a very large part of everyone's day-to-day existence. You can't escape inflation; you can't escape the possibility of purchasing a faulty product; you can't escape considerations of how best to spend your money. Hence, just from a personal point of view, it would seem that at least an introductory notion of economics and the economic way of thinking would prove useful.

But from a larger point of view, and one which we will go into in more detail in Issue II, if you don't understand some of the basic principles that economists have developed, you will have a difficult time understanding and either agreeing or disagreeing with numerous government policies. In particular, all you have to do is listen to or read the platforms of various political candidates to know without a doubt that they're mainly talking bread and butter issues. Moreover, once you have a basic understanding of some economic principles, you will realize that many of those issues on which campaigns are won or lost are not as complex as you used to think. What you'll find out throughout the rest of this book is that a little economics can go a long way. Of course, you won't be able to understand everything around you or everything that's happened in the past. But it can be hoped you'll be able to separate much of the rhetoric from the real issues.

The question remains, how best to acquire an introductory understanding of the subject.

USING HISTORY

We could take several paths to attain our final aim of a greater understanding of the economic world around us. The most difficult way would be to learn pure theory and to learn it well enough to be able to apply it to real-world situations. Another way is to integrate the theory with an analysis of current economic events. And still another way is to look at history through the eyes of an economist to extract situations in which

economic principles have been clearly demonstrated, at the same time learning those very principles over and over again. In this book, we will take this last course. But even more importantly, a major reason for studying history is to obtain a better understanding of the present. Many people have a tendency to view the past as essentially tranquil. Such people will have a somewhat distorted view of present events. However, even without an extensive understanding of economic history, an examination of what has happened in the past often leads to predictions of what will happen in the future. Take, for example, the history of price controls: Even a cursory examination reveals that almost all past attempts met with failure. After having looked at such a history, how much hope would you want to put on current attempts at controlling prices? Take another problem—regulating businessmen's behavior. A careful examination of the history of big business's reaction to various types of government regulation would certainly be helpful, wouldn't it, in predicting what will happen if the government proposes a new regulation?

An adequate understanding of what happened in the past will also help you better understand the real meaning of some of today's "anti-economic" slogans. Let's just look at one example.

THE GOOD OLD DAYS

For this example of how a careful reading of history might change one's analysis of a current situation, look at the clamor today for reduced economic growth and the desire for a less complicated life style. In other words, many people today contend that America should go back to the "Good Old Days," for then we were happier and less alienated from our environment. During its beginnings, this nation was presumably composed of happy yeoman farmers who all shared equally in the economic pie. Somehow, though, things have changed; today there is, according to some, an extreme maldistribution of income and wealth as compared to those Good Old Days. To be sure, to deny the extreme inequality in income that exists today would be denying the truth. However, we must put our views about the current situation in line with what actually existed in the past. It is only then that we can determine whether we are better or worse off in some subjective sense.

Go back, for example, to the year 1800, or to any year before the Civil War. There was certainly much more inequality in income then, partly because many people in the South were slaves. Their personal income was, in fact, very, very small. Go back to as far as colonial days and you'll find that over half of the working members of the population were either indentured servants or slaves. When you look at the wealth statistics—that is, information on how much of the tangible and intangible property was owned by what percent of the population—you get a striking picture: In 1860, the top 1 percent of families held 24 percent of the total wealth in the United States, the top 5 percent held 53 percent, and the top 10 percent held almost three-fourths of all the wealth in this country. That certainly doesn't sound like there was a bunch of yeoman farmers all getting their little share of the action, does it? Around that time, the sketchy information that we have seems to indicate that the top 5 percent of families were receiving about 10 times more income than the *average* income for the rest of the working members of society.

Income Uncertainty

Something else that wasn't so good in the Good Old Days was the extreme variability in income that was suffered by farmers. Remember that for a good many generations farmers made up a very large segment of our economy. And farmers, after all, were at the mercy of pestilence, droughts, bumper crops in other countries whose farmers competed in the world market, floods, hailstorms, frosts, and every other conceivable natural calamity which would cause their income to be great in one year and small in the next. Today, less than 5 percent of our population is engaged in agricultural pursuits. Compare this with over 90 percent back at the start of this nation. Even if we didn't have any special programs—which we do—to help out farmers, a much smaller proportion of our population is now subject to such variability in income.

Moreover, today income uncertainty is significantly reduced by numerous government programs. We have government relief at federal, state, and local levels. And we have government unemployment insurance. There are numerous salary continuation plans which guarantee steady incomes even when the wage earner is unable to work because of some disaster.

And Life Itself

Not only has income become more certain for the vast majority of Americans, but today life itself has become a more certain prospect. And this increased certainty about life has most likely been an improvement for most members of our society. Back in the so-called Good Old Days at the turn of the century, expected lifetime was perhaps 47 years. But by the beginning of the 1970s, it had risen to about 71 years, as we see in Figure 1–1. Certainly not all Americans participate to the same extent in improved health conditions. But even those who participate least still lead healthier lives than most of our forefathers.

The above sketch of the Good Old Days certainly wasn't intended to obviate a discussion of today's real problems, for indeed America is certainly not nirvana. Even if we are in some ways better off economically, this economic well-being has not been bought cheaply. With it has come a plethora of sociological and psychological problems, all related to our industrialized way of life.

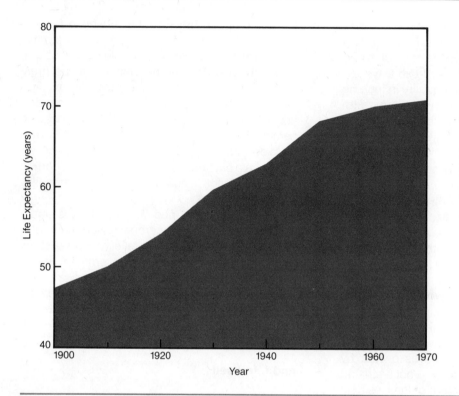

FIGURE 1–1

LIFE EXPECTANCY

At the start of the twentieth century the average American at birth could expect to live a little more than 47 years. By the middle of the century this number had jumped to almost 70. (*Source: Historical Statistics of the United States,* U.S. Bureau of the Census, p. 25, and Department of Commerce.)

ALIENATION

Increasingly it appears that economic growth in an industrialized world has brought with it the problem of alienation. When we used to till the ground, we were deeply attached to the production process itself. Even when we started out in small manufacturing plants, most of the workers had intimate knowledge of what they were doing, what it meant, and where the product was to go. Things have changed. We live in a world of conveyor belts and depersonalized production techniques, where many individual workers feel detached from the process that leads to the final product which their employers sell. This so-called alienation is of course a real problem, but not, unfortunately, one which economists have much to say about—except that it causes workers to become more inefficient.

We do know that when modern man becomes alienated from the production process, this indicates that we cannot equate economic welfare with happiness. We cannot equate economic growth—that is, increases in people's real standards of living—with a happier population. In fact, many will maintain that increased economic growth which leads to the increased alienation of modern man will lead to a decrease in happiness.

Some Solutions

There are ways around this increased alienation. In the last few years, companies such as Volvo and Saab in Sweden and Renault in France have started to introduce more personalized relationships between workers and the production process itself. These companies have started to deemphasize mass production techniques in favor of work teams which together assemble an entire product, such as an automobile. In this way, the workers can again identify with "the product." We can hope that this return to "inefficient" production techniques will at one and the same time increase the proficiency of the workers involved and also reduce the tensions and alienation that certain workers now feel.

THE WORLD AS IT IS AND THE WORLD AS WE WANT IT TO BE

Many who complain about the world as it is often point out how the world should be. Of course, everyone has the right to do this. But one must also be reminded about realism. We cannot usefully compare the real world with some ideal world that can never be attained. We must compare, as it were, the real with the real. We must be comparing the world in which we live with the world in which we could live given the makeup of the population, the resources we have at hand, and the institutional setting in which we live. We must be careful not to compare one model of a system with a model of another system. For example, what good does it do to compare a model of the U.S.S.R. with a model of the United States? Neither model exists in the real world. Alternatively, what good does it do to compare a model system with a real one? We won't get very far by looking at an ideal noncapitalist world and comparing it with the reality of capitalism, or by comparing an ideal capitalist world with the reality of modern-day socialism.

Economists, perhaps more than other social scientists, work under even greater constraints than we have just outlined. We have to look at the world as it is given to us in the statistics we use, the numbers we are able to gather in order to compare things within our economy or to compare our economy with another. Some say this is wrong, that we are on the wrong track, that we are prisoners of the data that are made available to us. That may indeed be true, but what are we to do? Perhaps the following story will give us a clue:

A man lost the keys to his car one night on a very dark street. Later that same night, a policeman spotted him on his hands and knees looking around under the street light on the corner.

"What are you doing?" asked the policeman.
"Looking for my keys."
"Where did you lose them?"
"Over there in the dark," replied the man.
"Then why are you looking here?"
"Because this is where the light is."

Our goal is to make the light bright enough to illuminate the spots now left dark. Before we even valiantly attempt this gargantuan task, we do have to face the problem that economics can't tell us everything.

(Roger LeRoy Miller, Inc.)

Definitions of New Terms

After every chapter and issue, there will be a short glossary of terms just introduced. Those terms will have been put into bold type, such as **inflation** on page 1.

INFLATION: a *sustained* rise in prices.

Chapter Summary

After every chapter, there will be a point-by-point chapter summary for you to use as a testing device to see if you've mastered the key points in the text, and also as a memory refresher. These summaries are not, however, a substitute for the text itself.

Questions for Thought and Discussion

After every chapter and issue will be some questions for thought and discussion. Many of these questions do not have one single correct answer. They are designed to stimulate your interest and thinking about the topics just covered. Even if they are not assigned by your instructor, you may wish to think about them yourself or discuss them among your friends.

ISSUE I

CAN ECONOMICS EXPLAIN EVERYTHING?

The Problem of Science

Economics and Other Sciences

Ask an economist why there is a shortage of, say, energy, and he'll tell you because the government-regulated price is too low. Ask an economist why there is a surplus of some product, and he will tell you because the government set the price too high. Ask an economist just about anything and he will come up with an economic answer. Does this mean that economics can explain everything, that sociology and psychology are useless? No, it does not. Political scientists, historians, sociologists, psychologists, and others who study man's behavior have just as much to say about the world around us as the economist does. Economics cannot explain everything, but for that matter, neither can any other science. There is no way that everything can be explained because

"everything" is a pretty big number, actually tending toward infinity. How can any one science explain an infinite number of phenomena? It can't. So in that sense, economics is no different from any other social science. All scientists must by necessity be content to analyze only a small part of the world around them at any one time.

Some Differences

There are some differences among social sciences. As one observer put it when comparing economics with sociology, "Economics is the study of how people make choices, and sociology is the study of why people don't believe they have any choice."

We'll have to get a little more sophisticated than that to see how much economics can help us in understanding the way history evolved and, perhaps, what will

happen in the future. All sciences rest on some body of assumptions that is the basis of theories or hypotheses. A sociologist will come up with a theory of why a certain event occurred, or why a certain subsector of the population acts in a specific manner. A political scientist will come up with a theory of why a nation acted in the way it did vis-à-vis an enemy. We can hope the political scientist's theory can be used to predict (both forward and backward in time) what will happen in a similar situation in other countries. Now, of course, this is exactly the same thing that a physicist or a biologist does.

Many people have the idea that in some real sense physics is a more exact science than economics or sociology or psychology. While that may be true, it is an oversimplification of the differences between these sciences. Physics is the study of physical phenomena. Physicists hypothesize theories which they test by either running experiments or observing physical phenomena in

(Roger LeRoy Miller, Inc.)

the real world. Economists examine the behavior of individuals and groups of individuals. Just as physicists hypothesize theories, so do economists. Both are empirical sciences. One problem in economics is that well-controlled experiments cannot normally be run. Economists must be content with observing what has happened in the past in order to test theories that have been devised.

These theories always rest on givens, or axioms, or assumptions. Many students balk at the assumptions used in economists' models. In fact, some of you may be in disagreement with the important assumption we will use concerning people's quest for betterment, or as economists like to put it, for **wealth maximization.** We'll be assuming throughout this book that this is indeed what underlies people's economic behavior.

The Role of Assumptions

Now it may be true that the assumption of wealth maximization or self-betterment on the part of individuals is an oversimplification. But of course everything is a simplification in any explanation of what has happened. If it weren't simplified, we wouldn't be able to do anything with it. If a theory or hypothesis is so complex that it can only refer to a very specific situation, it has no universality; it cannot be used to

analyze or predict what will happen in any other situation. We will put the various assumptions, including the one of wealth maximization, to good use in this book in our study of U.S. development. From this assumption stems, for example, the hypothesis that as the profitability increases in a specific area of economic endeavor, resources will flow into that area. And, conversely, if profitability is relatively low in a specific area, resources will flow out into other areas.

If you don't like the assumption that people are out to better themselves economically, that doesn't mean you can't still use it in your economic analysis. For what you would like to be able to do is predict how people will react to changes in their environment. If you can predict and analyze well using a hypothesis based primarily on an assumption of wealth maximization, you would not want to discard the assumption. If, however, that assumption leads your theories to predict things that didn't or don't actually happen, then you must ask yourself what assumption should be put in its place.

The Complexity of the World

Because we happen to have a finite capacity for reasoning and for understanding, and because our brains can only hold a finite amount of data, we are stuck with

making simplifying assumptions when we analyze any situation. Economists have a tendency to leave out political, sociological, and psychological aspects when looking at any particular problem. This doesn't mean those aspects are irrelevant—and indeed there are more and more tendencies for researchers to engage in what are called interdisciplinary approaches to social sciences. However, only occasionally will we in this book step out of the economist's shoes into those of another social scientist. For we are analyzing the economic events that have occurred in the United States and elsewhere. Always feel free, though, to add another dimension to the argument whenever you see fit. But before you do, ask yourself whether it would drastically change the predictive capacity of the economic analysis presented. If it doesn't, then you may wish to use Occam's razor and eliminate it for the moment.

Why Economics?

So economics can't explain everything. But neither can any other science. Why should you, then, bother with any particular one? We can offer one reason why economics might interest you, and that reason is fairly straightforward. In most cultures and during most periods, economic concerns take up an unusual part of everyone's lifetime. Perhaps in the future we will reach that glorious stage in history when we are truly the leisure class in which most of us have only to worry about how to spend all the free time we have. Certainly right now and even more so in the past, such has not been the case. Leisure time presents us with an allocation problem today, but certainly this problem is less important to most people than figuring out how to spend a limited budget, how to pay for a new house or a new car, how to react to rising meat prices, whether or not to join a union, what to do about the local bond issue for improved schools or sewers, whether or not going to college will pay off, what kind of job to take, or whether to change one's job, ad nauseam.

Man may not be an economic animal, but economics certainly haunts him for a good part of his life and his waking hours.

Now that you're convinced, let's get on with our study of history through the eyes of an economist by first examining some basic economic principles.

Definitions of New Terms

WEALTH: the scarce things that people value, such as land, houses, clothes, and cars. It is also possible to include one's inherent income-earning capacities as part of wealth.
WEALTH MAXIMIZATION: a behavioral assumption often used in economic analysis. If we assume that people maximize wealth, we assume that their behavior is meant to make their wealth as large as possible.

Questions for Thought and Discussion

1. We now consider it a "fact" that blood circulates throughout our body. However, at one time this "fact" was merely a theory that some scientist proposed. The theory had to be tested. Can you think of any other physical or biological facts that were at one time just theories presented by scientists of the day?
2. Are there any sciences which do not use assumptions?
3. If economics cannot explain everything, what can?

Viewing History by Way of Economics

2

As we survey the growth of the United States we are going to do it in a fairly specific manner. There will be quite a bit of emphasis on the economic aspects of the development of this country. That doesn't mean that political, scientific, sociological, psychological, and all the other ways of viewing the world around us and the world in the past aren't valid. In fact, we're not about to say that economics can explain everything, as you saw in the Issue at the end of Chapter 1.

WHAT *IS* ECONOMICS ALL ABOUT?

A commonsense notion about economics generally centers on money. That is, when asked what an economic view of the world is all about, most people will answer that it is one in which man's desire for money is held above all other demands. We're going to be a little more sophisticated than that and a little less emotional, because an economic view of the development of economic life has a lot more to offer than this stereotype of economic analysis would lead you to believe.

Basically, economics is about exchange: why people exchange things, in what situations they'll refuse to exchange things, which conditions in the world are more conducive to more exchanges, and the end results of all those exchanges. We know that people have been exchanging things since the beginning of time. While it is true that animals generally do not engage in such endeavors, since the beginning of recorded history we have evidence that exchanges took place between men. Moreover, archeologists tell us that during the Ice Age, hunters of mammoths in the great Russian steppes somehow got around to trading for Mediterranean shells.

You and I make exchanges all the time. We usually do it by way of an intermediary good called money. But we could—not as easily, of course—trade *things* for *things* instead of using money to facilitate this trade. You exchanged the purchasing power implicit in the price of this book for the book itself. If you hadn't used money and we were, in fact, involved in a system of **barter,** you might have had to exchange a couple of records or another book in order to get this one. But the fact remains that you are always engaged in these sorts of exchanges, whether or not you use money.

Choice

Economics is also about choice. Once there is the possibility of more than one exchange, people have to make a choice: Which exchange should obtain? When you have the possibility of exchanging your scholarship for records, food, housing, entertainment, books, or literally thousands of other things, you must make a choice among all these potential exchanges. That choice involves deciding which exchanges will make you best off. Economics tell us which alternative choices we can expect people to make in certain changing situations. We'll see below, for example, that generally if a product—say, records—suddenly becomes relatively cheaper than it used to be, we anticipate that people will start buying more records and fewer of other things. In other words, they will choose to make an exchange which involves the purchase of more records than before.

Voluntary vs. Involuntary Exchanges

In general, we'll be talking about voluntary exchanges among individuals and nations. By necessity, then, every voluntary exchange has to make both parties in the exchange better off: Exchange is mutually beneficial. Of course, we'll also have to talk about some pretty unpleasant

involuntary exchanges that have been made. These have occurred and continue to occur in situations in which coercive power is used to alter another person's or nation's behavior. When black persons were captured and shuttled aboard intolerably crowded slave ships going to the New World, they were forced by coercive power to submit to a new economic arrangement whereby they provided labor power to their owners and in turn were given the necessities of life (barely that much in many cases). When someone gets robbed, he is engaged in an involuntary exchange. While it's true that the robber might present you with a choice that you could voluntarily make—"your money or your life"—we generally don't consider that a choice situation, where one freely makes up his mind about what to exchange and what not to exchange.

The reason people from the beginning of history have wanted to exchange things with other people is to make themselves better off. And the reason they have wanted to make themselves better off is because they haven't had all of the goods and services they would like to have had in their lives. And why is that? Because we now, always have, and always will live in a world of scarcity.

SCARCITY

If we didn't live in a world of scarcity, you wouldn't have to read or even think about the economic aspects of anything because there wouldn't be any. Scarcity presents us with a problem: How do we allocate the available resources to all the competing demanders of those resources? For indeed there are many people in competition for scarce goods and services. And even if they decided really not to compete, they would still face the problem of how the available resources were to be allocated among members of society. So you see, it doesn't really matter what the situation is. Everybody can love everybody else and want to help everybody else, but the decision still has to be made: Who gets what and how much? Note that we are not saying that, for example, "frivolous" consumption doesn't exist today. It may indeed be true that today in the United States, the richest of all nations, we have far surpassed a level of subsistence living or even comfortable living and are now engaged in "superfluous" consumption activities. But even if that were true, the decision would still have to be made as to what to do with the resources used for "superfluous" activities if we were to use them for "non-superfluous" activities: Who would get what and how much?

Free Goods

There are some things around which are indeed free. We call them **free goods.** Not many are left. In old textbooks about economics air used to be called a free good, but now that's not really true in many cities where pollution makes air unfit to breathe. But it is still true that in many mountain areas in this country clean air is a free good. You can have all of it you want and so can anybody else who bothers to hike up to where you are. You and anybody else there don't have to worry about how this good, air, should be or has to be allocated among competing demanders. There is no scarcity involved. This is true also for running water in many areas in the United States. Who is interested in free goods, then? Certainly not economists. Perhaps in the case of air and water, physicists, hydrologists, biologists, and chemists might be. It is only when air or water becomes scarce, such as they are in cities, that the economist can step in and have something to say. Because here the problem of scarcity arises and here the problems of exchange come into play. We have seen throughout our history that as population and production increase over time, many goods pass from the realm of "free" to "economic," such as land for mining and water and air for industrial uses.

The Unhappy Truth

Since at any given moment, the total amount of resources available is fixed (but may grow over time), at that moment a choice has to be made. And, unfortunately for man, that choice always involves a cost. If you decide to do one thing, you cannot do something else. There is an old saying that is trite but true: You can't have your cake and eat it too. An economist would translate that into: To have something, you have to give up something—there is no such thing as a free lunch.

Take the example of the use of your time. For you, it is a valuable and scarce resource. You only have 24 hours per day, and only so many days per year, and only so many years per lifetime. Ignoring the possibility of life after death, we see that once you decide to do something, you can't do something else. While you are reading this book, you can't be reading *Time* magazine. While you are reading *Time* magazine, you can't be reading this book. During a one-hour exam, the time spent on one question could have been used on any other. When you generalize this situation, you realize that everybody has to make a decision about how to spend his time, and every decision will involve a cost, the cost being what that person had to give up in order to do what he actually is doing.

This same analysis holds in the realm of more concrete things. If a farmer in 1800 decided to plant all his farmland in, say, corn, he would be making a decision which involved a cost. The cost of that decision would be what he could get out of his land if he decided to plant an alternative crop, say wheat. The farmer has to choose among alternatives. He has to decide what the best use of his scarce resources is. And one of the ways he can decide is by looking at the cost of various decisions, the alternatives that are available, and the returns to those alternatives, for not all the alternatives can, in fact, be used. This leads us to an underlying assumption that we are going to make throughout this text. That assumption has to do with how people run their lives, how they react to various exchange situations, and how they react when things in their society are altered by laws, natural disasters, or the like.

MAKING ONESELF BETTER OFF

In our analysis of American economic life, we are going to assume that many people in the society generally attempt to make themselves better off. We know that making oneself better off can take many forms and can be ruled by many different aspects of one's life. For the purpose of economic analysis, though, we have to simplify things a bit. We're going to assume that people attempt to make themselves better off in their real standard of living, in their real command over leisure and goods and services which they would like to have. This means that we are going to assume for the purpose of our analysis that people in general will be attempting to run their lives so that they have the highest standard of living possible within the framework of their own society.

Now notice that we may be skirting a few important issues. Some people will feel better off if they know they are doing good for other people, even though they are not being paid for it. This is just one of myriad examples where people's emotions enter into their decision making about how they should act out their lives. But in the aggregate—that is, in the whole economy—we can effectively ignore such problems in our analysis if we want to make broad generalizations about the direction in which the economy has taken itself due to changes in the economic environment. Of course, if you were to analyze the economic behavior of a specific individual, you probably could not ignore the subjective and emotional aspects of his thinking.

When we take account of the unfortunate fact that scarcity exists and assume that people generally attempt to make themselves better off, we can

come up with some principles in economics that will help us better understand why our economy has developed as it has.

WHAT TO DO WITH ONE'S TALENTS

Since most people cannot have everything they want, they generally have to decide what to do with their productive talents. And in general, if people want to make themselves as well off as possible, they will apply their talents to productive endeavors which yield them the highest rewards. Now, it is true that part of this reward can be psychic. But as we mentioned above, we'll forget for the moment the psychic rewards that people get from doing different jobs and look only at their economic rewards. Today we can talk about how much money they make at doing different tasks. In the past, before people used money, we would talk about how much real output they could produce for their own consumption or for use in barter with other people.

It is pretty easy for a person to figure out what he does comparatively better than other people. All he has to do is look at his alternatives. A person decides what he can best do by finding out which productive endeavors give him the highest rate of return for his time spent working, i.e., the highest income or the highest command over goods and services which he would like to consume. He then specializes in this endeavor. This basic economic principle of **specialization** applies not only among individuals, but among nations as well. When people find out that they have advantages in doing specific, specialized tasks rather than other tasks they could choose, and in fact follow through on these realizations by actually doing them and then exchanging the fruits of their labor, we say that specialization has occurred. As we shall see throughout this text, the history of economic development in the United States (and in the world) is in fact a history of specialization. While it seems like an obvious way to act, man did not learn to specialize as he does today until very recent times. In fact, Adam Smith seemed to find it quite novel to observe what happened to the making of pins when specialization in the productive process occurred:

To take an example, therefore, from a very trifling manufacture; but one in which the division of labour has been very often taken notice of, the trade of the pin-maker; a workman not educated to this business (which the division of labour has rendered a distinct trade), nor acquainted with the use of the machinery employed in it (to the invention of which the same division of labour has probably given occasion), could scarce, perhaps, with his utmost industry, make one pin in a day, and certainly could not make twenty. But in the way in which this business is now carried on, not only the whole work is a peculiar trade, but it is divided into a number of branches, of which the greater part are likewise peculiar trades. One man draws out the wire, another straights it, a third cuts it, a fourth points it, a fifth grinds it at the top for receiving the head; to make the head requires two or three distinct operations; to put it on, is a peculiar business, to whiten the pins is another; it is even a trade by itself to put them into the paper; and the important business of making a pin is, in this manner, divided into about eighteen distinct operations, which, in some manufactories, are all performed by distinct hands, though in others the same man will sometimes perform two or three of them. I have seen a small manufactory of this kind where ten men only were employed, and where some of them consequently performed two or three distinct operations. But though they were very poor, and therefore but indifferently accommodated with the necessary machinery, they could, when they exerted themselves, make among them about twelve pounds of pins in a day. There are in a pound upwards of four thousand pins of a middling size. Those ten persons, therefore, could make among them upwards of forty-eight thousand pins in a day. Each person, therefore, making a tenth part of forty-eight thousand pins, might be considered as making four thousand eight hundred pins in a day. But if they had all wrought separately and independently, and without any of them having been educated to this peculiar business, they certainly could not each of them have made twenty, perhaps not one pin in a day; that is, certainly, not the two hundred and fortieth, perhaps not the four thousand eight hundredth part of what they are at present capable of performing, in consequence of a proper division and combination of their different operations.*

COMPARATIVE ADVANTAGE

Specialization through the division of labor, as outlined in Smith's famous example of pin-making above, rests on a very important fact—different people, different communities, and different nations are indeed different, at least when it comes to the ability of each to produce different goods and services. Take the simplest example, a two-person society. If each person were exactly the same in every respect and, hence, each person could do every job just as well as the other one, there would be no reason for specialization. The same is true for nations. If every nation had exactly the same resources and exactly the same talents, then the cost of producing any good or service would be the same everywhere. There would be no need or incentive to specialize. However, costs do differ. It is relatively less costly, say, for Japan to specialize in the production of, say, electronic equipment than it is for the United States under current circumstances. We say that Japan's current **comparative advantage** lies in the production of electronic equipment. The principle of specialization outlined above rests on the existence, the actual fact of comparative advantage. We know that it exists because we know that different people in different countries experience different relative costs of producing different goods and services.

The Wealth of Nations (1776), New York: The Modern Library, pp. 4–5.

Even if somebody could do everything better than everyone else, he would still want to specialize in his comparative advantage. A good example involves President William Howard Taft. Before he became president, he was probably the country's fastest stenographer. He could have been at the same time the country's best typist, best violin player, and everything else, but he decided to become president when elected, because that's where his comparative advantage lay. Had he declined the presidency in order to remain a stenographer, the implicit cost of that action would have been tremendous. To continue the example, consider the dilemma of the president of a large company. He can type better than any of his typists, he can file better than any of his file clerks, he can drive a truck better than any of his truck drivers, and he can wash windows better than any of his window washers. His advantage is *absolute* in all of these endeavors. However, his comparative advantage lies in managing the company, not in doing the aforementioned tasks. And since that's where his comparative advantage lies, it behooves him to specialize in that particular activity. How does he know that that is where his comparative advantage is? The answer is quite easy: He is paid the most for being president, not for being a typist or file clerk or window washer or truck driver for the company. Basically, then, one's comparative advantage can be found by finding out where one is most valuable to others. That is also where the greatest economic advantage to oneself lies.

DECISIONS ON HOW MUCH AND WHAT TO PRODUCE

Following along the logical implications of scarcity coupled with the assumption that people attempt to make themselves better off, we can predict which goods and services will be supplied, and when and where. If people want something very

badly, they will be willing to sacrifice more for it. In our money economy, we say that they will be willing to pay more for it. But if they are willing to pay more for it, then people who can or could provide it have a bigger incentive to do so. *Suppliers will supply more the higher the price that is offered to them.* And whenever some suppliers or producers are making lots of profit at doing something, others are going to have an incentive to enter that particular business to reap those high profits also.

On this basis, we can predict where resources will flow in an economy. In general, they will flow to areas where profits are highest, for these are areas not only where goods and services are made that people value the most highly, but also where individual businessmen and workers can make the most income. If we look at the development of any exchange economy, we will find that it is a history of resources flowing into areas that yield the highest rates of return, where there is constant specialization as individuals attempt to make the most income to have the best life possible.

HOW MUCH TO DEMAND

On the consuming side of the picture, again if we follow the logical implications of scarcity and people's attempts to make themselves better off, we can predict how people will react in different situations when faced with different alternatives of what they can do with their income. To start with, we know that everybody faces a fixed budget, even Rockefeller or Howard Hughes. This was true for the Neanderthal man, the Cro-Magnon man, the serf on a manor, the journeyman craftsman in a medieval city, the Renaissance painter, the New World explorer, the Great Plains farmer, and is true for everybody today. It is a universal problem. With a given fixed budget at any given moment, a person must determine how to allocate this budget over the different things that he wants to have, that he wants to be able to consume. In general, people are constantly comparing what they must give up in order to get a particular good or service. And what they must give up in our money society is purchasing power or command over other goods and services, which is represented by the price that has to be paid for anything that is bought. In a barter economy, what has to be given up is more obvious because things are directly exchanged for things: To get one pig it may cost two lambs, so it is two lambs that have to be given up.

When the price of something goes up, if a person chooses to continue buying the same number as he has in the past, he will find he has less remaining income, less ability to purchase all the other things he wants to have. In fact, if the price goes high enough, he won't be able to purchase anything else. Consider your purchase of records. Let's say you buy three albums a month, and they cost $4 apiece. If the price were to keep rising, at some point, if you continued to buy three albums, you wouldn't have any money for food or clothes or any other type of entertainment. So obviously, because of your budget constraint, you wouldn't be able to continue a rate of purchase of three albums per month. When we apply this thinking to the aggregate situation, we find that *as the price rises, the quantity demanded of goods and services will fall.* And correspondingly, *as the price falls, the quantity demanded will rise.* This is the so-called **law of demand.** And, since this is a universal law which seems to hold true at all times and in all societies, we will use it throughout the analysis which follows. It can be summed up in the following sentence:

Individuals respond to changing relative prices.

All that means is that when one thing becomes relatively more expensive than others, people will demand less of it. And when it becomes relatively less expensive than others, people will demand more of it. Notice here the stress on relativity. It is important to distinguish between *relative* prices of things and *absolute* prices. This is particularly true during periods of inflation, such as those that we have experienced in the last decade in the United States. If the price of all things goes up by 100 percent, do you think there would be much change in the relative cost of goods and services? The answer is no. After all, the relative true cost of every item in each person's budget will remain the same. One can make quite a few analytical errors by looking only at absolute prices in periods of rapidly changing prices. It is inaccurate, for example, for a newspaper to present the price of meat ten years ago and compare it with the price of meat today with the conclusion "See, meat costs 100 percent more today than it did ten years ago." What we want to know is, How much does meat cost today *relative* to other goods and services? Did the price of meat go up faster than the price of all other goods, the same, or slower? That's what's important to know if we are indeed worried about the price of that particular product.

CHANGING THE LAW AROUND

We can alter our simplified statement of the law of demand to apply to the supply side of the story. Basically, our **law of supply** will be:

People respond to changing relative rates of return; or as the price goes up, so too does the quantity supplied.

We therefore expect, if this law holds, to find more entrepreneurs, more businessmen, more workers, more capital, and all other resources flowing into areas where the relative rate of return is higher than in other areas of economic activity.

It is the lure of expected higher relative profits that induces businessmen to take their capital and move to a different industry. We will see, for example, that if we consider rates of return to labor also, individuals will move to areas where their expected relative rates of return are highest. The search for higher wages was one of the reasons (but, of course, not the only one) that so many immigrants came to our shores between the start of the colonies and the restriction on immigration during World War I.

WHERE IT ALL TAKES PLACE

So far we've talked about exchange, specialization, comparative advantage, demand, and a few other things. Where does all this economic activity take place, you might be asking. Generally we say that economic activity takes place in a **market.** Now, you are used to the concept of a market as being a place where you go to buy food, or, if you're familiar with the open-air markets in other countries and in certain areas in the United States,

Markets take many forms, all the way from desert trading . . .
(Marc Ribaud, Magnum Photos)

you equate the term market with a geographical point at which buyers and sellers get together. That's exactly what a market is all about. *It's an institutional device for bringing together the buyers and sellers of goods and services.* In olden times, almost all of these exchanges, or market transactions, took place face to face. Today, however, we don't even have to go to the place; for many things we can do it through the mail if we so choose. But the point is that economic exchanges take place in markets. These markets may be small or large, developed or undeveloped. We will see, for example, that very few developed markets existed during the Dark or Middle Ages. Cities were just starting to arise in many places. Wandering merchants had just started to expand the size of markets through their trading travels. We characterize such times as more or less pre-market system episodes in the history of Western man. Most of this book is concerned with market situations, with market societies, where exchanges take place on a broad front under conditions that

. . . to sophisticated stock exchanges.

(Leonard Freed, Magnum Photos)

have become increasingly more favorable to those exchanges.

Just by application of the few laws we learned above, we can predict that as the cost or price of actually making an exchange falls, the quantity of exchanges demanded will rise. These costs of exchanges are sometimes labeled **transactions costs** by economists. But whatever we want to call them, the fact still remains that the easier we make it for people to trade, the more trading they will do, the more specialization we will have, the more people will be able to engage in the activity that is most advantageous to them, and ultimately the better off everyone (or almost everyone) will be.

THERE IS OBVIOUSLY MORE TO ECONOMICS

In the last few pages, you haven't received a complete course in the basics of economics, to be sure. But you do have enough instruments stuck in your belt to be able to guide you in a trek through economic history. It's these kinds of simplified economic principles that allow us to unravel some of the great debates about the development of the United States. Many of these are presented in the historical issues which follow the chapters in this book. As I hope you will see, a little economics can go a long, long way (and it isn't dangerous).

Definitions of New Terms

BARTER: a system in which goods and services are exchanged for other goods and services without using the intermediary good called money.

FREE GOODS: goods that are so superabundant that everybody can have as much as he or she wants without preventing anybody else from doing the same.

COMPARATIVE ADVANTAGE: individuals find their comparative advantage by seeking out the highest yielding activity that they can engage in, relative to all other activities, during any given period of time.

SPECIALIZATION: the process of limiting one's activity to more and more narrowly defined processes.

LAW OF DEMAND: the quantity demanded of a good or service goes up when its price goes down, and vice versa.

LAW OF SUPPLY: as the price, and hence rate of return or profit, goes up for a good or service, producers will want to supply more.

MARKET: the geographical area in which economic exchanges take place and in which goods and services which are similar tend to have similar prices.

TRANSACTIONS COSTS: all of the costs associated with exchange, such as the cost of finding out the quality and price of goods, and so on.

Chapter Summary

1. Economics is the study of exchange and choice among exchanges. Exchanges can be made with or without the use of a medium of exchange called money. When things are exchanged for things, we call it barter.

2. Voluntary exchange benefits both parties involved.
3. At any given moment, the amount of resources available for our use is necessarily fixed; this is the age-old problem of scarcity. When a good is not scarce, it is then called a free good. Clean air used to be a free good but is now scarce in many polluted cities.
4. People generally specialize in the endeavor which yields them the highest income (part of which may be nonmonetary or psychic). Specialization is also called the division of labor.
5. Specialization depends on the ability of people to do different things at varying costs. Since the cost of doing things for different people differs, each will have a comparative advantage in at least one activity. This is also true for nations.
6. The law of demand can be simply stated as: The lower the price, the more of any product or service is demanded, and vice versa. Alternatively, it can be stated as: Individuals respond to changing relative prices.
7. The law of supply is similar: Suppliers will supply more the higher the price that is offered to them.
8. Economic activity takes place in a market, which is an institutional device for bringing together the buyers and sellers of goods and services.

Questions for Thought and Discussion

1. Can you think of instances where the law of demand fails? (Be careful, make sure you are talking about two different situations in which the product or service in question has the same quality and everything else is the same except that the price has changed.)
2. Can you think of a personal example where the law of supply holds? In other words, have you ever experienced a situation in which you were willing to take a job or to work longer because somebody offered you a higher wage rate?
3. There occasionally appear books claiming to show that scarcity no longer exists in the United States. Do you agree? Why?
4. Can you think of any truly free goods that exist?
5. It is often said that price doesn't matter; in other words, consumers don't react to higher prices. If you are spending all the income you have and the price of just one good or service you purchase goes up, will you still be able to buy the same amount of that good or service and also the same amount of everything else?

ISSUE II

IS ECONOMICS THE MIRROR IMAGE OF POLITICS?

The Nature of Political Action

Marx Speaks Out

The last chapter gave you a brief rundown of some of the major principles in economics that we will use throughout the book. Now that you have been exposed to them, perhaps it's worth a little thought to see if they make economics a science with some degree of universality. Hence, the title of this issue, which has been attributed to Karl Marx. We'll spend time later on looking at Marx's life and economic theories. Suffice it to say here that Marx was deeply involved in both political philosophy and economic questions. At a point in his life when he had in fact dealt extensively with both sciences, he came to regard economics as indeed the mirror image of politics.

The Politics of Scarcity

If we were to take a political journey starting from today going backwards until as far in the past as we cared to venture, we would find some striking resemblances in the political problems facing each generation of politicians in every society and every country.

For once we leave the area of decision making about moral behavior, we find that a not insignificant part of political action has involved giving one part of society something and, hence, by necessity taking away something else from another part. We say "by necessity" because of that age-old problem discussed in the previous chapter, scarcity. At any moment in any society, the amount of resources available is fixed. Whether it be today or 100 years ago or even 1000 years ago, if a politician decides that, say, more education will be provided "free" to children, someone ends up paying for that "free" education. Politicians, then, whether they be in democratic or totalitarian societies, end up deeply involved in economic problems, whether they like it or not and whether they admit it or not.

Politics Past and Present

If this were a book on the political history of the United States, the emphasis would certainly be different, many of the historical facts examined would be different, but nonetheless a basic similarity would still hold. In fact, if you want to have a little fun, take a glance at an abridged political history of the United States. You will find a tremendous number of topics discussed that are similar to those discussed in this text. And although there would certainly be more discussion of, for example, presidential candidates, the results of political elections, and so on, nonetheless, even this discussion of presidential candidates would involve an examination of their platforms. And without a doubt that examination would reveal numerous economic exclamations. Even though 100 years ago we were a lot poorer than we are today, it appears that as a nation we were nonetheless just as materialistic in the sense that citizens were concerned with what politicians would do if elected to improve the citizen's lot in life.

Today we are all well aware of the fundamental political problem of how the fruits of economic production should be distributed to various members of society. When a politician argues for increased medical care for the aged, he is in fact asking that more be given to the aged and less to others. If a politician demands that we spend three billion dollars more on pollution control, he is stating that $3 billion should not be spent on any other endeavor. The list will go on and on until all of the politicians' demands are exhausted. Fortunately—or unfortunately, depending on how you look at it—not all political desires can be translated into reality. Why? Because of our old enemy, scarcity. At any given time, the total amount of income in the United States that is available to purchase goods and services is fixed. Necessarily, the amount of income that the government has to spend is even smaller. Hence, any political problem about what should or should not be done generally involves the creation, expansion, contraction, or removal of a government program. Such action can be directly translated into either an elimination or an increase in the amount of funds available for other government actions to benefit other groups of people.

An Oversimplification, to Be Sure

Again, the reader is to be warned that we are indeed oversimplifying the political process. However, even a cursory glance at all the various government actions that politicians engage in every day in this country and elsewhere will reveal the economic nature of politics. Just as strikingly, though, an examination of economic phenomena oftentimes will result in the unearthing of political underpinnings. For example, the economic phenomenon of large grain surpluses during the 1950s can be explained by the government's supporting grain prices at too high a level. On the other hand, why the government would support the price at that level even though surpluses resulted necessarily involves the political question of why the farm bloc has had so much power in Congress.

Such intertwining of economics and politics leads us to conclude that, yes, economics is the mirror image of politics, but just as much, politics is the mirror image of economics. Now you know why the "dismal science" used to be called political economy.

Questions for Thought and Discussion

1. What other important features are there of political action?
2. Do you think Marx was right?
3. To be a good politician, is it best to study political science or economics? If neither of these two, what subject would be most appropriate?

Economic Systems before the Opening of the New World

WE MENTIONED in the last chapter that economics concerns itself with exchange and choice. Examples of early exchanges date as far back as the Ice Age. Archeologists contend that even as early as the Bronze Age, the universal phenomenon of the traveling salesman can be found. However, although some of the basic precepts of an exchange economy were evident from the beginning of social interaction among men, some important distinctions must be made. For we now live in a (modified) market economy. We use the market to solve many of our basic economic problems: Who gets what, where, when, and how much? But if we could go back (given more time and space) to study, for example, the economic organization of antiquity in Rome, Greece, and Egypt, we would find systems of massive slavery, long periods of technological stagnation, and the use of custom to guide the vast majority of economic activities that the ancients engaged in. Instead, however, let's start with the fall of the western part of the Roman Empire in A.D. 476. We will briefly trace the development of economic society to the opening of the New World.

AFTER THE FALL OF ROME

When Rome fell, the Huns and the German tribes started to invade everything in sight. For the next thousand years, the mislabeled Dark Ages were cast upon European society. Throughout this period, Europe depended on a **premarket economy,** otherwise known as a **traditional system.** The period, also called the Middle Ages or the Medieval Period, was one of extensive political fragmentation; this had important consequences for the economic organization of society. For, as we shall see, it takes a certain amount of consistent legal, political, and, more broadly speaking, **institutional arrangements** to be conducive to what we know today as a market-oriented economic system.

The Dark Ages Weren't Really Dark

While certain historians have classified the Middle Ages as a period when there was essentially no change in the structure of society, we shall see that this was not indeed the case. During this time there were periods of expansion and contraction, things were happening which were prerequisites to modern European and American societies of today. In fact, when we consider how long it took the Greeks and the Romans to develop their civilizations, the Middle Ages don't look so dark or so lacking in progress.

Just look at the technical innovations that occurred in Europe during this period. By A.D. 1100 the Moors had developed a paper-making industry. A mere hundred years later the Italians had sophisticated silk-throwing machines. By 1250 Milanese craftsmen had started making plate armor. During the same year in France and the Low Countries the great age of stained glass had started, the results of which can be seen in churches and cathedrals throughout Europe. By the thirteenth century broad-beamed fishing and transport boats had been built for northern trade. By the middle of the fourteenth century the cast-iron cannon had developed in Germany, as had the cast-iron furnace. And, of course, in the year 1440 Gutenberg began using movable type in his printing press. And during the same period, in the agricultural sector things were not stagnating either. Selective breeding of animals was spreading throughout Europe.

The Renaissance

The Dark Ages were certainly not utterly dark, and by the fourteenth and fifteenth centuries the Renaissance had started. This was a period when kings, queens, and nobles increased support of the arts. The University of Paris had already been founded in the twelfth century, and Kings College—the beginning of Cambridge University—was started in the early 1400s.

Now, it is true that change was relatively slow. In terms of the economic well-being of the population, there was probably on average no real change during much of this period, which is why it is sometimes called an age of stagnation. One of the best-known and most conspicuous institutions of this period, and basic to the organization of society, was the manor, a topic to which we now turn.

(Musée Condé, Photographie Giraudon)

LIFE ON THE MANOR

After the fall of Rome, continuous invasions brought the European countryside into chaos. Out of this chaos emerged a system of a large number of visually self-sufficient microcosmic societies, each formed around a manor. At the same time, there was not a complete collapse of all social institutions. In particular, there was a continuity of religious beliefs. They ended up providing the fundamental warrant for the feudal system, with its divinely instituted hierarchy of statuses and functions.

This was the era of feudalism. The manor, or farm estate, was ruled by a lord. In the feudal system, the lord was essentially responsible for whatever happened on his estate: He straightened out marital quarrels or arguments between anybody living within the estate's boundary, and he provided police protection. He was, indeed, the lord and master over all of his serfs.

Why Become a Serf?

The institution of serfdom arose out of the colonies of Rome. It developed fairly gradually, but became a ubiquitous feature of the feudal medieval society. Serfs were the lowest on the totem pole, which looked like the following:

Dei
The Pope
The Big Lords
The Little Lords
The Serfs or Villeins

Put yourself in the place of a European peasant in the tenth century A.D. Roaming the countryside were hoards of Huns and Germanic tribes, periodically raiding villages and anything else they could get their hands on. Your life wasn't worth much those days because it could not be easily protected if you were alone in the world, or even with a few of your friends. It was an era when might made right. As you're walking along in your travels, you've avoided all encounters with marauding Huns, and you come across a large estate where you seek refuge. The owner of the estate, the lord, offers you a deal. In exchange for a certain part of your labor services—that is, a certain part of your working week—he will provide you with protection and justice. This exchange is how serfs originally became serfs. And of course, once the system was well established, it was pretty hard for the son of a serf to be anything else but a serf. This arrangement lasted for a number of centuries until some external forces caused it to decline. But more on that later.

Types of Exchange

What's important to note in this discussion is that originally the arrangement between serf and master was, implicitly at least, a *voluntary* exchange. The serf exchanged labor services and perhaps a few "goods," like so many pieces of firewood per year, for the protection of the manorial master. Eventually, of course, the system grew to resemble more a slave/master relationship. Serfs could not marry—could hardly do anything—without the expressed consent of the manorial lord. And, in fact, it was usually the lord who decided on the type of crops that should be tilled and the type of labor that serfs were to engage in.

THE MANOR'S ECONOMIC ACTIVITY

You have to remember that well over 90 percent of the working population during medieval times was engaged in agriculture. The manor was the basic unit of organization for providing the agricultural products necessary for survival. In fact, during much of this time, agricultural productivity was close to the subsistence level, that is, barely providing enough for the subsistence needs of the population. There was little surplus in many of the centuries during the Middle Ages.

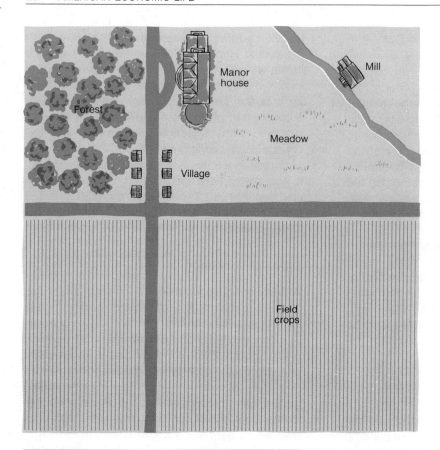

A TYPICAL MANOR ECONOMY

The manor economy was self-sufficient, the manor house being the most prominent aspect of the landscape. The field crops were generally tilled in extremely narrow strips with not much fertilizer being used. There would be a small village where the serfs lived, a river with a mill on it, and a forest and meadow.

The key to understanding the manorial life was that it was one of near *self-sufficiency*. The manorial estate looked like a small village in the midst of either a forest or some cleared land. If you look at Figure 3-1, you will see a schematic representation of what historians believe manors looked like. Notice that the field crops were all in strips. This was how agriculture was carried out in those times. It was a very primitive method, one that did not lend itself to increasingly efficient use of the land. Fertilizer was seldom used, and it wasn't until the development of the soft horse collar that horses could be effectively employed in plowing fields.

Positive Aspects of the Manor

Although, as we said, the manorial organization of agriculture prevented any attempt at increasing yields on crop lands, it did provide the basis of cooperation. We find the use of the gang plow, for example, and the rotation of crops and crop land on certain manors. In other words, the manor allowed for the sharing of equipment and labor. Moreover, this type of agricultural organization did provide a floor against famine. In fact, that is another reason why free men would choose to become serfs. For in addition to police protection, manorial lords provided food during periods of agricultural shortages.

Isolation of the Manor

We find ourselves, then, during this period of the early Middle Ages, with a feudal society characterized by manors that were more or less isolated and spread across a sparsely populated area of western Europe. Although nominally ruled by lords and Church people higher up on the hierarchy of feudal society, manors were really self-sufficient. They maintained extremely loose ties with any central political authority. It would be wrong, however, to say that in this period the manorial system was universal. For at the same time that feudalism was going strong in the west, there were some flourishing cities in the south, such as Venice, Pisa, and Florence, which, as we shall soon discuss, were chiefly commercial cities, and in the west and the north cities were developing which were much more self-sufficient.

THE RISE OF MEDIEVAL CITIES

Villages in England were almost totally self-sufficient except for a few items, such as salt, iron for plows, and millstones. They developed as walled fortifications for the lords of manors to inhabit, initially inhabited also by his attendants and by a fighting garrison. In times of danger, the population under the lord would also come behind the walls of the city. Eventually those living in these fortifications wanted to have certain manufactured products, so business as we know it started to become noticeable. Merchants, craftsmen, and artisans moved to these towns in response to increased demand for their products. Notice here that a rise in the relative rate of return induced movement of labor, or human resources, to these areas. So even in the medieval society, which was based largely on custom and which was thought of as a nonmarket-oriented organization, the simple economic rules and principles outlined in the last chapter still held.

As more and more people came to the city in search of economic gain and security, these cities became more and more crowded. We have evidence that as early as the tenth century, Cologne and Verdun extended their city walls. In the eleventh, so did Geneva, Rouen, Antwerp, and others. Then in the twelfth and thirteenth centuries, there was a veritable deluge of city wall

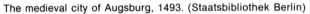

The medieval city of Augsburg, 1493. (Staatsbibliothek Berlin)

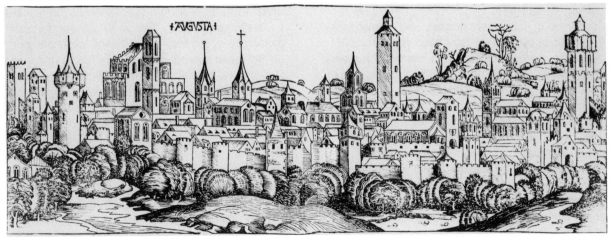

extensions; city populations were expanding by leaps and bounds. Cologne more than doubled from the eleventh to the thirteenth century, as did Strasbourg. (These population trends were later to be reversed, of course, when the Black Death hit.)

We find that during this time, as merchants, craftsmen, and artisans gathered inside city walls, the forerunners of modern-day business and labor organizations developed. One of the most prevalent was the medieval guild.

Combinations in Restraint of Trade

Guilds developed among craftsmen probably around the start of the 1200s. They were generally found in middle-sized towns of about 25,000 people. Here some division of labor or specialization prevailed. Italy had the strongest guilds until the cities became dominated by merchants or oligarchies. In France, guilds had to pay dues to feudal powers in order to exist. In England, they became so obvious and seemingly influential that political powers tried to prohibit them because they seemed inimical to the royal interests.

Now that we know where they were, let's find out what they were all about. **Guilds** were a special type of exclusive association of producers. Typically a guild was run by a master, or several masters. These were usually craftsmen who did their work in their own houses and sometimes in special shops. These so-called guild masters voluntarily agreed to set up a system of rules which would govern the conduct of each other, and more importantly, the conduct of anyone attempting to enter that particular craft in that particular town. Herein lies the restrictive nature of guilds and why we titled this section "Combinations in Restraint of Trade." To prevent entry into the particular calling that the guild masters were making money at, they required a long apprenticeship for anyone who wanted to become a journeyman (master craftsman). The apprenticeship was ostensibly designed to insure the

adequate training of journeymen, but as an aside, it also prevented "too" rapid an entry into the profession itself, hence maintaining the incomes of the guild masters at levels that they thought appropriate to their station in life.

There were many types of guilds: the glovers' guild, the hatters' guild, the scribners' guild, and so on. Guilds also were designed to control the social conduct of their members. Members could be fined for improper behavior and for not contributing enough to charitable organizations. Basically, however, we can view the guilds as economic units which were used to establish monopoly positions for the guild masters and those who were lucky enough to enter the guild later on.

We can define a monopoly as an organization which has control over the selling of something. (The term actually means, in Greek, single seller.) The guild masters were essentially establishing themselves as the single seller of a particular type of service and its product, such as hats. They attempted to prevent entry by specifying criteria for apprenticeships and by changing the length of the apprenticeships.

They attempted to prevent competition *within* the guild by specifying how many threads per inch had to be in a piece of cloth, how the cloth had to be shrunk, how much buttons had to weigh, and what type of production techniques could be used. In fact, in certain places it was necessary for craftsmen to keep their windows open so that passersby could easily see if they were cheating on the guild's production-technique restrictions. Ostensibly, these monitoring techniques were used to establish "standards" and to protect the guild's "good name."

Using Law of Demand

The restriction on the number of guild members can be easily understood by using our simple law of demand given in the last chapter. There is an inverse relationship between the price of a product, say, hats, and the quantity demanded. In other

Glassblowing needed training and skill, and tended to be a specialty of certain districts. This drawing from Bohemia shows the process, from digging the raw material, sand, through the final examination and packing of the finished vessels. (British Museum)

words, if members of the hatters' guild produce more hats, the only way they can get rid of them is by in effect lowering the price. Looked at another way, if the guild members produce very few hats, they can effectively charge a higher price per hat and sell all of this smaller quantity supplied. If the guild master were to let in lots more hat makers, all of the hat makers would have to accept a lower price if everybody is to get rid of their hats. By restricting the number of producers of hats, the guild master and members made sure that what they received for their hats provided them with a steady, relatively higher income. Of course, there are problems of monitoring all the members of the guild. What if some of them started to make more hats than they were allowed or started to offer a different style of hat? These hatters might start taking away business from other people. It is not hard to figure out why there were so many restrictions on guild members.

AND MERCHANTS TOO

Merchants also started to band together in what were called merchants' guilds. These organizations were not, however, the same as craft guilds. Merchant associations, which were known in Italy and England during the twelfth century, were interested mainly in self-regulation of trade and, of course, in peripheral social interactions among the members. They often found themselves in competition with craft guilds. In fact, in London in 1200, one succeeded in persuading the King that the weavers' craft guild should be abolished; the King gave a monopoly to the merchants. Merchants in those times were known as freemen, to be contrasted with craftsmen. A craftsman could become a freeman only if he gave up his craft and got rid of all of his equipment from his house.

A lot of merchants banded together in what was to become the most far-reaching kind of international organization among foreign merchants during that era. It was called the Hanseatic League, which we depict in Figure 3–2. The best-known members of this league were the Hansa of London and those of the Teutons. The Hansa of London, for example, had by the end of 1350 gotten all of its members royal protection and a special privilege to trade whenever and wherever they pleased in England for a period of 40 days. In other words, any member of the Hansa League could go to any particular spot in England and stay there for 40 days, all the while trading and making income. We shall see below that the increased trade among towns and nations was one of the contributors to the downfall of the feudal society.

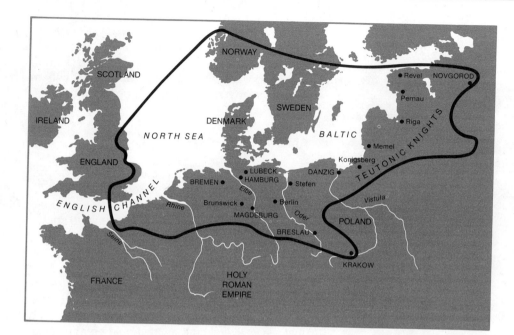

FIGURE 3–2

**THE GREAT
HANSEATIC LEAGUE**

The Hanseatic League
during the Middle Ages
encompassed over 70
towns throughout
Europe and England.
It was the most
far-reaching
international
organization of foreign
merchants.

THE DECLINE OF FEUDALISM

By the beginning of the seventeenth century, feudalism had largely disappeared in Western Europe. In its place was a developing market-oriented economy which was spreading throughout the world. What accounted for the decline of such a pervasive way of life for such a large sector of the world? Historians have often looked to the Church, religious life styles, and the Crusades to explain at least part of this decline. Let's turn now to the supreme religious adventure in medieval times. The end result of that adventure was a society that the Church had opposed for centuries.

Spreading the Faith

If we ignore for a moment the religious aspects of the Crusades, it is obvious that those hardy Crusaders who made it to the East found a startlingly different way of life, one that they were not used to in the medieval economy. For in the East,

people were far more civilized in some senses of the word; there were luxuries that were unheard of in the West. The Crusaders also came upon a much more money-oriented economy. In other words, a medium of exchange commonly accepted by a majority of the people was in wide use.

We might say that the Crusades had a *demonstration effect;* knights in shining armor tasted a little bit of the "good" life and wanted to continue it when they returned to the West. Urban living seemed much more appealing after they saw what it was like. When these valiant men returned to their homelands, some left the countryside; they wanted city life. This demand for an urban environment created one of the impetuses for increased urbanization and all that comes with it. It is perhaps responsible for fostering the growth of towns, the increased number of town charters, and the development of an important middle class.

The Crusades were also a source of increased demand for certain products, such as arms and clothing. This was thought to be a stimulating influence on the medieval economy. It at least induced these industries to grow at a more rapid rate than they would have otherwise, and also accounts for royal government support for merchant guilds instead of craft or producers' "locals."

Changing Religious Attitudes

The Church had lots of rules against market exchanges used to obtain "excessive" personal gain. For example, there were rules against **usury**—lending out money at interest, even very low interest. Today it is hard for us to imagine such a rule. Perhaps exorbitant interest rates are out of the question, but a zero rate? Why would anybody continuously be willing to give up the use of his own money for a certain period of time if he is not paid for it? Voluntary exchange must be mutually beneficial. Perhaps some people would be willing to give up the use of their money for a while because of love or philanthropy, but most didn't then and still don't. Strictures on interest rates are no different from strictures on a positive price being charged for any good or service.

During medieval times, the Church attempted to instill in the populace the notion that life on this earth was only temporary, ephemeral, and one should look to the hereafter. There was extreme disapproval of wealth seeking. Life on earth should be a preparation for eternity, not a time to make things better for the present. Life on earth was supposed to be unimportant.

The Protestant Ethic

The Reformation changed all this for many people. According to some economic historians, the advent of **Calvinism** was responsible for the tremendous growth in a capitalistic system where pecuniary gain was the main guiding force of individual economic actors in society. John Calvin preached the Puritan ethic, or the Protestant ethic, as it is sometimes called. He rationalized the change to bourgeois economic life by teaching the necessity of pursuing intense worldly activity. In so doing, a person would be fulfilling his duty to God. One was to be known to God only by the fruits of his gainful labor. In working harder, he could strive for higher status in the eyes of the Lord. Calvin reinterpreted the so-called **division of labor**—that is, specialization—as a way of allowing each person to do his best according to God's calling. And further, for Calvinists it was a sin to be idle. Also, Protestants were imbued with the idea that abstinence from consumption was a virtue; therefore, it was a virtue to save, to be thrifty. And, of course, when one saved, one was supposed to do whatever he could to make his savings as productive as possible. All of these new ideas that were soon to be accepted by many in society may have been a factor in causing the breakdown of feudal life. But there were certainly other reasons for this to happen, and it is to those we now turn.

THE ULTIMATE DECLINE IN THE MANORIAL SYSTEM

Cities started to develop in Western Europe even during the beginning of the Middle Ages. In fact, it was within the city walls that many serfs found their freedom when they decided that they could do better outside the manorial estate, for it was a rule in most situations that if a serf stayed away from the manor for a year and a day, he became a free man. During this time, a commercial expansion started throughout Europe. Fairs were held in different parts of the countryside. The Crusades also added to the desire for wealthy individuals to acquire the finer things in life that were present in the Orient. This induced traveling salesmen to visit towns and manors throughout the countryside to barter or trade for money with interested villeins and noblemen alike. And introduction of the use of money was an important catalyst.

Money is not, of course, necessary for trade. Things can be bartered. A pair of shoes can be traded for 15 buttons. A pot can be traded for four pieces of cloth. Most wandering merchants, however, wanted to get a more universal medium of exchange for the goods they traded with the villeins and the noblemen. They didn't want to be hampered with additional bulky goods that they would have to trade later on. Money, whether it be coins, dollar bills, or some convenient durable commodity, is generally defined as a *medium of exchange.* It is also a *store of purchasing power* if it is commonly accepted, and that's why its use is so widespread. It is extremely inconvenient to resort to barter when trying to obtain what one wants. You need to find someone else who has what you want and wants exactly what you have. It's just a lot simpler to sell goods or labor services for a payment in some medium of exchange and then to later on buy whatever goods or services you want. *The use of money allows for increased specialization.* Increased trade was dependent on the acceptance of money as a means of exchange, and that's exactly what happened in medieval society. The use of money became more widespread and trade continued to expand. However, money brought with it problems that were previously unknown to the manorial economy.

A JUST PRICE AND INFLATION

Previously everyone was used to a "just" price that was charged for goods and services. Economic activity had been ruled by custom. And this is a logical and economical way of doing things in a stationary society. The just price was generally set such that there were no shortages or surpluses for the goods involved. And why not set such a price if, after all, nothing changes? However, once money was introduced and trade became more widespread, just prices simply weren't good enough any more. One of the main reasons was the ubiquitous phenomenon we know today as inflation—a sustained rise in prices.

Rising Prices

For example, during the sixteenth century the general price level more than tripled because of the tremendous influx of gold and silver from the Americas. Now, why should an influx of precious metal cause prices to rise? Remember first that money is not only a medium of exchange but a store of purchasing power. People want to keep it because they can exchange it later on for goods and services. Suppose that the only form of money is gold. Noblemen and villeins, as well as numerous other people in medieval society, have learned to accept gold in payment for goods and services. Later on they pay for other goods and services with this gold. Now suppose that all of a sudden the supply of gold in existence doubles because of shipments from the New World. The people who bring the gold in exchange it for goods and services. Now, before they came all of the other gold that was used would merely change hands; the supply was fixed, or constant. That is no longer the case. A lot of people end up with a lot more gold than they used to have. But gold is what they use to buy real goods and services. When lots of people have a lot more gold and there's the same quantity of goods and services around as before, something's got to give. Individuals end up bidding against each other to get what they want. The price of those fixed supplies of goods and services has to go up in terms of gold. Throughout the rest of this book, you'll find other examples of how a large increase in the supply of the medium of exchange has led to an increase in the price level, or inflation.

Inflation Unexpected

The manorial lords, just like everybody else, were caught off guard. They wanted to buy some of the finer things in life which were available outside of the manor. These things had to be purchased with the medium of exchange, and in terms of that medium of exchange, they became more and more expensive. The lords were no longer satisfied

This fifteenth century print from an illuminated manuscript shows the traffic in the front courtyard of a castle. (Staatsbibliothek Berlin)

with their previous relationships with their serfs. Up until then, serfs had been required to do a certain amount of each day's work for the lord. Now the lords wanted them to pay a certain amount of money in exchange for the land and protection that the lord provided. In the absence of any inflation, the lord could set a particular mutually agreeable price for the use of his land and the serfs would willingly agree.

With the rise of a market economy, established prices for goods and services were increasingly known by everyone. Hence, the translation of the value of a certain amount of each day's work into a fixed money payment was relatively easy. The wage payment, however, had been fixed before the unanticipated inflation of the sixteenth century. So, during this period of unprecedented rises in the prices of goods and services that the lords wished to buy outside of the manor, they experienced a loss in their economic power. In other words, the value in *real* terms of the money payments received from the people using their land was falling. This is an important relationship:

Prices determine the real value of money payments. When we talk about real value, we're talking about purchasing power. Take a concrete, present-day example: If the price level goes up 10 percent and your scholarship remains the same, the real value of that scholarship has dropped by 10 percent. The same thing happened to the manorial lords.

At the same time, the merchant class was gaining more power. Unanticipated inflation provided an opportunity for profitable sale in markets, thus whetting commercial appetites and rewarding producers. Additionally, we must realize that the manorial system could not support a rising population.

A GROWING POPULATION

At the beginning of the Middle Ages, fertile land was relatively abundant. As population grew and manors became overcrowded, new ones could be formed in the untilled regions of Europe. Population continued to grow until the middle of the

1400s, when the Black Death came. Population stagnated for a while, but then started taking off again. Population pressures started to be felt by the increasingly crowded manors which could no longer easily expand or multiply into regions where land was still fertile. All of this was happening at a time when merchants were becoming an increasingly economically powerful class.

THE MARKET ECONOMY EMERGES

Workers started to be paid with money instead of being required to do a certain amount of work in exchange for use of land. In other words, this factor of production—labor—was monetized, as it were. Around the same time, especially in England, another factor of production—land—was also being monetized. As land became more valuable, lords attempted to make a higher income by making better use of their lands. In England, for example, there was the beginning of what was later termed the Enclosure Movement. The English had an immensely profitable trade in wool. That meant that land which could be used to raise sheep was more valuable than other land. Hence, it was decided that those peasants who might use land to the detriment of sheep raising should be prevented from such acts. Land was therefore enclosed with fences. A certain number of landless peasants were therefore unable to make a living using the lord's **common property** grounds as they were used to doing. This led to the English Poor Laws, which essentially involved a tax to raise revenues, to round up the poor and put them to work.*

Land, like labor, was no longer conceived as a certain aspect in an explicit social and material relationship within a society. Labor, for example, had become a good or commodity to be disposed of in the marketplace just like any other good.

*This is not completely unlike current workfare programs.

One man did not have to work for a lord or guild master in return for the mere assurance of subsistence. He could attempt to shop around in order to get the best price or wage possible for his labor services. The same was true for land. Land used to be thought of as inviolable, the territory of some great master. Now it had become another commodity to be sold or rented.

A monetized market economy brought with it a lot more than the explicit creation of factors of production such as land and labor. It brought with it a system in which *information* became less costly to obtain. The information we are referring to is considered completely natural today—the prices of goods and services, where they can be bought and sold, what their quality is, and so on. Prior to the development of the market economy, such information was extremely difficult to obtain. In other words, the cost to individuals of obtaining it was sometimes prohibitive. In a market economy, the sources of information are myriad. Mainly, though, they come from the producers, who wish to sell their products at the most favorable prices. To do so requires that many potential buyers be aware of price and availability. Moreover, such information provides clues to producers as to where greater profits might be made. If it is well known that a certain type of hat is selling for a specific price in Pisa and a hat maker in Venice had discovered a way to produce them cheaper, he knows immediately where potential profit-making opportunity lies.

A RECAP

The Middle Ages lasted for a millenium. During that time we saw constant change: clearing of the land, extension of agriculture, and a rise of resources. We also saw very little that was dramatic except occasional famines and plagues. Cities developed gradually, trade developed gradually, the rise and subsequent decline of the manor were gradual, and the so-called commercial revolution was spread over several centuries. During this period of ups and downs a pervasive phenomenon occurred: Population seemed to increase to some natural limit and then fall back, due to some natural phenomena. Several centuries later one astute person developed a theory after observing these phenomena, and, of course, his name was Malthus—the Reverend Thomas Robert. His specter haunts us even today, so let's go back to find out what his ideas were and where they seemed to make the most sense.

Definitions of New Terms

PREMARKET ECONOMY OR TRADITIONAL SYSTEM: a system in which most economic activity is based on custom or tradition, generally where money is not widely used as an intermediate good in exchange, and a situation in which very little trade or exchange takes place relative to more modern times.

INSTITUTIONAL ARRANGEMENTS: the customs, laws, and institutions which determine how individuals may conduct themselves in economic and also in noneconomic matters.

CRAFT GUILD: an exclusive organization of producer craftsmen. Guilds were run by guild masters who ruled with an iron hand in setting up a system to govern the business and social conduct of all the members.

MONOPOLY: in its strictest sense, a single seller of a good or service, but more generally, a seller of a good or service who has considerable control over prices and output.

USURY: lending money for interest; today usury generally implies lending money at "excessive" interest rates.

CALVINISM: a set of beliefs handed down by John Calvin; a rationalization of bourgeois economic life in which a person fulfilled his duty to God by working hard and saving lots of his income, which could be invested in profitable outlets.

DIVISION OF LABOR: a situation in which individual workers take on specialized tasks instead of attempting to do everything necessary to produce a product or service.

DIMINISHING RETURNS: a situation in which as more of one input—say, labor—is added to a fixed amount of another input—say, land—the increase in output does not rise in proportion.

COMMON PROPERTY: property which is in a sense owned by no one but also owned by everyone; the opposite of private property.

Chapter Summary

1. The Middle Ages was a period of several centuries during which a traditional or premarket system was in existence. This period was not, however, one of stagnation; numerous innovations appeared, as well as many of the prerequisites for the market economy that later followed.

2. The manor was an economic and social institution which was found throughout large parts of Western Europe. This was the age of feudalism, during which the manor was ruled by a lord.

3. The manorial lord provided his serfs with police protection, justice, and food during famines.

4. The manor was basically self-sufficient and fairly isolated from any central political authority.

5. Within the cities of the day, combinations in restraint of trade grew up. These were known as guilds, which were a special type of exclusive association of producers. Guilds limited the number of craftsmen allowed to produce a product, and also set standards for production techniques. Guilds acted as monopolies.

6. Merchants had guilds also. Oftentimes these merchant guilds found themselves in competition with craft guilds.

7. One of the most far-reaching organizations of merchants was the Hanseatic League, which encompassed over 70 towns throughout Europe during the Middle Ages.

8. The decline of feudalism until its ultimate disappearance around the seventeenth century can be traced to a number of factors: (1) Some scholars believe that the Crusades had a demonstration effect—returning knights had tasted the "good" life and wanted no longer to live in isolated manors; (2) Calvinism became popular and rationalized economic specialization and accumulation; (3) A monetary economy grew up.

9. Money came to be used as a medium of exchange and also as a store of purchasing power. Money can be anything that is commonly accepted as a medium of exchange. The use of money allowed for increased specialization.

10. An influx of precious metal from the New World caused prices to rise in the Old World. This inflation was unexpected and therefore caused a disruption in the economic relationships among the lord, his serfs or workers, and the outside market economy.

11. A monetized market economy saw the explicit rationalization of the factors of production, such as land and labor. It also brought with it a system in which information became less costly to obtain and disseminate.

Questions for Thought and Discussion

1. Even though money may not have been used at the beginning of the Middle Ages, does that mean that the economic principles studied in the last chapter were not valid? Why or why not?

2. Do you think that the original "voluntary" implicit contract that workers entered into with manorial lords can truly be treated as voluntary?

3. Why would merchants want to band together into an exclusive type of organization?

4. Why couldn't people anticipate the inflation that actually occurred when gold and silver were brought in from the New World?

ISSUE III

A Gloomy Future

Essay on Population

In 1798, a little-known English man of the cloth named Thomas Robert Malthus published *An Essay on the Principle of Population, as it Affects the Future Improvement of Society.* The uncomfortable and, indeed, depressing conclusion of that 50,000-word treatise was that "population, when unchecked, goes on doubling every 24 years or increases in the geometric ratio," but according to Reverend Malthus, food production—or more generally, the means of subsistence—only increases at an arithmetic ratio. We can see what Malthus meant about geometric as opposed to arithmetic rates by looking at Figure III-1. Here the gold line would represent something, say population, rising at a geometric rate. Notice how it starts slowly and then gradually gets steeper and steeper. Compare this with the black line, which represents, say, food growing at an arithmetic rate. It remains equally steep throughout its path.

Revising His Ideas

A few years later, in 1803, Malthus put out a second edition of his now-infamous essay on population. Instead of talking about population doubling at a geometric ratio, he indicated that the human species was destined to poverty and a life of misery unless the rate of population-growth was retarded by **positive checks** or **preventive checks.** He listed as preventive such things as late marriages or no marriage at all, sexual abstinence, and moral restraint.

Even though Malthus preached moral restraint, he realized that "hot passion leads to surplus souls and cold reason leads to sin." And since he was of strong moral character, he appeared unimpressed by the low fertility of prostitutes for "a promiscuous intercourse to such a degree as to prevent the birth of children seems to lower, in the most marked manner, the dignity of human nature. It cannot be without its effect on men, and nothing can be more obvious than its tendency to degrade the female character, and to destroy all of its most amiable and distinguished characteristics."

It's understandable, then, that Malthus put much more faith in such positive checks as wars, pestilence, and famine.

As you can imagine, Malthus was criticized severely. His fellow clergymen thought he was crazy; politicians and journalists called him a heretic. But then again,

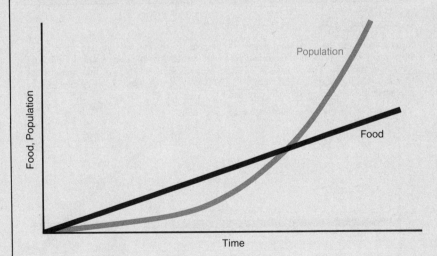

FIGURE III-1 THE MALTHUSIAN DILEMMA

Population increases at an exponential or geometrically increasing rate, as evidenced by the heavy gold line, whereas food production only increases linearly or arithmetically. Eventually population outstrips the food supply.

others, especially a famous economist of the time named David Ricardo, made good use of the Malthusian theory. Let's delve a little deeper into why Malthus came up with such heretical ideas; we shall see that although his theories didn't predict very well in the industrial society of his time, they did do a great job of describing what happened during the preindustrial European episode that we have just studied in the previous chapter.

A Product of Traditional Europe

Even though the Reverend Malthus grew up during the Industrial Revolution, he was a product of traditional Europe—

that is, preindustrial, pregrowth society. He believed, as did Adam Smith, the father of much modern economic thinking, that economic life depended on the productivity of land, so that ultimately it was the land which determined the level of our existence. Malthus was convinced, being the clergyman that he was, that the "passion between sexes" would cause men and women to breed so long as there was enough food around to feed a growing family. We might depict the Malthusian cycle, as it is called, graphically in Figure III-2. Here we show the population size on the horizontal axis and the real wage rate per person on the vertical axis. Notice here the emphasis on the word *real*. The real wage rate is essentially

the wage rate expressed in purchasing power over real goods and services. Real wage rates are, therefore, an indication of a person's ability to purchase the things he wants. We don't have to then worry about problems of inflation, or rather, general changes in the price level. Notice that we have drawn in a heavily shaded line that we call subsistence. This is the so-called subsistence level of income, or real wages, necessary for a family to survive. Presumably, if he does not obtain at least this high a level of income, his children will die because he cannot feed or clothe them. Once the population reaches the point D, widespread famines occur; there are numerous deaths in the society, according to the Malthusian doctrine. This was the period of "positive" checks: disease, famine, wars, plus an increase in vice which, according to Malthus, was degrading but resulted in fewer births.

Key Assumptions

Malthus made some key assumptions on which his theory was based. The most obvious is that population decisions were dependent only on maintaining the real wage rate above the subsistence level of wages. So long as people could obtain a real wage which gave them more than subsistence, the "passion between sexes" would take over and the

---

FIGURE III-2   THE MALTHUSIAN CYCLE

Population is on the horizontal axis and the real wage rate or standard of living on the vertical axis. The heavy horizontal line indicates the subsistence level of real wages that the population must receive in order to survive. Real wages will first increase, but after diminishing returns set in, they will fall until point D. Then positive checks come into account—famines, pestilence, and the like.

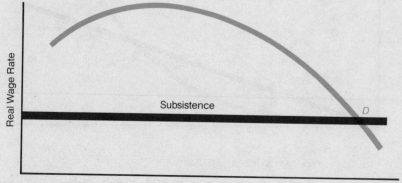

(Staatsbibliothek Berlin)

Malthus and Traditional Europe

It turns out that Malthus came up with a pretty good description of how things happened throughout Europe for many centuries before he wrote his essay—for example, there were recurrent periods of famine and pestilence. In fact, we can use the Malthusian doctrine to discover what happened during the age of feudalism described in the previous chapter. Population would increase on a manor until it was no longer worthwhile for the manorial lord to have any additional serfs—for a reason that has to do with an important economic principle called diminishing returns.

Diminishing Returns

With a fixed amount of land and fixed technology, after a point additional increases in the number of workers will result in reduced productivity for each additional worker. That is, the additional output brought about by the additional worker will not be as much as by the previous worker. This is sometimes referred to as **diminishing returns** or productivity of the additional workers. To better understand this concept, look at the situation in which the manor lord has a fixed piece of land of a given fertility. He also has a certain number of plows, which we assume also for the moment is fixed. He has a

world would become more peopled. While this may have been true in many situations, which we will describe below, it has not always been the case. There are many primitive societies in which Malthus' "preventive" checks were used, the most obvious being infanticide.

The second key assumption that the Reverend used was one of fixed technology. As we said above, Malthus was growing up in the Industrial Revolution, when this assumption certainly did not hold, but he was a product of an era when technology in fact did not change very quickly. This was certainly true with agricultural societies; technological changes were very slow. For example, English crop rotation and fertilization methods were only slowly adopted during the commercial revolution. This is one of the reasons that Malthus viewed agricultural output as growing at an arithmetic rate, instead of at a geometric rate like the population. But, according to Malthus, even if there were some once-and-for-all increase in the food base of a society, this would only lead to inexorable pressure of the population on the increased resources. He felt that when everything got sorted out, the average level of living would be just as low as it was before the great increase in the food base.

certain number of seeds, and whatever else is necessary to grow his crops. The only thing that the manor lord can vary in our little example is the number of men working on his plot of land. After a certain point—say, when he has ten men—he'll run out of plows for each of them. That means that the eleventh man will have to do some other task besides plowing. Or perhaps he will take turns with somebody else. When the twelfth man comes along to work, he also will have to share a plow, and the thirteenth, and so on. Finally, if the manor lord hires on more than 20 men, each will only be able to use a plow less than half the time. So you see that with a fixed amount of land and tools to work with, as additional men are hired on, it is inevitable that their contribution to productivity or to the total amount produced must diminish. We find, then, that for a given amount of other factors of production, the larger the number of workers in the specific occupation, the smaller the productivity of each one.

The value of each worker to the manor lord is also determined by the value of the output that the workers produce. In a market situation—say where the manor lord has started to sell some of his crops to city dwellers—the higher the price those city dwellers are willing to pay for his crops, the more valuable each worker becomes. If the market situation is extended to money payments to workers, the manor lord would be willing to raise his workers' wage payments if in fact the price he got for his product in town had gone up.

When to Stop Adding Serfs

Before money payments were made to serfs on the manor, they exchanged a certain amount of each day's work for lodging and use of the land and anything else that the manor lord provided. What the lord provided had some value. The labor services that the serf provided did also; the value, as we mentioned above, was determined by the value of the output attributable to each serf. If the manor is fixed in size and there are no increases in agricultural technology, as more and more serfs are added diminishing returns set in: At some point, the additional output attributable to an additional serf would not be equal in value to the services the manor lord would have to offer the serf. Hence, it would no longer be worthwhile to add serfs to the manor.

Of course, this assumes a fixed amount of usable land with fixed fertility. Manors could extend themselves, and, indeed, they did. However, at some point there would be no more relatively fertile land for manorial extensions. It was more difficult for further increases in population to then spread out into previously uncultivated acreages. The specter of diminishing returns was something that could no longer be further escaped by expansion into other territories. At this time land became relatively more valuable than labor. Since the value of an agricultural worker was dependent upon how much output (and its price) could be attributable to that worker, as relatively fertile land became more scarce, labor became relatively less valuable. Real wages fell in the agricultural sector. This led to an incentive for people to move into nonagricultural pursuits, which constituted a relatively small part of the economy during the pre-1800 European scene.

Plagues and War

When looking over the history of European population during the Middle Ages, we find recurrent periods of famine, pestilence, and war.

In the early 1300s, Europe experienced some of the most serious famines that had ever occurred, and, to top it all off, the famous Hundred Years War between England and France was started before complete recovery was possible. This is when we saw an early example of germ warfare: The enemy got a disease-laden missile sent by catapult.

In the middle of the fourteenth century, the Black Death came. The first wave started in 1347 and continued until 1351. It was of a pneumonic type, which was the most infectious and most deadly form of plague. The plague germs were carried by rats and fleas. Relatively dense city centers were the homes of these plague-laden creatures.

During this period, the population was reduced by as much as one-third during a single year over hundreds of thousands of square miles. From the middle of the fourteenth century on, population was reduced as pestilence continued to recur. For example, in England the plague returned in 1360, 1369, and 1374.

Such horrible crises tended to weed out the physically weak, so after a pestilence occurred, mortality was down, marriages and births were up. Many societies therefore saw surges in population for each generation to come. In fact, if we look at the population before the industrialization of Europe, fluctuations were erratic and sometimes violent, as evidenced by what happened during the Black Death. However, these fluctuations were around some sort of trend. The trend could be stable—up, or down.

It is interesting also to note that those who lived in the cities were more susceptible to pestilence than those who didn't. As real incomes rose and the population

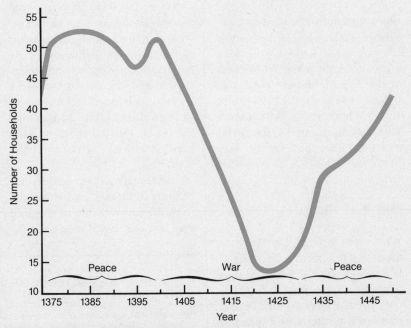

FIGURE III-3   THE RELATIONSHIP BETWEEN POPULATION AND MILITARY MANEUVERS IN OUGES, BURGUNDY

We see a distinct correlation between what happened to the population in this small town and the fighting of wars. (*Source: Cambridge Economic History of Europe,* Volume 1, p. 676.)

became more urbanized, the population was more subject to violent death by disease because of the spreading factor that is proportional to population density. The denser the population, the faster infectious disease will spread. In the seventeenth century, for example, the immense town of London lost one-sixth to one-fourth of its population during a period of disease, while in many rural parishes during this period, there wasn't one death attributable to the plague.

Wars

War activities had a lot to do with what Malthus called "positive" checks on population increases. Looking at Figure III-3, we see for example, the relationship between military operations and the number of households in Ouges, Burgundy. There was a distinct correlation between the fighting of wars (plus the Crusades) and the reduction of population. (There may have also been a correlation between population growth and the start of wars.)

We could go on with further illustrations of periods when population grew until war or pestilence reduced it to some previous level, and then it started to grow again. The Malthusian cycle was indeed at work during the Middle Ages. However, Malthus missed the boat in terms of industrial societies, like the one he was living in.

What Went Wrong?

What went wrong with Malthus' thesis was that he assumed a fixed technology. He also assumed that population size was a function only of real income, and in fact that survival rates were a function of income level. In the first instance, we know that starting in the seventeenth and eighteenth centuries the technological capacity of society increased; whether it was due to the Industrial Revolution, to increased schooling of the population, or to other determinants, it did increase, and that is what the rest of this book is about. Malthus ignored the possibility that the curve in Figure III-2 could rise. Look at Figure III-4. Here we show three separate curves, one with a certain productivity of the population, another with a higher produc-tivity, and a third with an even higher productivity. These increases in productivity are a result of increases in technology. The real income per capita of the population can rise even though the population is growing if the curves shift up fast enough. In this particular simplified model, there need never be a Malthusian positive check.

Additionally, it turns out that in many situations, as real income rises, the survival rate of children may increase, but the demand for children might fall, or at least might not rise as fast as income does. Stable populations are not unknown in the world today: Witness, for example, Japan and France. We do still find, however, the Malthusian cycle acting up in various less-developed countries in the world today. But more on that topic in Issue XV.

Malthus was right, but only for before his time and perhaps under similar conditions existing today in certain countries.

FIGURE III-4 POSSIBILITY OF IMPROVED TECHNOLOGY

In this diagram, which is similar to Figure III-2, we have the same level of subsistence real wages but the curves now move to the right as technology improves productivity. We have labeled those curves successively Productivity 1, 2, and 3. If productivity rises fast enough the population can grow without real wages falling to subsistence levels.

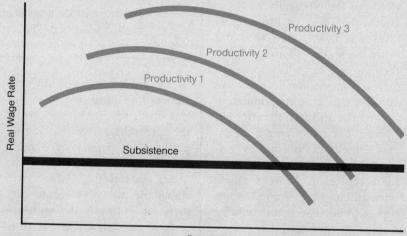

Definitions of New Terms

POSITIVE CHECKS: according to Malthus, these were the necessary checks on population growth that came about whenever the subsistence level of living was reached. These include famines, plagues, and the like.

PREVENTIVE CHECKS: these, according to Malthus, involve birth control and other actions which would prevent population from outstripping the food supply. If enough preventive checks were taken, positive checks would not occur.

DIMINISHING RETURNS: usually called the law of diminishing returns: After some point, successive increases in labor, for example, added to fixed amounts of land and other things used for production, will not cause an equal proportionate increase in output.

Questions for Thought and Discussion

1. Why did Malthus' predictions go awry?
2. After the plague, workers' wages (whether explicit or implicit) increased. Why do you think this occurred? (Hint: Remember the law of demand and turn it around.)
3. Why do you think there might be a correlation between population growth and the start of wars?

The Opening Up of the New World

AFTER THE Black Death brought a temporary halt to the rise in the population of Europe, growth resumed its long-run upward trend. At the same time, a market economy was developing, and the rise of the nation-state in the fifteenth century brought forth poles of power. These poles of power were political in nature but economic in exercise. Crucial to the development of political power was the development of economic power. One of the ways to obtain economic power was to establish trade with the Far East, and originally world adventurers set out on sometimes-subsidized sailing adventures in order to establish a direct route to the East. One of the results of these ventures was Columbus' discovery of the Americas in 1492. Soon, however, the nation-states abandoned their attempt to find a fast route to the East and settled down to the job of colonization, for this was the era of mercantilism.

MERCANTILISM

Many economic implications flowed from the basic political preconceptions of the time. It was assumed that the only way to obtain political power was to obtain wealth. The greater the wealth that a nation had, the more power it had. It was also assumed for some reason that the world's resources would not grow, so that for one nation to be better off, another nation had to be worse off. The idea was to increase the flow of wealth into the mother country. Hence, besides increasing a nation's territory, the colonies themselves were to be a source of wealth by their economic exploitation, such as their export of precious metals, and their provision of resources that were not available in the home country. The success of Spain in obtaining gold and silver from South America that was shipped back to the mother country further encouraged the development of colonies by the great nation-states of Europe during the seventeenth and eighteenth centuries.

The main precept of mercantilism can be stated in a few words: Obtain more wealth, particularly in the form of precious metals. In order to assure the mercantilist goal, it was necessary to have government intervention. As we will see, this government intervention took the form of taxing goods coming into a nation, expanding colonial territory, and providing incentives to encourage the sale abroad of domestically produced goods. In other words, there was an attempt to force exports to be greater than imports into the mother country. The difference would be in the form of gold or silver. However, mercantilist precepts ignored a common principle: Both parties gain from voluntary trade, whether that trade be between individuals, states, or nations. Ex post, we might say that the goal that government intervention should have had was the increase in both exports and imports, in other words, a balanced increase in all trade with all nations.

THE FIRST COLONIES

England was slow to establish colonies. The Dutch were already in North America and in the East and West Indies; the Spanish were in North and South America; and the French were in Canada and the West Indies, all before the English set themselves to the task of developing outside territorial bases. The first English attempts at colonization were dismal failures. Sir Humphrey Gilbert and Sir Walter Raleigh just couldn't hack it during the 1580s in Newfoundland and the Carolinas. It wasn't until 1607 that the Virginia Company of London succeeded in establishing the first permanent colony in Jamestown (Virginia, of course). Then by 1620 the Plymouth Company had established the first New England colony. In 1630, the Massachusetts Bay Company established its

own outpost. Then followed Rhode Island, Connecticut, New Hampshire, and the rest. It wasn't until 1732 that the last of the thirteen colonies, Georgia, was established.

Differences in Colonization Techniques

The English colonies were somewhat different from the Spanish, for the English decided to people their colonies, whereas Spain decided to exploit an existing population, using the infamous *encomienda* system, which was almost feudal in its workings, using an indigenous labor force.

Even though some of the original English colonies were started with government help, most of them were private ventures in which the Crown did not participate. The lure of profits induced joint stock companies, such as the Virginia Company

Sir Walter Raleigh was a daring man who originated colonizing expeditions to America. He is also credited with introducing potatoes and tobacco to England.

The lower deck of a Guinea slave ship used during the eighteenth century.

and the Plymouth Company, to raise money to finance these colonies. The companies were in a sense quasi-public and the stockholders felt they were entitled to a return on their investment. It turned out, however, that none of these ventures was actually profitable. Several colonies were started as individual proprietorships, such as Maryland by Lord Baltimore, and Pennsylvania by William Penn. They, too, were unable to turn a profit. In an attempt to make some money, they tried to secure revenues from the settlers by annual payments, but that didn't work out very well.

It may seem incongruous that the original profit-seeking entrepreneurs who set up colonies in the New World were unable to make any income. After all, wasn't the New World filled with untold natural riches? Weren't there abundant lands full of timber and rich soil? Yes, and yes, and even more so. But it takes more than one factor of production to yield a product.

The Problem of Scarcity

Land was abundant, but labor wasn't. Neither was capital. Originally there were few machines around, very little equipment for clearing land, and almost no manufacturing implements: It was, indeed, a bleak situation (although in a pretty setting). We expect that when land is abundant relative to labor and capital it will be relatively low-priced. Using the same line of reasoning, labor and capital were relatively scarce and, hence, relatively high-priced. The colonists originally could do nothing with all of the land around them except pick away at some already-cleared areas that the Indians had abandoned. Later, as a few tools, horses, and mules were imported, better crop-planting methods could be used and more land could be tilled. But even then there was a limit to productivity that was dependent on the number of hands available. There was always a problem of obtaining relatively inexpensive labor. There were several methods used to induce more people to come over to the New World. After all, that's what England wanted, for that's how England thought it would get rich and politically powerful—by having strong colonies in America that transferred wealth to the motherland.

Ways to Get Workers

There were basically four methods used to get manpower into the New World.

Headrights. Under the headright system, approximately 50 acres were promised to each person who landed in the colonies, and additionally, the same amount was due to any person for every other person whose trip he paid for. These land grants of 50 acres usually went to individuals who had enough money to pay for their own passage, and perhaps a few other people, and provided as well for the necessary tools to cultivate the land.

Land Grants. Whole groups of settlers could obtain land grants for organizing their own communities. Generally, this happened when a religious minority wanted to escape persecution in the Old World. The Pilgrims are a good example.

Indentured Servants. These were servants who in exchange for passage to the New World agreed to work, usually for seven years. At the end of the seven-year period, they were sometimes given some land, a little money, and a few farm implements to start their own free life. Sometimes prisoners were sent to the New World as indentured servants. Generally, these prisoners were of a special type: They came from debtors' prison and were not therefore real criminals as we think of criminals today.

Slavery. Last but not least, slaves began appearing in the New World, brought first in Dutch ships in 1619. Eventually they were imported in British ships. As we shall see later, slavery was most popular in the South, where the plantation system grew up in the relatively warm climate.

Title page from a 1609 booklet promoting emigration to Virginia.

At this time, elsewhere in the Western Hemisphere slavery was expanding at a rapid rate.

Remember that there was really no big desire for many people to leave England. There was increasing prosperity, so that most people who came to the New World either sought economic returns or had to be paid to do it. During the colonial period, two-thirds of the colonists were from England, but within individual colonies, there were other nationalities. For example, in Pennsylvania Germans made up one-third of the population, and in the South there were many Scots.

BACK TO SLAVERY

Slavery was actually unimportant in North America for almost the first century of settlement. Before 1740, for example, there were less than 140,000 slaves in the colonial economy. But between 1740 and the Revolution, that figure grew to over 300,000. Slave trade during this time was rampant. The slave trade was very profitable, and England desired a market for the slaves they shipped from the Gold Coast. They found a market in North America. Even after the Revolution, over one-half of the slaves were still coming in European ships. The South especially wanted slavery as the plantation system developed. It was difficult to get workers from other colonies because each man was himself a landowner. Indentured servants during this period cost as much as two times per year what a slave did. Slavery may have developed slowly, but by the beginning of the nineteenth century, it had taken firm root, and only the bloodiest war in the history of the United States could uproot it.

WHAT TO PRODUCE AND WHERE?

At first, of course, there was no question about what the colonists should do with their time. It was either do or die, produce enough food to survive or go down as a casualty in the first colonization attempt in the New World by the English Crown. Later on, however, it was no longer a question of just surviving, but of making oneself better off, of getting above the subsistence level. This question is generally answered for each individual and each region by looking at where one's comparative advantage lies. It was obvious in the colonies that, at least at first, their comparative advantage lay mainly in agricultural production. And so, indeed, over 90 percent of the population engaged in this endeavor. The colonists were not, however, self-sufficient. They may have been able to produce the agricultural products they wanted, but there were certain manufactured goods that they had no way of obtaining unless they could somehow trade with other countries.

The most obvious country to trade with was, in fact, England. There the colonists spoke the language, were familiar with the customs and the prices, and could do business in a relatively easy manner. We might say, then, that the transactions costs involved in trading with England were generally less than those in trading with other countries. An English trade soon developed, and with it specialization in the different colonies depending on their comparative advantage. England was obviously in a mood for trade with the colonies, because that's one of the reasons they were set up. For many items, England was happy to have the colonial exports because they allowed the Crown to be self-sufficient within its own political sphere in just about all goods and services. Remember, one of the tenets of mercantilism was to obtain wealth, and in particular, specie or precious metal in the form of gold or silver. Precious metal could not be obtained, thought the mercantilists, if the mother country imported goods from other political units, because these goods generally had to be paid for with specie.

THE SOUTH

The South had a relatively high concentration of population. By 1770, there were 1.5 million Southern colonists as opposed to half a million in the New England colonies and half a million in the Middle Colonies. (We probably could have predicted, then, that Virginia would be the "mother of presidents" because of the predominance of population and, as we shall see, the economic surplus of certain agricultural products in the South.)

The South developed exports which were complementary to English production. These included tobacco, indigo, and rice. By 1770 over half the exports of all the colonies were accounted for by Southern production. In fact, up until the Revolution, trade with England was dominated by Southern staples.

Tobacco

The use of tobacco, which started out very slowly in the English population after its European introduction by traveling Spaniards, soon became ubiquitous. When it was found that in Maryland and in Virginia cheaper and better quality tobacco could be grown than in most other parts of the world, the English were ecstatic, for they had then developed their own cheap supply of good tobacco.

It is not hard to see why the plantation system developed when tobacco was found growable in southern, warm climates. It required only very crude implements and much unskilled labor. It could be raised on newly cleared land as the old land lost its fertility. The plantation system with its large numbers of poor, unskilled laborers was perfect for such production. Here the task system could be used. Supervision over each slave's "piece work" was relatively easy.

Mercantilism was not only rampant among the great nation-states of that time, it also reared its ugly head in the Southern colonies. There was not going to be the allowance of a free-enterprise environment if it was thought to hinder the wealth of the Southern colonists. For example, one-half of the tobacco crop was burned in order to maintain prices in 1639. And again in 1733 there was a restriction on the growing of tobacco. The burning and restricting were not as inane as they may sound.

The demand for agricultural products is relatively **price inelastic.** That is, the quantity demanded of agricultural products is relatively unresponsive to changes in the price. Therefore, a rise in the price of, say, tobacco or rice would not lead to a drastic reduction in the quantity of those products demanded. Conversely, a fall in the price would not lead to a drastic increase, either. Given this type of demand situation, a bumper crop of tobacco or rice could only be gotten rid of if the Southern colonists were willing to accept an extremely large decrease in the price. They didn't

like this idea, and hence the burning of the tobacco crop in 1639. Periodically such "burnings" have reappeared. Americans have occasionally seen newspaper pictures of dairy farmers pouring milk in the road to illustrate their desire for higher prices, or pig raisers slaughtering whole herds of piglets to demonstrate their refusal to sell at prevailing low prices.

Rice

The cultivation of rice became a major export crop for South Carolina by 1700. It was grown in low-lying fields and sometimes in swamplands. These could be irrigated with some control by allowing tidewater rivers to inundate them. Like tobacco, it required a warm climate and quite a bit of unskilled labor. It was conducive to a plantation system also.

Indigo

Indigo was useful to the British as a dye for their textile industries. In fact, the British were so keen on obtaining supplies of indigo that they paid a special subsidy, or bounty as it were, to its producers. In other words, anybody who would make so much indigo could be assured of a specific subsidy payment from the British in addition to whatever the crop fetched on the open market in the British economy. Indigo proved to be a useful and convenient crop to grow because it was complementary with rice in its demand for labor services: That is, the peak seasonal periods when lots of unskilled workers had to be in the indigo fields were different from the peak seasonal periods when lots of workers had to be in the rice fields.

THE MIDDLE COLONIES

The Middle Colonies were made up of the fertile agricultural areas of Pennsylvania, New York, and

New Jersey. Here livestock and grain could be more cheaply produced than in New England or the South. That is, the Middle Colonies' comparative advantage lay in the production of these goods. There was very little direct trade with England from these colonies because their comparative advantage was essentially the same as that of the English, for England also produced livestock and grain relatively cheaply. The Middle Colonies, in fact, tended to import more than they exported to England. What they did to balance that trade deficit was trade with southern Europe and the Indies.

NEW ENGLAND

This area consisted mainly of very small farms which produced only for local town markets. The comparative advantage of the New England colonists lay in their proximity to ocean waters, which were filled with fish, and the vast acreage of forest lands. Hence, we find them exporting ship timbers, whale oil, and codfish. Later on, the New England colonists became extremely efficient shipbuilders, and many New Englanders became world traders as well as sailors directly in competition with the mother country.

TRADE, TRADE, TRADE

From the very beginning, the colonists were reliant upon foreign trade. Even at the beginning of the nineteenth century, foreign trade comprised 15 to 20 percent of American incomes. This figure was probably even higher during the colonial period.

From the very beginning, the colonies were not allowed to trade unimpeded in the world market. And, in fact, the intensification of British restrictions on their trade finally led to the outbreak of the Revolution.

RESTRICTING THE COLONISTS

The earliest restriction on colonial activity dated back to 1660 with the passage of the infamous Navigation Acts. These Acts were passed in response to an attempt by the Dutch to get the shipping trade. Around 1600 the Dutch had developed a fast commercial sailing boat called a flute, which was as good as anything developed for many years to come. The Navigation Acts required that English ships, and only English ships, could be used for trade with England. Since the colonies were part of England, this applied to them also.*

There were several other things that the Navigation Acts required, but we'll leave those for the following issue, when we discuss whether or not the colonists were getting a raw deal from the British Crown.

From 1763 onward, there was a period of intensification of British restrictions. After the Seven Years War between the English and the French, a series of edicts on the political and economic freedom of the colonists was handed down by the British Crown. For example, the Proclamation of 1763 indicated that no colonial settlement was allowed west of the Appalachians. In order to get some money from the colonists to pay for the wars that Britain had waged on their behalf, the Sugar Act of 1764 assessed a tax of three pence per gallon on molasses. However, very little of this duty was ever collected: The colonists were very unsympathetic to the plight of the British treasury.

Still attempting to get more money out of the colonies, the Stamp Act of 1765 provided for

*Note that this Navigation Act was to be repeated years later with the passage of the Jones Act in the United States, which requires that shipping among American ports must be done in American flag carriers. If you want to know the results of that act, all you have to do is see how expensive food and manufactured goods are in Hawaii. The shipping costs are outrageously high relative to what they would be without the Jones Act.

From the Royal American Magazine, 1774. (Historical Pictures Service, Chicago)

internal taxation—as the Stamp Act Congress called it, "taxation without representation." The British backed down, Pitt made his famous speech to the Parliament to repeal the Stamp Act and also to modify the Sugar Act. Note that the Stamp Act crisis generated a feeing of unity within the colonies because the act applied uniformly to all of them. When the Townsend Acts were passed in 1769, putting duties on glass, and lead in paint, the colonists boycotted English commodities. The results were impressive. The purchase of British goods was reduced by about 50 percent. This caused the British to back down again and to retreat into an uneasy truce which lasted until the Boston Tea Party of 1773. The colonists were boycotting the British East India Trading Company so that the company was accumulating larger and larger stocks of unsold tea. In order to help it out, the British Parliament lowered the duty on East India tea so that it had the same price as smuggled tea. The colonists didn't like this at all because they didn't want a British monopoly on the sales of that product. They showed their wrath by dumping a shipload of tea into the water.

Essentially, the period of negotiation ended in 1773. The colonists first found out that they were a united group after the Stamp Act got them riled up enough to hold the Stamp Act Congress. They also became cocky when they found out after the boycott of British goods that they could do without 50 percent of English imports. The colonists demanded and got sovereignty. The "shot heard 'round the world" on April 19, 1775, finally led them to what they wanted. A question remains, however, regarding their economic situation. Were the mercantilist restrictions placed on the colonies by the British Crown actually detrimental to their economic health? To this we now turn.

Definitions of New Terms

MERCANTILISM: an economic doctrine which preaches that a nation becomes better off by acquiring wealth, generally in the form of gold or silver. Modern-day advocates of mercantilism indicate that it is better to export more than one imports.

PRICE INELASTICITY: a characteristic of the demand for some goods and services. If that demand is price inelastic, a large change in price leads to a relatively small change in the quantity demanded. In other words, the quantity demanded is very unresponsive to price changes.

Chapter Summary

1. As Europe developed its market economy, a philosophy of mercantilism emerged in which the only way to obtain political power was supposedly to obtain wealth consisting mainly of precious metals. Such a mercantilist philosophy led European nations to desire new colonies.
2. Most colonies in America were private ventures that were started by individuals who were lured by profits.
3. Relatively inexpensive labor was always a problem in the original colonies. In order to get manpower into the New World, a combination of the following different methods was used: headrights, land grants, indentured servants, and slavery.
4. In the beginning, the colonists' comparative advantage lay in agricultural production.
5. The colonies developed differently, however. The South had a relative concentration of population; it developed exports which were complementary to English production, such as indigo, tobacco, and rice. The plantation system was particularly suitable for the production of rice and tobacco.
6. The Middle Colonies specialized in livestock and grain production but did not trade with England so much as with southern Europe and the Indies.
7. New Englanders started exporting codfish, whale oil, and timbers and then later on became efficient shipbuilders.
8. Foreign trade was an important source of American income from the very beginning. However, England started restricting certain aspects of that trade as early as 1660 with the passage of the Navigation Acts.
9. Other British restrictions, such as what the colonists called "taxation without representation," eventually led to rebellion against the Crown's rule.

Questions for Thought and Discussion

1. Can you translate current attempts at increasing America's exports and decreasing America's imports into mercantilist philosophy?
2. Although the colonies had relatively few slaves in the beginning, what do you think was happening in the rest of the Western Hemisphere? (Actually, slavery was much more important in the Caribbean Islands and in South America.)
3. Why would someone voluntarily become an indentured servant?
4. Colonial America had huge quantities of land; relative to other countries, America still does. Does this mean that her comparative advantage was and still is necessarily in the production of agricultural products?
5. Why would a dairy farmer pour milk into the road to illustrate his desire for higher prices? What economic principle would he be demonstrating?

A MAN OF COMMON SENSE

Benjamin Franklin (1706–1790)

Statesman, Printer, Scientist, and Writer

"REMEMBER THAT *time* is money. He that can earn ten shillings a day by his labour, and goes abroad, or sits idle, one half of that day, though he spends but sixpence during his diversion of idleness, ought not to reckon *that* his only expense; he has really spent, or rather thrown away, five shillings besides." Such were the words of Benjamin Franklin in his *Advice to a Young Tradesman,* published in 1748. A better example of keen understanding of the opportunity cost of one's time would be hard to find. Franklin was a practical thinker and came up with what we can now interpret as some pretty good economics.

To be sure, his aphorisms must have been colored by his strict Calvinist upbringing. The true Calvinist was a driven man, described by British economist R. H. Tawney as: "Tempered by self-examination, self-discipline, self-control, he is the practical ascetic, whose victories are won not in the cloister, but on the battlefield, in the counting house, and in the market." Calvin himself referred to God as the "great task maker," and looked around for tasks man should undertake. Ben Franklin claimed that he was a freethinker, but the continual exhortations he got from his father —"Seest thou a man diligent in his business. He shall stand before kings"—must have had some effect.

The young Ben was born and raised in Boston. Family funds were insufficient for him to aim at Harvard, so he turned his hand to printing and went to Philadelphia in 1723, then decided he needed to perfect his printing knowledge in London, where he spent two years doing so and living like a bohemian. Within a few years he began to prosper as a master printer. His simple style and great clarity in writing also started to bring in its just rewards. *Poor Richard's Almanac,* published annually between 1732 and 1757, was one of Franklin's most profitable enterprises, selling 10,000 copies a year. At the tender age of 23, Franklin wrote his first words on economics: *A Modest Inquiry into the Nature and Necessity of a Paper Currency* (1729). Coincidentally, Franklin was the first one to start printing Pennsylvania's paper currency, and he stayed in this business for quite some time.

Franklin was a crusader and also a good businessman. He introduced printing and newspaper publication to many communities throughout the colonies. He also helped start the present University of Pennsylvania in 1751. Then he was named Deputy Postmaster General of the colonies, a post that he held until fired from his job because of the Hutchinson's letters scandal in 1773 and '74. The scandal involved letters written by one Thomas Hutchinson, who at the time of their writing was Chief Justice of Massachusetts. They contained pleas to a member of the British government for troops and abridgment of American liberties. Franklin had obtained the letters and sent them to a friend late in 1772. The friend was not supposed to publish them, but he did, and during the ensuing scandal the House of Commons quickly got rid of the Deputy Postmaster.

During this period Franklin started much of his scientific study and also his political, philosophical, and economic training. Venturing abroad once again, he spent six weeks in Scotland with the philosopher/historian David Hume, and on at least one occasion was able to converse with Adam Smith, the author of *The Wealth of Nations.*

Franklin continuously argued for the advantages of trade with the British Empire. He was convinced, perhaps after his discussion with Adam Smith, that voluntary trade benefits both parties, and that the more trade there is, the better off people will be.

Franklin, along with Samuel Morris, was an original signer of the deed of settlement of the Philadelphia Contributorship, an insurance plan, dating back to 1752, for members against all fire hazards. The ingenious Franklin and Morris got the contributorship to offer rewards to those organizations which put out fires on their insured properties. But competition became so great that a notice was issued: No more rewards would be given unless fire fighters started paying more attention to fighting the fire than to fighting each other.

Ben Franklin was also one of the first advertisers in America. When he started his *General Magazine,* he became disappointed that businessmen did not believe that advertising could bring better results. Franklin himself advertised his own Pennsylvania Fire Place. The copy he wrote was persuasive: He criticized ordinary fire places because they caused drafts that made "women . . . get cold in the head, rheums, and defluxions, which fall into their jaws and gums have destroyed early many a fine set of teeth."

During the Revolution, Franklin helped draft the Declaration of Independence, which he signed. He was also the diplomatic agent sent to France for the new republic. Then he was chosen commissioner in 1781 to negotiate peace with Great Britain. Finally, he took part in the federal Constitutional Convention.

To practical men, especially the officers of savings banks ("a penny saved is a penny earned"), Ben Franklin seemed the summation of good sense and morality. To others he appeared to be a colorless and materialistic opportunist. But as John Adams once said, his "reputation was more universal than that of Leibniz, Newton, or Voltaire and he was the first civilized American."

ISSUE IV

WAS ENGLAND RIPPING OFF THE COLONISTS?

Mercantilism and Its Effects

The Navigation Acts

The setting is seventeenth-century England. The Dutch have just invented a more efficient sailing ship. The British are afraid that they will lose out in the developing shipping industry throughout the world. The Navigation Acts are passed. They require that all goods entering English ports must be carried either by ships of the exporting nation or by British ships. This was the beginning of a number of mercantilist restrictions that England placed on not only her trading partners, but her colonies.

The Rest of the Restrictions

Note that the Navigation Acts were originally intended as a response to the attempt by the Dutch to get control of worldwide shipping trade. Additional restrictions on trade and colonial economic life soon were imposed, however. After 1660, tobacco had to be shipped to England, where it was either consumed or reexported to other countries. Prior to this date, the colonists could engage in direct trade with all who wished to buy the tobacco that

came from Virginia and Maryland.

Tobacco was just one of a list of so-called **enumerated articles** that had to be shipped only to England. There were further restrictions which required certain enumerated articles to come first to English ports from other countries before they could be shipped to the colonies.

There were out-and-out prohibitions on the production of, for example, fabricated iron and hats. This was England's attempt to limit domestic manufacturing in the colonies in order that manufacturing in the mother country would not face competition from colonial entrepreneurs.

Part of the mercantilist credo required that tariffs be put on the imports of many goods into England proper. However, for such items as tobacco, lumber, pig iron, and silk, the colonies got a preferential tariff. The Navigation Acts were not solely, therefore, negative for the colonial population. This also was true for the bounties or subsidies that England provided for certain products that it lacked; as we mentioned in the previous chapter, the growth of indigo that could be used in dye was fostered

by per-unit bounties paid for production. This was also true for naval stores in the South and for silk.

How to Answer the Question

While a simple enumeration of the mercantilist restrictions on colonial trade would lead one to the immediate conclusion that the colonists were being exploited, it is not necessarily correct to assume this. We have to look at all aspects of the problem. The colonists, of course, generally only saw the negative side of British rule. As dispassionate observers, however, we should be able to come up with a balance sheet showing not only the costs that were incurred by colonial rule from England, but also the benefits. Moreover, we cannot compare what actually happened to the colonists with what the colonists would have liked to happen. For in order to come up with a valid analysis, we have to compare what happened with what realistically *could* have happened. We want to ask ourselves, "Would the colonists have been better off if they had been independent at an earlier date compared to what actually happened to them by remaining under the thumb of England?" Otherwise stated, would the growth of material living standards in the colonies have been faster if they had had independence at an earlier date under the same world trade conditions? In order to find the answer to this question, one of the things we can do is compare the economic activity after the Revolution to the economic activity before the Revolution. And that is what we will do now.

The Navigation Acts Again

Remember that the Navigation Acts required that one of the two nations dealing in trade had to ship the goods. The colonies were considered part of England and they, therefore, *benefited* from this aspect of the acts, for the acts were meant to keep the Dutch out of world trading competition as a shipping nation. Of course, to the extent that the American colonies were efficient shippers relative to other countries in the world, the restriction was simply irrelevant: They would have underpriced the Dutch and got all the business anyway.

After the Revolution they were worse off than before because they were very limited in terms of how much they could trade with other parts of the world, such as the British West Indies, after they left British rule. Because of this particular aspect of the mercantile restrictions, then, we can conjecture that colonial shipping incomes would have been lower had independence occurred at an earlier date.

Tobacco

The colonists were convinced that the requirement to ship tobacco to England for reexport to the rest of the world was detrimental to their wealth positions. However, we found that after the Revolution, when in fact the colonists were no longer under this restriction, they continued to ship 90 percent of their tobacco to England, some of which was later shipped to Western Europe. Compare this percentage with the 98 percent that they shipped while they were under the British rule. It is obvious that England possessed a certain amount of monopoly power in the purchasing of Virginia and Maryland's tobacco crop. But this was not necessarily true with other items. Nonetheless, after the Revolution, two-thirds of the exports to Britain were reshipped to other countries. The explanation for this phenomenon is not hard to find: The colonists were by and large of English stock; they spoke English; and they were familiar with English customs, laws, and prices. The transactions costs of dealing with English commercial interests were indeed lower than those that would be incurred when dealing with non-English commercial organizations. With or without mercantile restrictions, the colonists would probably have shipped just about as much as they did to England anyway. So on this score,

we cannot attribute very high costs to the colonists for remaining under British control.

Direct Prohibitions

The direct prohibition on the production of fabricated iron, hats, and other manufactured goods certainly had some influence on the way the colonies developed. However, we cannot expect that they had very much influence. After all, rich, fertile land was the abundant resource in the Americas, certainly not capital and labor, which were extremely scarce. Industry could not have started even without specific restrictions on manufacturing in the colonies. After the Revolution there was a continuation of imports of fabricated iron and other restricted items anyway. Moreover, it's hard to imagine that if beaver hats had been produced in the colonies, an industrial revolution would have begun.

Incidentally, the urban population during the late colonial experience numbered at most 6 percent, so an industrial society couldn't have been built up much sooner anyway. There was at that time a great deal of home manufacturing, which was not touched by any of the mercantilist restrictions. On the whole, then, the specific prohibitions against manufactured goods cost the colonists very little in terms of a reduction in their economic welfare.

The Benefits of Being a Colony

We have yet to enumerate the possible benefits that the colonists reaped from being under the colonial rule of the British Empire. We have already briefly mentioned what some of the specific benefits under the mercantilist regulations were, the most obvious being a bounty on indigo, naval stores, silk, and to a lesser extent, lumber. Although the direct payments to colonists in bounties do not indicate the actual net gain to them, we can get an upper limit on the benefit from this system. The data obtained by Lawrence Harper* show that, in total, the bounties paid on colonial products added up to about 65,000 pounds, or at the exchange ratio of pounds to dollars in those days, $324,000. This particular benefit is dwarfed by an even larger one which comes under the title of military protection.

Military Protection

Before the Revolution, the colonists had little or nothing to do with protection of their property and life, for all of this was provided by the British government.

*Lawrence Harper, "The Effect of the Navigation Acts on the Thirteen Colonies," in *The Era of the American Revolution*, R. B. Morris, editor, New York: Columbia University Press, 1939.

In the beginning, the British helped to fight off the Spanish, the Indians, and the French. Moreover, American ships were allowed to sail to the Barbary Coast without fear of the infamous Barbary pirates, for Britain had in effect bought off the pirates from attacking its own ships as well as those of its colonies. We can get some idea of what the benefit of British protection should have been valued at by looking at what the new government spent for national defense after the ratification of the Constitution. Its annual outlay was in excess of $2 million, an outlay which continued to grow as the population grew. Had the colonists become independent earlier, they would have had to provide for their own military and naval protection. The burden of defense would have been on them alone.

Additionally, Britain took care of much of the administrative work in the colonies. The colonies did not, for example, have to conduct their own foreign policy, pay for missions abroad for ministers, and the like.

The Actual Cost of Mercantilism

If we were to look only at the figures presented by Lawrence Harper, we would find that the total cost of mercantilism to the colonists was about $1 to $3 per

capita. When we compare this figure to the $60 to $70 of income per capita of the day, we realize that mercantilism at most cost 5 percent, according to Harper's figures, and at least 1.5 percent. There were many things wrong with what he did in obtaining these statistics, so we might regard the above estimate as an upper bound. Harper, for example, gave no dollar figure to the value of military aid and naval protection bestowed upon the colonies by the British Crown.

More complete computation yields a *net* cost of $2,600,000, or $1.20 per capita, in 1770 and an average *net* cost of $2,255,000, or $1.24 per capita, over the period 1763–72.* This amounts to only 1.2 percent of estimated national income.

That is not to say that the colonists would have been economically better off if they had never obtained independence. And in fact we really don't have enough data to answer categorically the question posed by the title of this historical issue. In any event, the colonists were not getting ripped off as much as many historians believed before the actual data were carefully investigated. The

*R. P. Thomas, "A Quantitative Approach to the Study of the Effects of British Imperial Policy upon Colonial Welfare: Some Preliminary Findings," *Journal of Economic History,* December 1965, Volume 25, Table 2, p. 637.

costs of mercantilism range between 1.2 percent and 5 percent of per capita income. This figure doesn't seem so bad when one considers the benefits. The colonists were quick to take advantage of any gain that mercantilism allowed them, but they were even quicker to complain of any costs that came along with such advantages. It is only when looking at all the facts that we can determine a correct conclusion. It is rarely useful to ask someone what they think has happened to them, or what they feel actually happened. A researcher must somehow dispassionately look at what actually happened and then compare it with what *could* have happened given the *actual* situation of the time.

Don't Look at Just Averages

We also have to be careful about looking only at averages. Above we have calculated that the average net cost of British imperialism was probably close to 1 percent, but in any event never exceeded 5 percent of estimated national income. This doesn't seem like enough to warrant a revolution. However, the costs that we outlined above bore differently on different sectors of the economy. For example, the restriction on no further colonization west of the Appalachians hurt New England merchants the least and Southern landowners the most. Not only did it eliminate the possibility of obtaining increased land for cultivation, it destroyed the possibility

for continuing speculation in land sales. It is not surprising, then, that George Washington, who was one of the biggest landowners in the colonies and who had wished to own lots of land in Ohio, was one of the staunchest supporters of the Revolution. In fact, if we were to look at who organized the Revolutionary War, we would find that they were the ones most hurt by the mercantilist restrictions. They had a lot to gain and little to lose by shucking off British rule.

At the time, Samuel Adams observed that fully one-third of the population opposed the war, one-third supported it, and one-third were the "great silent majority." The vocal "minority" obviously got what it wanted.

Definitions of New Terms

ENUMERATED ARTICLES: articles which had to be shipped only to England from the colonies. Also articles which had to be shipped to England and then reshipped to the colonies as imports.

Questions for Thought and Discussion

1. Can you think of a case showing that English rule greatly retarded the growth in income in the colonies?
2. Why do you think Samuel Adams called the one-third who didn't say anything about the Revolution the "great silent majority"?

From Unification to Secession

T HE YEAR 1776 produced the Declaration of Independence, but it wasn't until 1783 that the Treaty of Paris saw the termination of hostilities with England (which hostilities, as we shall see, broke out again some thirty years later in the War of 1812). During the Revolutionary battles, the new nation was continuously faced with the economic problems of war—among the most pressing of which was how to finance it.

FINANCING THE WAR

Even though the war cost the United States only $100 million in gold (a mere pittance to us today when our defense budget exceeds $80 billion per year), the Continental Congress had difficulty raising even that sum. For in the very weak Articles of Confederation which it drew up, the Continental Congress did not give itself the power to tax. However, Congress was able to borrow almost $8 million in gold from abroad, over three-fourths of it coming from France and the remainder from Holland and Spain. Domestically, about $10 million was raised through loans from individuals and businesses. Then the Continental Congress began requisitioning the states, but it obtained less than $6 million in that manner. The states were very quick to ignore the request of Congress.

The States

The states themselves started to raise funds for the war by selling bonds and issuing paper money. Then, in 1777, the states began levying taxes, but the amount obtained was indeed trivial. And, even though later on the states promised to reimburse the losers, they confiscated Tory property. In this manner they were able to raise a considerable amount of money.

Continental Dollars

The Continental Congress authorized an issuance of almost $200 million in paper currency during the four-year period commencing with the Revolution in 1775. But during that period this paper money actually accounted for a little more than $40 million of the central government's income. Since nobody was really sure whether these "Continentals" were going to be redeemed in gold or silver after the Revolution, their value steadily declined. Congress was not strong enough to declare that these notes could be used as legal tender. Instead, it merely asked the states to penalize persons who refused to take them in exchange for goods and services. By 1781, Continentals were worth 1/500th of their original face value. Quite an inflation! Part of it was caused by people's lack of faith in the dollars, but part was caused by the large increase in the number of them issued.

Generally there is a relationship between large changes in the money supply and the price level. It's been called the **quantity theory of prices.** Basically, it states that for a relatively fixed amount of output, if people don't change their habits about using money (or cash), a change in the money supply will lead to a proportionate change in the price level. (Remember that we talked about this in reference to the sixteenth-century influx of New World gold and silver into Europe.)

Looked at another way, the quantity theory tells us the obvious: If the supply of dollars goes up drastically, the value (purchasing power) of those dollars will fall. The same, of course, is true of any good. The more abundant the supply, the lower the price that can be obtained for that good. The price of dollars is merely what one gives up to hold them. If one gives up less than formerly, the price, or value, of dollars has fallen.

STRUGGLING UNDER THE ARTICLES OF CONFEDERATION

The Treaty of Paris gave the United States all the territory east of the Mississippi between Canada and Florida, in addition to the right to navigate the Mississippi, even though this was not necessarily worth very much since Spain controlled the mouth of the river at New Orleans. Additionally, the United States got fishing rights within British territorial waters in the North Atlantic. As we shall see, the Articles of Confederation did not provide a strong enough political framework in which the American states could grow to become one of the richest nations in the world. There were also lots of economic hardships suffered after the war because of certain things that had happened. To these we now turn.

Traditional trade patterns had been disrupted because, for one thing, the Treaty of Paris ended the era of mercantilism for the colonies. As we stated in Issue IV, American ships could no longer trade legally with the British West Indies, and ships built in America could not be bought by England because of the Navigation Acts. (Remember, New England was no longer part of the British Empire.) There was also an attempt by the West Indies to reduce its imports from the United States. The result was that our export trade fell off drastically during and after the Revolution. But we still had many things that we needed to import because we were far from being a self-sufficient nation. Consequently, there was a deficit in our balance of trade with the rest of the world. The value of our exports was less than the value of our imports.

In order to pay for this excess of imports over exports, we shipped out large amounts of specie—gold and silver—to other countries. The result was a reduction in the U.S. money supply and with it a fall in prices. This made American merchants unhappy because they had not anticipated the intensity of the **deflation**—continuous falling prices—that occurred after the Revolution. Moreover, they were unhappy because the British resumed large-scale exports to the United States. In fact, the British were accused of **dumping**—that is, selling their goods in our country at lower prices than they were sold at in Britain.

What we saw in the United States was a "depression" between the years 1785 and 1786. One should be careful, however, in equating the depressions in the early years of U.S. independence with depressions and recessions of more modern times. Today a recession or depression is usually felt by the vast majority of Americans. But in those early years most of the population was engaged in farming. A fall in prices hurt them, but they didn't become unemployed. Changes in business activity weren't generally catastrophic.

The export sector was, however, indeed hurt. It has been estimated that the value of per capita exports after the Revolution was one-half the value of those before the Revolution. It is important to note that we had very little political power at the beginning of the 1780s. Very few foreign countries had yet accepted us as a viable nation in the world economy, and they therefore would not engage in treaty discussions with us. There were financial difficulties throughout the world when we engaged in trade.

THE EFFECTS OF DEFLATION ARE SOON FELT

As the price level fell unexpectedly, there was growing unrest among debtors in our nation. It is not very hard to figure out why. Let's say, for example, that farmers had borrowed money to purchase land and tools at, say, a 10 percent rate of interest. Had the price level remained stable, that 10 percent rate of interest would have been paid off in dollars that had the same value when the loan was repaid as when the loan had been taken out. The **principal** of the loan—that is, the total amount borrowed—when repaid would also have the same value in purchasing power as it had when it was borrowed. Now look at the situation when we have an *unexpected* fall in the price of goods and services in our economy. Debtors found that they had to pay interest and repayment of the loan with dollars that had a higher purchasing power than when they borrowed them. The actual (real) rate of interest that they were forced to pay for the loans they had taken out before the deflation started was now actually higher than stipulated in the contracts they had signed. Notice that the key to understanding the unrest of debtors during this period of deflation was the fact that the deflation was *unanticipated*. Had it been fully anticipated, debtors would have only been willing to pay a lower rate of interest, and creditors would have been willing to accept that lower rate, knowing full well that they would have been paid back in dollars with a higher purchasing power.

SHAYS' REBELLION AND THE NEED TO REVAMP THE ARTICLES OF CONFEDERATION

By 1786, in the city of Concord, Massachusetts, the scene of one of the first battles of the Revolution, there were three times as many people in debtors' prison as there were for all other crimes combined. In Worcester County, the ratio was even higher—20 to 1. The prisoners were generally small farmers who couldn't pay their debts. In August of 1786, mobs of musket-bearing farmers seized county courthouses and did not allow the trials of debtors to continue. The rebels got Daniel Shays, a captain from the Continental Army, to lead them. Shays' men launched an attack on the federal arsenal at Springfield, but were repulsed. The rebellion didn't stop there but continued to grow into the winter. Finally, George Washington wrote to a friend:

For God's sake, tell me what is the cause of these commotions? Do they proceed from licentiousness,

British influence disseminated by the Tories, or real grievances which admit to redress? If the latter, why were they delayed until the public mind had become so agitated? If the former, why are not the powers of government tried at once?

What Shays' Rebellion did was demonstrate economic chaos and also show the weakness of the government under the Articles of Confederation. In order for the nation to grow and prosper in the world economy, it was necessary that a stronger central government be organized. So the Constitutional Convention was convened in Philadelphia in May 1787. The completed Constitution went into effect in March 1789. It was a necessary doctrine for the economic development of this nation.

THE ECONOMIC ASPECTS OF THE CONSTITUTION

Contained in Article 1, sections 8, 9, and 10 are the main economic provisions in the Constitution, without which it probably would have been impossible for many things to occur in this country. The Constitution reaffirmed the permanent nature of private property in terms of federal support of the institution. The additional three major categories of the economic provisions were taxation, control over money and credit, and restrictions over commerce, as well as the ability of the federal government to establish treaties with foreign powers which were to be held paramount over all laws made by the several states.

Taxation

One of the major weaknesses of the Confederation had been the inability of the Continental Congress to levy taxes against the population. Although this was perhaps more of a political problem than an economic one, without this ability the United States never could have had a large, organized central government.

Money and Credit

Even though state banks were still allowed to exist, the federal government was empowered to "coin money, regulate the value thereof, and of foreign coin, in addition to fixing the standard of weights and measures."* Implicit in this section of the Constitution is the ability of the federal government to issue a national currency. This was important for the development of commercial activities and a market in which the buying and selling of debts and shares in companies could occur. This kind of trading occurs in a **capital market.** The Constitution also allows the federal government to redeem the debts of the "several" (individual) states. This further allowed a capital market to develop. As an aside, Congress decided to redeem state bonds at their original par value, even though they were selling at a substantial discount. In the process, they created a larger national debt than would have existed otherwise. What the government could have done was purchase those bonds on the open market. Then nobody would have been hurt and nobody would have been treated to a windfall gain by being paid more for the bonds than had originally been paid for them by the then current owners. Note, however, that approximately 80 percent of the debt at that time was held by U.S. citizens, so the redemption of the debt at par value in effect only meant that there was a redistribution of wealth in favor of bond holders. We did not, in fact, give much of it away to foreigners. Also, the bond redemption helped restore the faith and credit of the central government.

Regulation of Commerce

The Constitution decreed that all import duties should be the same for all of the several states, and further, that there could be no export duties. This was to insure that the states could not set

*This power is the basis for the forced conversion to the metric system of measurement that is soon to be made.

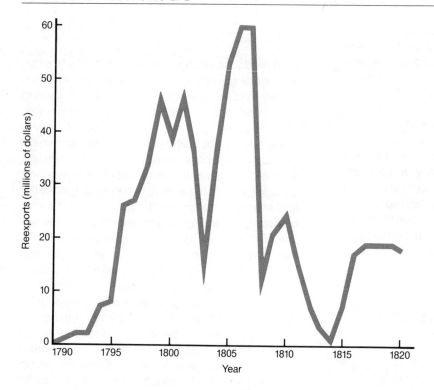

FIGURE 5–1

REEXPORT CYCLES

Reexports were merchandise sent to the United States and not used here, but instead sent on to another country. When the French and English started fighting, our reexport trade started to jump by leaps and bounds, reaching a peak just before the Embargo of 1807.
(*Source: Historical Statistics,* p. 538.)

up barriers against trade between each other. This was a way of fostering *inter*regional trade, as well as *intra*regional trade. The Constitution effectively gave the federal government the right to police interstate commerce, which was at that time limited mainly to coastal trade.

RECOVERY AND THE GROWTH OF SHIPPING

The situation at the end of the 1780s was one of economic recovery from the depression of 1785 to 1787. In 1789 a revolution began in France. Then, in 1793, the French and English started battling again. The series of wars between the two arch enemies lasted until 1815. Their demand for American exports quickly rose; by 1795, exports of American goods had doubled over the 1793 level. The French were at this time unable to ply the Atlantic in trade, so the United States became one of the main shipping concerns in the world.

We began to reexport numerous goods because we were a neutral power. That is to say, nations would ship goods to us which we would then reship to the belligerents. For example, in 1790 we reexported only 3 percent of the goods which we imported, but by 1805 we were reexporting 60 percent.

As can be seen in Figure 5–1, the reexport trade grew by leaps and bounds. So too, of course, did total exports, until certain political actions prevented us from exporting any more. In 1790, almost 60 percent of our trade was carried on in American ships; in the years 1805 and 1806, it was just about 100 percent. This was, in fact, an era of unusually intense commercial and trading activity, as well as shipping activity. For Americans the war in Europe was indeed lucky. It stimulated the U.S. economy and brought us prosperity just when we needed it most.

We were benefiting from our neutral position in a world of belligerents at that time. There was also demand for new ships by both American and foreign merchants. American ships were bigger and better built in those years than they had been earlier, and we were prospering from shipbuilding. All of this additional activity in the commercial and transportation sector added to our national income. In fact, by 1800 income from all forms of trading and transportation was more than 25 percent of total national output.

We must remember, however, that the prosperity of these times was not necessarily a basis for subsequent development. There was no similar increase of prosperity in the interior of the United States. And, of course, a nation as large as ours cannot generally grow by merely becoming an efficient shipper for the rest of the world. But note that some historians contend that the profits made from commercial endeavors during this period were the source of investment funds that brought on later development.

THE END OF THE COMMERCIAL BOOM

England and France had a temporary peace during 1803 and our commercial shipping boom slowed down for a while. When they started fighting again, things started improving for Americans, until both sides decided to deny neutral ships access to enemy ports. About 1500 American ships were seized. So Congress enacted the Embargo of 1807, which prohibited American vessels from sailing to foreign ports. This was an attempt to force England and France to respect American neutrality. The results of the Embargo were impressive: As we see in Figure 5–1, reexports fell drastically; total exports dropped by almost 80 percent

when the Embargo was enacted. Pressure from merchants, sailors, and commercial interests led to the repeal of the act in 1809. Instead, the Non-Importation Act was passed, which prohibited trade specifically with Great Britain, France, and their territories.

Eventually all sides got carried away and the War of 1812 was declared. England was our enemy again. It was largely a naval war, one in which the British navy blockaded the entire coast of the United States and seized more than 1000 American ships. Exports fell to practically nothing.

THE RISE OF INDUSTRY

The blockading of American waters gave a shot in the arm to American home industry. Before 1812, there had been almost no manufacturing in the United States. Only 7 percent of the population lived in urban areas. We did have a textile industry to speak of in 1800, but even by 1810 two-thirds of it was done in the home. There had been some heroic attempts by Samuel Slater to develop a mechanized weaving industry in Providence, Rhode Island, in the 1790s. None of the increased commercial activities or promise of fortunes got anybody really interested in the potential of the textile industry until the Embargo of 1807. After all, as we have pointed out many times in this book, resources will flow into areas where they have the highest relative rates of return. Entrepreneurs in the days before the Embargo saw their highest rates of return in reexporting, shipbuilding, and general trading. It was commercial rather than industrial or manufacturing interest.

Development of the Textile Industry

The salutary effects that the Embargo had on manufacturing were quickly felt: In 1808 there were only 15 textile mills, but by 1809 there were almost 90. This rapid multiplication of mills demonstrated how little capital was needed to start one. Few of these new mills survived, however, after the Peace of Ghent in 1814 terminated the War of 1812. For Britain started massive exports again and was again accused of dumping—selling goods at a lower price in America than was charged the English public. The textile industry had to wait until the Waltham system of cloth weaving developed by Mr. Lowell was better refined. His use of power mills and a system that used relatively low cost, well-supervised labor is what caused the growth of the industry later on.

Britain had already been experiencing an Industrial Revolution. American businessmen started to borrow the English know-how for producing certain products. We had to adapt their techniques, however, to suit our situation. There was a relative scarcity of labor in this country, so labor-saving machinery was desired by entrepreneurs. This may have led to our initial desire to standardize parts for the things we made. The British were to follow us, for example, in standardizing the parts for firearms. In fact, they were amazed when they saw what we were able to do.

Iron Industry

Our iron-making industry got off to a very slow start but eventually developed into one of our major manufacturing activities, although we lagged behind in the production of bar iron. After the introduction of puddling and rolling techniques (which had already been in use three decades before they were picked up in the United States), our technology of iron making did not change until the introduction of the Bessemer converter in the late 1860s and the open-hearth furnace method in the 1870s and 1880s.

By the start of the Civil War, manufacturing produced a substantial part of national income. In fact, it had risen to 60 percent of the product generated by the agricultural sectors. By 1850, the productive capacity of the United States which was devoted to the making of **capital equipment**—machines and the like—represented a higher percentage of total production than in any other nation in the world. By the beginning of the Civil War, we were indeed on the way to becoming fully industrialized.

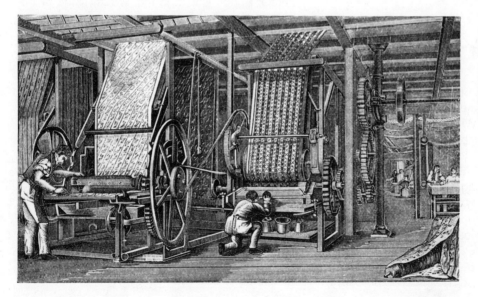

The cotton textile industry became a part of New England industrial life. This scene shows calico being printed. Calico was a coarse, plain-weave cotton cloth first imported from Calicut, India to England. (Historical Pictures Service, Chicago)

Transportation Network

Two important features on the economic landscape added to the increased industrialization of our country, which in turn further increased the real income that was available for Americans: They were the development of a transportation network and the expansion of the capital market. The development of a transportation network expanded the size of the market and allowed for increased specialization—for, as Adam Smith once said, "The division of labor is limited by the extent of the market": the larger the market, the larger the degree of specialization possible. Generally, increased specialization leads to higher real income. Of course, that is not the sole reason we had an income of $150 per capita in 1860—perhaps the equivalent of $600–700 in today's money, which was at that time higher than that of any other place in the world. But it did have something to do with it. The second feature which allowed for the growth of the economy from the Revolution until the Civil War was, as we said above, a large expansion in the capital market—in the credit flows and in the money available for industrial expansion. Let's first look at how things developed in the world of money.

MONEY, MONEY, MONEY

Remember that a key provision of the Constitution is that the federal government regulates the money supply. It didn't do a very good job of this at first, but there were some important attempts at providing for a stable monetary system in the early United States. In 1791, when Alexander Hamilton was 34 years old, he was appointed Secretary of the Treasury (not bad). He wielded a power in this nation that was second only to that of the President. His financial program reflected his belief in a powerful national government. He wrote a lot and had great influence, particularly in commercial and banking sectors. In the thirtieth Federalist paper, he pointed out that:

Money is, with propriety, considered as the vital principal of the body politic; as that which sustains its life and motion, and enables it to perform its most essential functions.

He suggested that a basic unit of value be established, and so the Mint Act of 1792 was passed. The dollar was to be that basic unit of value, and the decimal system was to be used (we fortunately didn't use the old British pounds, shillings, and pence).

Hamilton also wanted a national bank:

The tendency of a national bank is to increase public and private credit. Industry is increased, commodities are multiplied, agriculture and manufacturing flourish, and herein consists the true wealth and prosperity of a state. (Letter to Robert Morris, 1781)

FIRST U.S. BANK

So the First Bank of the United States was chartered in 1791 for a period of 20 years. It was a private corporation governed by 25 directors and had a capital of $10 million, of which the federal government provided 20 percent. This bank served as the government's depository. It also made loans to the government and to private individuals and companies. It was profitable, averaging 8 percent per year rate of return for those who invested in it. It died, however, when its charter was not renewed in 1811; the assets of the bank were bought by one Stephen Girard of Philadelphia.

This was an unfortunate time for the bank to close its doors because during the War of 1812 treasury finances were in bad shape, since no central depository existed. At that time, there was a great increase in unregulated local banking. In general, specie payments were abandoned: That is, nobody was willing to pay off their debts in hard currency—gold or silver. So the cry went up for another bank, which appeared in 1816.

THE SECOND BANK OF THE UNITED STATES

This bank was also chartered for a period of 20 years. It started out with a capital stock three and a half times that of the First Bank of the United States. The government again provided 20 percent. The Second Bank was established with the condition that it would not intervene in the expansion of the economy that had already started. From the very beginning, the Bank acted perversely against the welfare of the economy. Right after it had been chartered, trouble started in the economy. The price of cotton dropped, and farmers began to have troubles. Instead of countering these problems with expansionary activities, the Bank from 1818 to 1819 contracted its deposits. This wasn't the only thing that happened, because at the same time we had to pay off the debt for the Louisiana Purchase. So quite a bit of specie flowed overseas, helping contract our money supply in a way that the public did not anticipate.

Finally, there was the Panic of 1819. The Bank completely stopped the payment of specie and there were bank failures throughout the economy. The price level was falling drastically at the time. However, the extent of this crisis should not be exaggerated in a country that was highly agricultural. True, the commercial sector was hit very hard, but certainly not the largely self-sufficient agricultural sector. The first president of the Bank, who was considered incompetent, was ousted after the Panic of 1819. Two later presidents, Langdon Sheves (1819–1823) and Nicholas Biddle (1823–1836) were considered more competent. In fact, during their two terms, there was an attempt by the Bank to increase the money supply by issuing bank notes for the whole country.

Jackson Attacks

However, there were political currents set up, particularly at the end of Biddle's appointment, to get rid of the Second Bank. President Jackson took office in 1829. He began immediately to attack the Second Bank of the United States. But a committee that was formed in the House of Representatives affirmed the constitutionality of the Bank in spite of Jackson's request that it do otherwise. The Bank of the United States had indeed developed some sort of national currency because it had a large number of branches, and U.S. bank notes were in circulation everywhere. The rate of exchange between U.S. bank notes and all other currencies was the same throughout the nation, more or less. Congress apparently saw this as a good thing, and Jackson's attempt at that time to get the Bank closed down for unconstitutionality failed.

He therefore had to develop another strategy. He made the Bank into a national bank that was different from what it was originally intended to be. He forced it to become a noncredit-creating institution, not unlike the savings and loan associations of today. What he wanted was a 100 percent reserve bank. That is, no credit or bank notes could be issued that were not backed by a sound deposit within the Bank itself. The Bank, then, would just become a transfer institution, although it could still do some regulation.

The Second Bank of the United States was, of course, not like a modern central bank because it couldn't really regulate the reserves of commercial banks and it couldn't generally support others in periods of financial crises. But by virtue of its size and the number of branches it had, it could exercise some control over the economy. It would ask for specie redemption from other banks from time to time to keep them "honest."

Biddle's big mistake was to apply for a recharter four years before the end of the Second Bank's original charter. The Act was passed in Congress in July 1832, but it was vetoed by Jackson. In 1836, the Second Bank was no more.

Inflation

The demise of the Second Bank brought with it many changes in the American banking scene. However, what happened after its failure may not necessarily have had anything to do with that particular event. We are speaking about the contraction of 1834 and the inflation of 1835, 1836, and part of 1837. Many historians believe that the inflation was caused by the fall of the Second Bank, which allowed for a rapid increase in the amount of paper currency available through a proliferation of wildcat banks. (These banks got

FIGURE 5-2

PRICES AND THE MONEY SUPPLY DURING THE DEMISE OF THE SECOND BANK

Prices rose sharply in 1835 and 1836. Although this rise has generally been attributed to the demise of the Second Bank and the proliferation of circulating money from wildcat banks, much of it was in fact due to increased specie, as can be seen in the bottom line. There had been a 100 percent increase in the 8 years prior to 1835. (*Source:* Hugh Rockoff, "Money, Prices, and Banks in the Jacksonian Era," in R. W. Fogel and S. L. Engerman, eds., *The Reinterpretation of American Economic History,* New York: Harper & Row, 1971, Table 1, p. 451.)

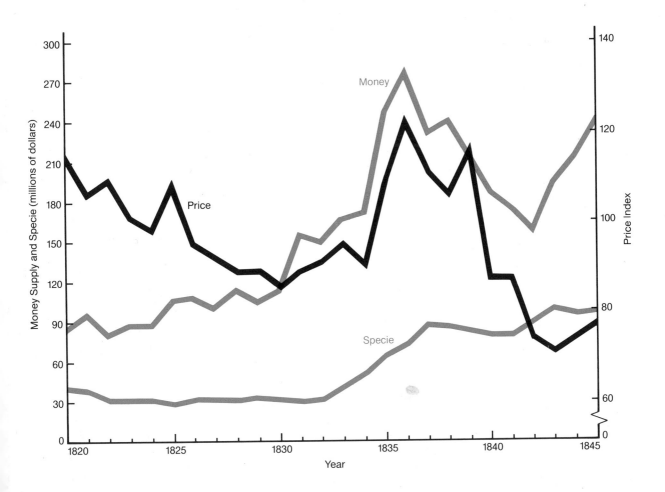

their names from the fact that they were so far out in the boondocks that only wildcats frequented them.) The evidence concerning the increase in the money supply and the increase in prices is fairly impressive. We see, for example, in Figure 5–2 that the money supply did indeed increase in 1835 and 1836. Then it dropped a little bit thereafter. In fact, from 1834 to 1835, the increase was almost 50 percent. Does this alone, however, mean that the U.S. Bank's demise was responsible? No, it doesn't: Other events were taking place.

International Economy

We were part of an international economy at that time. We had a gold standard which we adhered to, and this involved shipments of gold in and out of the country. These formed the basis of our circulating money supply, so it is here that one must also look to see if there was some sort of increase during the inflation that occurred at the demise of the Second Bank of the United States. Indeed, we find that there was a large increase in specie imports from Mexico. Britain and France were also periodically sending us specie, and we had stopped sending it out of the country to the Orient. If we look at the bottom line of Figure 5–2, we see that there was a tremendous specie jump between 1833 and 1834, and then again between 1834 and 1835, and 1835 on through 1837. We can say, therefore, that the demise of the Second Bank did not cause the inflation of 1835 and 1836.

TRANSPORTATION ON THE MOVE

One of the main deterrents to interregional trade in colonial times was the lack of cheap transportation among the colonies, except along the coast. This had to change if the United States was to become an integrated and ever-expanding market in which specialization could continuously occur. At first we turned to development of the most obvious methods of transportation: water-

ways and roads. There was rarely any federal assistance for the development of highways in those days because of some constitutional objections. Nonetheless, private companies did build a number of turnpikes. By 1810, there were 180 turnpike companies in New England alone. By 1813, there were about 1400 miles of privately built roads in New York, and by 1832 Pennsylvania had over 2000 miles.

Canals

Canals had disadvantages, such as freezing in the winter, but they had many advantages also. Mainly, they allowed for relatively cheap transportation among fixed points. The earliest canals weren't much, but they were a start. The greatest canal-building activity occurred between the War of 1812 and the Panic of 1837. The most famous canal, of course, is the Erie, which ran from the Hudson River near Albany, New York, to Buffalo on Lake Erie. Completed in 1825, it extended some 360 miles, and could accommodate 30-ton barges. There were, of course, many other canals, like those built in Pennsylvania, Delaware, Maryland, Ohio, Illinois, and Michigan.

The Steamboat

At the same time, the steamboat was being developed for upstream travel along the larger rivers, such as the Mississippi. In fact, the rapid development of steam engines was due to this use in transportation. Steam-powered ocean vessels were also used, but their effects on international trade were far less than previously thought by earlier historians. Sailing ships were to dominate the seas for many years, for trading at least.

The Railroads

By tapping the interior, New York's successful Erie Canal posed a threat to other eastern cities and their commercial interests. Baltimore emphasized

When the steam engine was married to the paddlewheel, big rivers took on a new life. Here we see "The Champions of the Mississippi" sometime during the nineteenth century. (Historical Pictures Service, Chicago)

the railroad because the canal was not completely practical for its needs. Of course, there were to be many mistakes with the use of this new transportation mechanism. For example, Baltimore tried to build its railroad over a mountain pass in a period when steam locomotives were not completely worked out in their design and application. Railroads did have advantages, though, and they were soon to be realized. They were speedier than canal transportation, they could be used in almost all weather, and they certainly had advantages for overland routes.

For a variety of reasons, railroads were soon to become the predominant means of transportation in the United States. In the following issue, we examine whether government action on the behalf of, for example, the railroads was important for their development and the development of the United States, and in Issue VIII, we look

at the critical questions of whether or not railroads were indispensable for American growth. In that issue, we will treat the period from before the Civil War to World War I. We note here briefly, though, that the transportation improvements seen before and after the Civil War were important for forging a national economy. The lower transportation costs *per se* made it possible to cultivate new lands and to extend the size of the market to allow for increased specialization. The improved transportation had secondary effects on the economy by expanding existing capacity to supply a larger market made available by improved means of getting things from one place to another. This, of course, also includes the transportation of people, and we will discuss in the following chapter the causes and effects of western migration. But let's first see how much the government had to do with getting economic growth rolling.

Definitions of New Terms

QUANTITY THEORY OF PRICES: a theory that can be used to predict changes in the price level. Basically, if we assume that people's habits concerning the use of cash (and the number of transactions) remain unchanged, then a change in the quantity of money in circulation will lead to a proportionate change in the price level.

DEFLATION: a continuing fall in the price level.

DUMPING: selling goods abroad at a lower price than they fetch at home.

PRINCIPAL OF A LOAN: the total amount borrowed that must be repaid when the loan becomes due.

CAPITAL MARKET: a market in which loans can be obtained, or in which shares in companies can be bought and sold.

CAPITAL EQUIPMENT: term applied to machines, buildings, and other productive goods.

Chapter Summary

1. Congress had a difficult time financing the Revolution. Part of the war expenses were paid for by Continental currency notes. However, when a sizable amount of currency is issued in a relatively short time, the value of that currency usually falls. In part this is why Continentals were worth only 1/500th of their original face value in 1781. Also, people had lost confidence in them.

2. The Articles of Confederation provided a very weak framework for the Union. Shays' Rebellion demonstrated economic chaos and the weakness of the government under these Articles. Hence, the Constitution was drawn up as a substitute.

3. Besides reaffirming the permanent nature of private property by granting it federal sanction, the Constitution also gave Congress the ability to tax, issue money, and create a credit market. Moreover, the Constitution prohibited discriminatory import duties and all export duties, thus fostering trade among the states.

4. The outbreak of war in Europe and the subsequent inability of the belligerents to sail the high seas brought a veritable commercial revolution in the United States. However, it came to an abrupt halt in 1807 with the passage of the Embargo Act.

5. Before the Embargo, highest rates of return were found in reexporting, shipbuilding, and trading. After it, however, industrial and manufacturing endeavors became relatively profitable; hence, we saw a rapid development in our textile industry.

6. In the monetary sector, the First United States Bank was chartered in 1791. It was not really a central bank, nor was the Second Bank of the United States, although the latter's actions had significant effects on the economy.

7. The inflation that followed the demise of the Second Bank was probably not caused by that event. Rather, large amounts of specie were entering the nation at that time, thus increasing the money supply. This increase in the money supply would lead, according to the quantity theory of prices, to rising prices.

8. Our transportation system started with canals and roads, and then saw the beginning of the railroad network. Since the division of labor is determined by the extent of the market, the lower transportation costs are, the greater is the market, and, hence, the greater the division of labor.

Questions for Thought and Discussion

1. Who suffered from the loss in value of the Continental dollars?
2. Why would the Constitution's reaffirmation of the permanency of property rights be important for economic expansion? Would it have been possible to have the same expansion without this reaffirmation?
3. Can you imagine how commerce would be in the United States if each state could set up its own import taxes and export duties?
4. If our comparative advantage lay in shipping, was the Embargo of 1807 beneficial for the general economic welfare of the nation?

THE MAN WHO FACED THE JACKSONIANS

Nicholas Biddle (1786–1844)
President, Second Bank of the United States, 1822–1836

FAULTY STRATEGY in his fight against President Jackson and the Jacksonians certainly was not in keeping with the brilliant career that Nicholas Biddle had led up until the time he took over the presidency of the Second Bank of the United States in 1822. Biddle came from a prominent Philadelphia family. James Biddle, his father, was a U.S. Naval officer, commander of the *Ontario,* and the man who took formal possession of Oregon Country for the United States in 1818.

Young Nicholas was a precocious student; he entered the University of Pennsylvania at 10 and graduated at the tender age of 13. He also received another degree from the College of New Jersey (now Princeton) at age 15. He was a student of the classics and French literature and became the editor of America's first literary periodical, *Port Folio.* In 1815 he helped prepare Pennsylvania's reply to the Hartford Convention, in which numerous proposed amendments to the Constitution had been offered. Most of these proposals attempted to limit the power of Congress and the Executive. He went on later to compile for the State Department a digest of foreign legislation affecting U.S. trade.

Among his published works was *A History of the Expedition Under the Command of Captains Lewis and Clark,* which he prepared from the explorers' notes and journals.

By the time Biddle was appointed a director of the Second Bank of the United States in 1819, he was considered brilliant, debonaire, and versatile. At the age of 37 he had already been a child prodigy, a writer, a lawyer, a state senator, and a diplomat. And Biddle added to these traits tremendous pride and an uncompromising attitude towards others. These latter two qualities seemed to serve him well when he took over the presidency of the Second Bank.

As president he showed that he could discipline any other bank by forcing it to pay debts to the Second Bank of the United States and its branches in hard specie. But such behavior did not win Biddle many friends in the newer sections of the country or in the Old South.

Biddle's cavalier demeanor did not enhance his chances of winning over President Jackson. The President was a man of the people who felt that a national bank was merely a monopoly that used public funds to enrich a few already wealthy men—the common people were bound to get hurt. Jackson eventually won and from 1834 to 1836 Biddle had his Bank concentrate on how to liquidate itself. This, of course, meant moving all of its capital to the East, where the banking center of the nation still lay. However, a state charter was drawn up allowing the Bank to continue in existence. With this new lease on life, Biddle attempted to peg the world price of cotton because he felt it was crucial to American credit abroad. His first cotton pool earned a cool $800,000. The second one, however, failed to the tune of over $900,000. The Second Bank of the United States closed its doors in 1841.

Biddle died disgraced and discredited by many, but he left behind him principles that could be used later in the formulation of a true central banking system in the United States. Some observers believe that the monetary and banking reforms of FDR and the original creation of the Federal Reserve System were in part based on some of the principles established by Biddle.

ISSUE V

DID STATE INTERVENTION SPUR THE GROWTH OF THE ECONOMY?

Private vs. Public

Government Was Small

Nowadays, when about 25 percent of national output is consumed by government at the federal, state, and local levels, it seems almost unthinkable to question whether or not the government has any serious impact on the economy. However, this relatively high percentage of government involvement in economic activity was unheard of in the earlier days of this nation. In the nineteenth century, for example, we estimate that no more than 5 percent of **gross national product** could be accounted for by government expenditures. However, it would be a mistake to merely look at this small figure and conclude that government intervention in the economic affairs of the nation had no, or even little, impact on subsequent growth in the economy. From the very beginning of our country the government was active at all levels. It was responsible in one way or another for some of the development of our transportation system and our manufacturing sector. How important it was is, to be sure, another matter, and one which is the key to understanding this issue.

Helping out the Canals

Overland travel was a relatively expensive form of transportation for shipping goods across country. Therefore, the idea of a network of canals was thought of very early in American history. One of the earliest and the most successful of the canals connected the Hudson River with Lake Erie, a distance of 363 miles. The state did indeed intervene in this particular venture—100 percent. The Governor of New York, DeWitt Clinton, was an early advocate of the Erie Canal. In 1817 he got the state legislature to set up a fund to build that famous waterway. They estimated the cost then would be a little bit under $6 million. "Clinton's Ditch" was finally completed in 1825, costing closer to $8.5 million. Even before the canal was completed—that is, while only sections of it were being used—the tolls exceeded the interest costs on the debt used to pay for its construction. In the first nine years of its existence, the tolls summed to almost $17 million.

The effect of the canal on the movement of goods was dramatic. Much of the produce of Illinois, Indiana, Ohio, and western New York could have an easy route to the Atlantic Coast. Freight rates from Buffalo to New York fell by almost 85 percent and, more important, the shipping time was cut to one-half of what it had been previously. By 1853 tolls reached a cumulative value of $94 million on the great Erie Canal.

In the beginning of the canal construction period after the War of 1812, state intervention was great. Between 1815 and the start of the Civil War, almost $140 million was provided by state governments. This amounted to almost three-fourths of the total investment in canals during that period. Some states used other than financial aid. For example, instead of giving money directly New Jersey provided a banking privilege to get some of its canals going. After an auspicious beginning, however, direct state intervention in canal efforts dwindled and there was a tendency to have a mixed government-private system, or merely some government aid to businessmen who were attempting to build these waterways for transportation networks.

Possible Effects

Although it is true that after a while government had little to do in the development of canals, we must not forget that the original underwriting of canals by the states possibly had a side effect which would cause us to ascribe

77

ISSUE V   DID STATE INTERVENTION SPUR THE GROWTH OF THE ECONOMY?

a much greater role to this early state activity. The fact that the government had originally taken upon itself to provide the capital for many of these canal adventures, coupled with the great success of the Erie Canal, made foreign capital more available for investment in these canal ventures in exchange for purely private securities. While it is difficult to quantify the benefits from this aspect of state help for the canal system, we can be assured that it was important, for it provided a demonstration effect and leadership. Moreover, we know that

some of the earlier canal ventures would have been simply out of the question for private enterprise to undertake all alone. For example, the total amount expended on the Erie Canal was 15 times as great as the largest private transportation improvement, the Middlesex Canal, that had been made to that date. It was also more than ten times as great as the largest authorized capital of any manufacturing corporation then in existence. American businessmen were obviously not ready for such a quantum leap in the amount of capital that had to

be expended for these early transportation networks.

We cannot stop our analysis of state intervention with the development of canals, for even more important was the activity on behalf of railroads.

Helping the Railroads Along

Just as with the canal system, state aid was greater at the beginning of the development of railroads than at the end. In fact, toward the latter part of the nineteenth century, there was almost no government help for railroad systems.

In the 1830s, however, the government engaged in some less ambitious and less successful railroad schemes which may have set the foundation for further development of the Iron Horse. In the South, for example, during the period between the Revolution and the Civil War, state financing accounted for 55 percent of total railroad expenditures, of which 75 percent was directly in cash. By the 1850s, private financing of the railroads had taken over for the most part what the states had done in the beginning (although after the Civil War land grants were impressive). The only assistance from government was at the local level. Notice here a change also in the amount of intervention: When a state financed a railroad, it provided entrepreneurial aid. When the local

The Erie Canal. (The Buffalo and Erie County Historical Society)

level government helped finance a railroad, it did no such thing.

The plethora of local aid in the South and the North during this time seemed to induce some weird configurations of railroad lines. One historian, commenting on a railroad in the state of New York, said that it zigzagged across the countryside "in search of municipal bonds."

Government Investment Small

If we look at Table V–1, we find that government investment accounted for a not very large part of total investment in railroads during the period before the Civil War, and for even less after the war. However, this would be a misrepresentation of the benefits derived from state intervention. It

TABLE V–1

GOVERNMENT INVESTMENT AS A PERCENTAGE OF TOTAL INVESTMENT

ACTIVITY	TIME SPAN	PERCENTAGE OF TOTAL INVESTMENT
Canals	1815–1860	73
Railroads	To 1862	25–30 (plus some public land)
	1862–1872	10–12 (plus huge public land grants)
	1873–1890	1

As a proportion of total investment in railroads to 1862, government investment was at most 30 percent plus some small amount of public lands. This percentage fell to about 10–12 percent during the decade of the Civil War and after, but some extremely large land grants were added to this. After 1873, there was almost no contribution by government to railroad investment. (*Source:* Goodrich Carter, "Internal Improvements Reconsidered," *The Journal of Economic History,* Volume XXX, Number 2, June 1970, Table 1, p. 297.)

is quite clear that without government help a number of railroads would not have been built when they were. Moreover, just as with canals, government support for railroads may have provided an atmosphere that induced private investors to risk their capital in this new transportation adventure. And there were some states which provided a much larger share of the total capital invested in railroads, such as Georgia, which during the decade 1841 to 1850 allocated more than one-third of its state budget to the Iron Horse.

Land Grants

States and the federal government did allow certain numbers of land grants to help the railroads. We have not yet discussed them, and, in fact, before the Civil War they were not very important: During that period only two railroads were completed with the assistance of land grants. However, a total of 130 million acres was eventually given to railroads by the federal government and over 50 million by state governments.

Steam-engine railroads had a slow start but became a major transportation mode by the turn of the century. Here we see a trial run of the *De Witt Clinton.*

79

ISSUE V   DID STATE INTERVENTION SPUR THE GROWTH OF THE ECONOMY?

Are There Any Answers Yet?

We still haven't come up with any assessment of whether or not state intervention spurred the growth of the American economy. Many historians have labeled the system of mixed government-private enterprise building of canals and railroads "The American System." Some historians maintain that during this period the government "everywhere undertook the role put on it by the people, that of planner, promoter, investor, and regulator."* It is quite clear that this in fact was perhaps only the case in certain very specific examples, like the Erie Canal. At any rate, the government's role in the transportation system declined as we approached the Civil War. This still doesn't answer our question, however; we want to know whether the rate of growth in the United States would have been lower had the government not participated even to the limited extent it did. Using economic data, historians have yet to come up with a definitive conclusion. Certain very obvious examples would lead one to believe that this intervention did yield innumerable positive benefits. Some have said, for example, that the Erie Canal had effects upon the development history of the United

*Robert A. Lively, "The American System," *The Business History Review*, Volume XXXIX, Number 1, March 1955, p. 81.

States which "ramify almost into infinity." But we can just as easily find some spectacular failures of government intervention, such as occurred with the Pennsylvania Canal System. We also can look at the history of other countries to find out whether government intervention there brought definite differences in rates of growth as compared with the United States. In England, for example, during the same period almost all transportation investment was done by the government. England's rate of growth, however, was certainly no greater than ours and, in fact, has been estimated to have been lower.

What About Helping Manufacturing?

From the very beginning the government did not carry through Alexander Hamilton's suggestions as outlined in his "Report on Manufactures," in which he suggested that the state undertake a number of promotional activities, such as subsidizing important industries. Up until the Civil War there was very little subsidy of manufacturing. There was also not an overwhelming amount of "protection" in the form of relatively high tariffs, although for a short period we did have rising tariff rates. (As you will recall, these are the duties or taxes that have to be paid to the United States government when foreign

goods enter this country to be sold.) We had our first tariff on July 4, 1789, with an average rate of only 8.5 percent. It grew steadily larger, reaching a peak in the late 1820s and then falling thereafter to considerably lower rates. This can be seen in Figure V–1. Our mercantilist policies did not last very long, so no particular emphasis on home manufacturing was brought about by this government intervention.

What we see in the United States during this period was a system of no quotas, no currency regulations, very little allocation by the government of our scarce resources, and few subsidies paid to manufacturing. We had a more or less freely functioning market mechanism in which changes in relative prices and relative rates of return would induce resources to flow in directions that would yield the highest rates of return, both to the individual and to the nation. Where the state did have some effect, and probably the most important effect of all, on the growth of the economy was in its original provision of an atmosphere conducive to the development of large and well-functioning markets.

Establishing the Atmosphere

We might well go back all the way to the Constitution to find out where state intervention did the

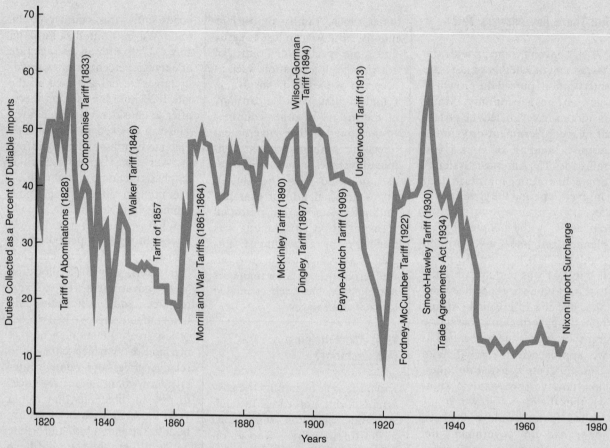

FIGURE V-1 TARIFF RATES IN THE UNITED STATES SINCE 1820

Tariff rates in the United States have bounced about like a football, and indeed in Congress tariffs do represent a political football. Import-competing industries prefer high tariffs. In the twentieth century, the highest tariff we ever had was the Smoot-Hawley Tariff of 1930, which was almost as high as the Tariff of Abominations in 1828. (*Source:* U.S. Department of Commerce.)

most good for the development of the U.S. economy. We find that the key articles—giving power to Congress to tax, provide for a common currency, regulate tariffs, and so on—allowed for the development of a framework for a large market system. The Constitution also provided for an atmosphere of political stability in which the states would not be fighting against each other and could not impose restrictive duties on each other's goods, and in which generally there was a lowering of transactions costs for those who wished to engage in exchange. Some of the outcomes of Hamilton's great work in government economics led to the development of a large credit market—that is, we had from the very beginning a developing market for the buying and selling of bonds and stocks. This allowed resources to flow more freely into areas where they not only could make the most

81

ISSUE V   DID STATE INTERVENTION SPUR THE GROWTH OF THE ECONOMY?

profit for the investors, but also to where they were most needed by the population.

It was perhaps in the develop-ment of an atmosphere in which everybody knew what the ground rules were, who owned what, and how well it would be protected that the growth of the nation could continue for years to come.

Definitions of New Terms

GROSS NATIONAL PRODUCT: the market value of all final goods and services. When GNP is corrected for price level changes, it is called *real* GNP.

Questions for Thought and Discussion

1. If private industry was unwilling to build, say, the Erie Canal, why might general economic welfare be improved if the government took on the task?
2. Can we tell the extent of help given to the canals and railroads merely by looking at the total amount of government financing?
3. Can you think of who might wish a high tariff?

The Role of the Cotton Economy in Provoking National Growth

6

Fᴿᴏᴍ ᴛʜᴇ ᴠᴇʀʏ beginning, the staple crops from the South accounted for a large percentage of the total exports from America. In the colonial era, rice, tobacco, and indigo accounted for more than one-half of the exports of all of the colonies combined. These came from the Southern colonies. After the Revolution, the trend was somewhat reversed. However, a new staple crop was soon to take the place of all the others and to become the leading source of national export income for many years to follow.

KING COTTON

Back in 1793 cotton was an insignificant feature of the Southern landscape. In fact, since the importance of tobacco and rice had fallen after the Revolution, there was little Southern furor when the Constitution stipulated that international slave trade could be stopped after 20 years. This was all to change, and part of it may be due to Eli Whitney's invention of the cotton ginning machine, which removed the bottleneck in the preparation of cotton and enabled one worker to clean more than 50 pounds of it a day, thus lowering the cost of American cotton at the same time that England's textile industry was growing by leaps and bounds. King Cotton was on its way to the top.

Jumps in Cotton Production

The South increased its production of cotton at a phenomenal rate, doubling almost every decade until 1840, after which it still continued to grow but at a slower rate. We see in Figure 6–1 that by the start of the Civil War, cotton production was up to 4 million bales a year.

A New Source of Export Income

Cotton became the new source of export income for not only the South, but all of the United States. We see in Figure 6–2 that cotton exports as a percentage of all U.S. exports rose from 38 percent during the period 1815 to 1819 all the way up to 65 percent just before 1840, then falling down to 51 percent by the start of the Civil War.

REASONS FOR THE DEVELOPMENT OF COTTON IN THE SOUTHERN ECONOMY

Of course no one knows exactly why the South ended up relying on cotton as its main source of income, but we can conjecture a few possibilities. In the first place, the Southern climate and terrain were suitable for such a crop. There were numerous new lands in the South that were both more fertile and more easily cultivated than other areas of the country that could be used when the rapacious cotton plants reduced the natural fertility of older lands. Moreover, the plantation system of cultivation had already been set up for the growing of rice and tobacco during colonial times. This system was just as well suited for the production of cotton, which required large amounts of land and of unskilled labor. In the South, slaves were imported and bred as unskilled labor. It is fairly obvious that cotton was what the South would produce best. Since there was the possibility of not only interregional but international trade, the South was able to specialize in its comparative advantage endeavor, which happened to be cotton production. Easy transportation was another important reason why cotton could become king in the South. It had a vast network of waterways that could carry the cotton

FIGURE 6–1

BOOMING COTTON PRODUCTION

Starting out with the mere 3,000 bales produced in 1790, cotton production increased to its peak prior to the Civil War at 4.5 million bales. (*Source: Historical Statistics,* p. 302.)

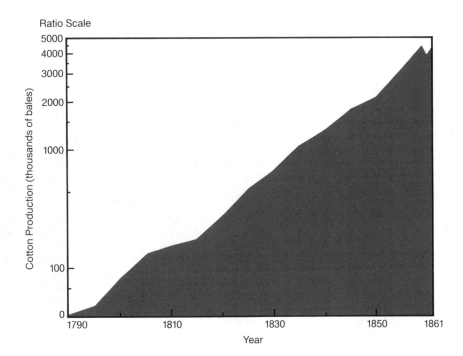

Ratio Scale

Cotton Production (thousands of bales)

Year

A sophisticated version of the cotton gin. Its invention was to change the face of America: cotton became King and the institution of slavery became firmly entrenched in the South.

FIGURE 6–2   **COTTON EXPORTS ON THE RISE**

The export income from cotton produced in the South became increasingly important in the United States, rising from 38 percent after the end of the War of 1812 to 65 percent during the period 1835–1839. (*Source: Historical Statistics,* pp. 538–547.)

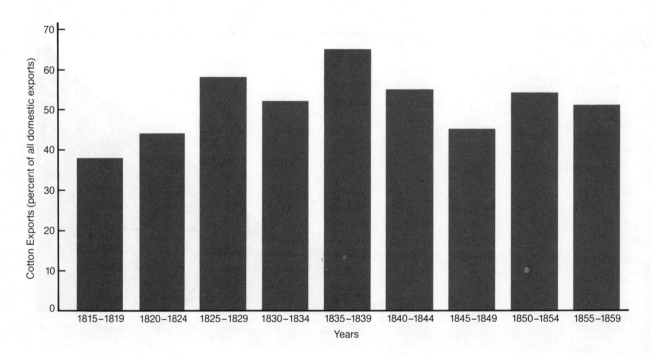

down to ocean ports, the main one being, of course, New Orleans. This well-established transportation system allowed cotton farmers to merely cart their bales of cotton to a nearby river and have them shipped down to the large vessels waiting at the dock in New Orleans, Charleston, or Mobile.

Before we get into answering the question of whether or not the cotton economy spurred national growth, we'll first take a look at how the Southern situation compared with the rest of the country in the pre-Civil War period.

THE ANTEBELLUM SOUTH

Although cotton was king and there were numerous plantations around the Southern countryside, the vast majority of people were engaged in yeoman farming that was either subsistence or left a slight surplus which could be sold to the plantation owners for their own consumption and that of the slaves.

There was very little urbanization in the South, with the obvious exception of New Orleans and perhaps Charleston and Richmond. This meant that there were few local industries, but that didn't mean that the South was stagnating, as many historians have said. In fact, in 1840 and even in 1860, the per capita income of free people in the West South Central area was higher than the national average. Moreover, the per capita income was growing all the time, at a rate equal to those of other parts of the nation. The South was far from being an undeveloped region. It was, for example, in the vanguard of railroad investment until the falling price of cotton brought an end to this aspect of its expansion.

Cotton was not the only crop that was grown in the pre-Civil War era: Corn accounted for the most acreage, but it was not a commercial crop; and there was rice in South Carolina and sugar in Louisiana and Texas, as well as tobacco in Virginia. In fact, sugar was one of the staples that

was grown on the new lands of the westward migration, which we'll talk about in the following section.

It is fairly obvious that the South had no need to diversify in its economy. In fact, it was quite clear to Southern plantation owners that their comparative advantage lay in cotton production or, to a lesser extent, the production of sugar, rice, or tobacco. We find, for example, that in the Old South, where the costs of producing cotton were much higher than in the New South, there was almost no shift to other types of production. Cotton was still the best thing that a landowner could produce, even when the cost of producing went up. So during the pre-Civil War era there was little tendency for industry to grow up in the South.

Diversity of Incomes

Although the **per capita GNP** of free people in the South was, in fact, as high as or higher than that of most other regions of the country before the Civil War, there was probably more diversity or inequality in income and wealth than in other

(Historical Pictures Service, Chicago)

sections of the country. To be sure, one of the main reasons for this great inequality was the large number of slaves in the Southern economy. Much of their income surpluses accrued to their owners, not to themselves.

In the period just before the Civil War, almost one-half of Southern personal income went to just 1000 families. There were some egregious examples of concentrated wealth. The Hairstons had 1700 slaves on all of their plantations. In Georgia, a Mr. Howell Cobb had over 1000 slaves on his lands. In rural Louisiana, the top 10 percent of families had 96 percent of all wealth!

Little Investment in Education

An aspect of the Southern economy which was not at all favorable to its further development was the lack of investment in the education of its populace. To be sure, this was partly because much of the population consisted of slaves. It was not generally worthwhile for a slave owner to provide education for the people he owned (and in some states it was even illegal!). Most were bought specifically to do tasks that required very few skills. However, it is not certain why the free white population in the South lagged so far behind the rest of the country in obtaining educational resources. This would have grave consequences in the post-Civil War era even up to the present, for, as we shall see in later sections of this book, **investment in human capital,** as it is called, is important for increasing the productivity of individuals, regions, and the nation as a whole.

Schools available for the white population in the South were almost 20 percent fewer than in the North. And there were almost 50 percent fewer students going to school in the South than in the North. So small an investment in education was perhaps understandable if most persons in the South felt that cotton would remain king. After all, there was little need for a highly educated populace if the only productive activities would involve growing staple crops and exporting them

for needed imports. In fact, the data that we will present in the next issue demonstrate that most people (at least those who owned slaves) felt that cotton would remain king and that the price of cotton would remain high enough to justify continuing production in that area.

THE COTTON ECONOMY AND WESTWARD MIGRATION

Now to grapple with the problem of whether or not the cotton economy helped increase the growth in the national economy, we look at how cotton spurred the westward movement that would not otherwise have occurred at such an early date. Whether or not this westward movement was responsible for increased national growth is, of course, a debatable issue which we cannot answer at this time. But it is clear that cotton caused westward migration on a scale that far exceeded what would have happened in its absence.

As we mentioned above, cotton of course required fertile lands; and like most crops, cotton, when cultivated for a long time, takes fertility out of the land. And once the natural fertility of the soil has been depleted by cotton cultivation, it is necessary to move on to new lands. Moreover, in the quest for increased profits, Southern cotton growers would move on to more fertile lands as the price of cotton rose relative to other crops. We find that there was a year or so lag between increases in the price of cotton and a new thrust in westward migration. The main surges to the West occurred during the periods 1816–1819, 1833–1837, and to a lesser extent in the 1850s. This corresponds fairly closely to the information we have on cotton prices presented in Figure 6–3.

There was a little scenario that would be followed every time the relative price of cotton rose in the American economy:

1. The relative price of cotton goes up.
2. New plantations are started, taking three to four years to clear.

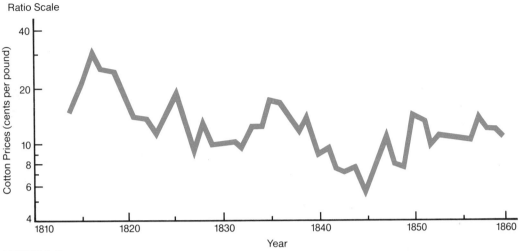

FIGURE 6-3

COTTON PRICES PER POUND PRIOR TO THE CIVIL WAR

A rise in cotton prices in 1815 led thereafter to the surge to the West during the period 1816 to 1819. Another rise in cotton prices starting in 1833 brought the next surge to the West which lasted until 1837. A relationship again occurred to a lesser extent in the 1850s. (*Source: Historical Statistics,* p. 124.)

3. The supply of cotton rises.
4. The relative price of cotton falls.
5. Some of these plantations shift to growing corn, but whenever the price of cotton goes up, they shift back to cotton.
6. The demand for cotton rises so much again that most of the cultivated land is being used for cotton production.
7. The relative price of cotton goes up again as the demand grows faster than the supply.
8. A new cycle starts again; more thrust into the West.

So there is little doubt that in fact the cotton economy did spur the growth of the population into the Southwest. It also had some effect on the development of manufacturing in the North, but to a decreasing extent as the North branched out into industries other than textile manufacturing.

EFFECTS ON THE NORTH

The availability of relatively inexpensive cotton for the development of the New England textile industry is, of course, a well-known historical fact. Moreover, each fall in the price of cotton in the South was an additional stimulus to the North because cotton was a major input into its manufacturing sector. So to some extent we may say that the cotton economy did encourage the growth of industry in New England. Also, Southern demand for cheap textiles to clothe slaves further spurred the Northern textile industry.

WAS THE SOUTH RESPONSIBLE FOR INTERREGIONAL TRADE?

Many historians have maintained that the demand for foodstuffs by the South spurred the development of the Western regions by providing them a ready market for their products, such as wheat. The scenario goes as follows: The South would export cotton to New England and foreign ports, buying imports from New England and the West; the West would sell foodstuffs to the South, and some to the North, buying certain imports from the North, thus allowing for a very complete and ever-increasing trade among all parts of the new nation.

However, when closely examined, the data indicate that even prior to the Civil War the South was an increasingly isolated part of the United States. While it is true that in 1839 50 percent of the West's exports went to New Orleans, only one-third of them stayed. And by 1850 only 17 percent of the West's exports flowed to New Orleans, but at that time almost 85 percent of them stayed in the South. By the beginning of the Civil War New Orleans was no longer a major domestic reexport center. But, in any event, the South was never a major market for Western foodstuffs. The large plantations raised most of their own corn and pork, and hence, relied very little on the West for food, and this reliance diminished steadily to 1860. For example, in 1840 the importation of Western corn into the South added a grand total of 1 percent to the Southern supply.

What actually happened was probably that Western development came mainly from increased Eastern demand. Much of what the West produced went through the South in the earlier years before the Civil War to be reexported—most of it, to Eastern coastal cities and some of it to European ports. A closer look at the available data gives every indication that there were fewer and fewer ties between the South and the West. And by 1850 the Southern economy was almost going it alone. The national economy no longer depended on the South as it had in the earlier years of this nation. Secession seemed economically acceptable to the South at that time. Moreover, it was certainly far from clear that slavery would have died out of its own accord. That is what we look to next when we explore whether or not slavery was profitable and viable. Surprisingly enough (and contrary to popular belief), we will find that not only was the system of slavery viable and would have lasted much longer had the Civil War not occurred, it also was profitable, at least when compared to the other investments that plantation owners could have made with their capital in those days.

Definitions of New Terms

PER CAPITA GNP: GNP divided by the total population. When corrected for price level changes it becomes per capita *real* GNP.

INVESTMENT IN HUMAN CAPITAL: the training, schooling, and medical attention of human beings which yields higher incomes in the future. Investment may be formal, such as going to college, or informal, such as on-the-job training.

Chapter Summary

1. The growth in cotton production in the South was phenomenal; cotton became a new source of export income for the entire United States.
2. Cotton developed in the South because easy transportation was available, the climate was suitable, and Southern plantation owners were able to import and breed slaves.
3. Corn accounted for more acreage than cotton, but was not a commercial crop. Sugar and rice, as well as tobacco, were also raised.
4. There was an extreme inequality of income and wealth in the South, much more so than in the North.
5. Southerners showed a proclivity to small amounts of formal education.
6. Western migration followed the price cycle of cotton; when the price of cotton rose, migration to the Southwest increased.
7. Up to the Civil War, the South became increasingly isolated from the rest of the United States in its trading arrangements.

Questions for Thought and Discussion

1. Why do you think Southern whites spent less on formal education for their children than Northerners? Can you give both economic and sociological answers to this question?
2. Have you ever invested in your own human capital? If so, do you expect to obtain a high rate of return on that investment?
3. Why did an increase in the price of cotton lead to Westward migration?

THE MAN WHO MADE COTTON KING

Eli Whitney (1765–1825)
Inventor and Manufacturer

IN 1790 cotton production was about two million pounds. Ten years later, it had risen to 35 million. In 1790 the trend towards voluntary abolition of slavery was increasing: Washington and Jefferson provided in their wills for their own slaves to be set free. This trend was soon to be reversed. Slavery thrived up until the Civil War.

Why did all this happen? What was responsible for the tremendous increase in the production and sale of cotton and for the newfound profitability in slaves? A simple but monumental invention—the cotton gin. And it was invented by an inveterate tinkerer, Eli Whitney.

The young Eli used to putter around in his father's workshop on their family farm in Massachusetts. He then started to make and repair violins in the neighborhood. When he was only 15, he was a manufacturer of nails in his father's shop, even hiring helpers to fill part of his orders. Then he turned to hat pins. But by the time he was 18, he decided he wanted more education. Working his way through Leicester Academy in Massachusetts, he finally was able to enter Yale in 1789 at the age of 23. Not able to live on the funds offered by his father, he repaired equipment and apparatus around the college. A carpenter who had lent Eli his tools remarked after watching him work, "There was one good mechanic spoiled when you went to college."

Then he decided to go into law. Having been invited as a tutor to stay with the widow of General Nathaniel Green, he overheard a conversation at one of her dinners on the Savannah plantation. The men there pointed out the deplorable state of cotton cultivation in the South. Except in certain coastal areas the only variety that could be grown was short-staple, upland cotton, which was extremely difficult to clean, requiring one whole day to obtain a pound of lint. A machine was needed to remove the tenacious seed from the cotton. In ten days Whitney had invented that machine: a cylinder barely two feet long and six inches in diameter with rows of combing teeth to separate the lint from the seeds and a brush with a fan to remove the clean cotton. This little model was 50 times as efficient as hand labor. News of the cotton gin soon spread and a myriad of the curious and interested came to find out what it was all about. It was soon stolen, carried off, and copied. Patent laws weren't what they are today.

Whitney was never able to make much money from the invention which changed the entire history of the South and, indeed, the United States. Virtually every Southern planter went into cotton production. Land that was once considered worthless soon became valuable. Slaves were now a much sought after part of the cotton production process. The price of field hands doubled in less than 20 years.

Whitney didn't stop at the cotton gin, for he had to find something else to provide his living. He invented another process which perhaps proved to be even more important for the history of the United States. Whitney looked at the manufacture of firearms and decided he could do better. Having never built a gun before, he brashly contacted Treasury Secretary Oliver Wolcott in 1798 and took on the task of manufacturing 10,000 or 15,000 stand of arms at a price of $13.40 each. Whitney proposed to make the guns by a new method and in so doing invented the standardization of parts. He once wrote, "One of my primary objects is to form the tools so the tools themselves shall fashion the work and give to every part its just proportion—which when once accomplished, will give expedition, uniformity, and exactness to the whole. . . . The tools which I contemplate are similar to an engraving on a copper plate."

After a slow start, Whitney perfected his method. He was able to use relatively unskilled mechanics to fashion the precise parts that when put together made a very good gun. As it was, Whitney took eight years to fulfill a contract that he promised would be done in two. During this period he had to withstand prejudice and ridicule, but in the end he won out, and his method of machine milling of parts that could be used interchangeably revolutionized the entire manufacturing process used throughout the world. As late as 1840 the British were amazed at the use of interchangeable parts, which had already begun to revolutionize industry in America.

College apparently did not spoil the mechanic in Eli Whitney.

ISSUE VI

WAS SLAVERY PROFITABLE?

How Necessary Was the Civil War?

(Library of Congress)

Common Views of Slavery

Many historians are convinced that on the eve of the Civil War, slavery was not only unprofitable, but a moribund institution. In other words, the Civil War was apparently unnecessary as a means of eradicating the last vestiges in the United States of coercive control over individual freedom. Additionally, the common view of the slave society was one

in which the power of the lash ruled, the slaves' total income was expropriated by the slave master, and carnal licentiousness between slave masters and female slaves abounded. Such things no doubt occurred, and with a frequency that humanitarians of the day and afterward could rightly deplore. However, recent evidence indicates that the typical representation of the plantation slave life was somewhat of an oversimplification. This is not to say, of

course, that we should have allowed slavery to continue. As an economist one cannot answer such a question, although as a human being one's answer is quite clear.

The Rise of Slavery

Slavery was relatively unimportant for almost the first century of settlement in colonial America: Before 1740 there were fewer than 150,000 slaves in all the colonies of that time. However, between 1740 and the Revolution, that number more than doubled. The interest in slavery was, of course, economic, pure and simple. The discovery that tobacco could be grown cheaply in Maryland and Virginia necessitated large numbers of unskilled workers to cultivate many acres of land. The same held true for growing rice in South Carolina.

The Dutch were the first to develop the slave trade with the American colonies, but soon England entered this highly profitable venture. Slaves were much cheaper than their next best substitute—indentured servants.

While the Southern contribution to total exports remained high until the Revolution, there was a reversal in the trend immediately thereafter until cotton became king in the South. At the time the Constitution was written, it was relatively easy for the forefathers of this nation to foresee outlawing the importation of slaves into the United States, for then it did not appear that the institution of slavery would continue to be profitable or viable.

All of this changed, however, as cotton became the most important Southern crop. The plantation system was the most suitable for the raising of this staple, and with it the demand for unskilled labor grew.

Not Everyone a Slaveowner

It was far from true, however, that everyone in the South had slaves. By the start of the Civil War, there were 1.4 million free families in the Southern states. Only 380,000 of them owned slaves, which meant that about one-fourth of all

Southern families were indeed slaveholders. Now, of this particular group, less than one-fourth held ten or more slaves, which means that it wasn't even 4 percent of the Southern white population which had ten or more slaves on their farms. This 4 percent held over three-fourths of the total number of slaves at that time. Hence, slavery was not the all-pervasive institution that one usually thinks it was in the pre-Civil War South. However, those who held power in the Southern states were more likely than not to be the owners of slaves, for slaves were part of Southern wealth. It is therefore understandable that they would object to any threats by the North to emancipate the black man.

The Incentive System within the Slave Economy

While it is generally assumed that in the Southern slave system might made right, there were other, more economic ways of obtaining high productivity from bondsmen. Some historians have pointed out that one in five slaves was in a skilled or managerial position, such as field foreman, within the slave economy itself. Hence, there was an occupational hierarchy which created a social hierarchy in the bondsmen's society itself. This gave slaves an economic incentive to be more productive than they would otherwise have been. In other words, slaveholders were able to use economic incentives in addition to whatever

(Historical Pictures Service, Chicago)

corporal incentives they found necessary to obtain what they considered "correct" slave behavior. There is no reason not to expect bondsmen to react to economic incentives in the same way that free men did. And indeed, when the evidence is carefully examined, we find that there was mobility within the ranks of the slaves themselves as bondsmen strove to attain higher occupational and, therefore, social status within their institutional constraints.

Was Slavery Going to Die Out?

It is generally assumed that the South was stagnating before the Civil War and that, since slaves seemed to be unprofitable and less productive than their free brothers, the institution of slavery would have died of its own accord. But if we examine what was actually happening in the South, slavery does not appear to have been moribund, for the South itself was far from stagnating. A look at Table VI-1 shows that per capita income in the South, though more unequally distributed, was certainly not much lower than the national average, and in some cases, such as in the West South Central area, it was quite a bit higher. It was also higher in all cases as compared with the North Central region of the United States, a region which historians

have customarily indicated as one having a very high level of living at that time. And if we treat slaves themselves as "intermediate goods," we find that in both 1840 and 1860 the per capita income of the free population in the South exceeded the national average.

Moreover, we see that the South was certainly not stagnating if we look at its rate of growth in per capita income. It grew at an average rate of 1.7 percent a year, which exceeded the national average of 1.3 percent a year. It also exceeded the growth rate of the North Central states. The South was a growing economy, one in which its inhabitants anticipated that things could only continue to get better, not worse. We will find below that the price of slaves was rising generally

throughout this period, indicating that their value was increasing, not decreasing, so even if they were unprofitable (which they weren't), their increasing price indicated that they had some value to Southern plantation owners, even if it be only for prestige. Farm and household slaves also provided leisure time for owners—another reason, then, why they would be desired.

Were Slave Owners Losing Money?

Until quite recently, historians hypothesized that by the end of the 1850s, slave owners were losing money on their investment in slaves. To understand first of all how the price of slaves is deter-

TABLE VI-1

PER CAPITA INCOME BEFORE THE CIVIL WAR

	TOTAL POPULATION 1840	1860	FREE POPULATION 1840	1860
National Average	$ 96	$128	$109	$144
North	109	141	110	142
Northeast	129	181	130	183
North Central	65	89	66	90
South	74	103	105	150
South Atlantic	66	84	96	124
East South Central	69	89	92	124
West South Central	151	184	238	274

We see that the South was far from stagnating before the Civil War. In fact, its per capita income was higher in some of its subregions, such as the West South Central, than the national average. (All expressed in 1860 prices.) (*Source:* R. W. Fogel and S. L. Engerman, "The Economics of Slavery," in *The Reinterpretation of American Economic History,* New York: Harper & Row, 1971, Table 8, p. 335.)

mined, we have to look at them (unfortunately, in some people's eyes) as a **capital investment.** That is, the potential owner would decide how much he was willing to pay for the slave by determining what the *current* value of the slave's *future* net income was.

This is fairly easily done, although one can only make guesstimates of such things as future rates of profitability on any asset, whether it be a slave or a machine or a stock or a bond. Now, don't get upset because we are treating human beings as capital assets; this is merely an analytical device that we will use to show that slavery was indeed profitable. This has nothing to do with whether slavery was good or bad or should or shouldn't have been abolished or whether or not the Civil War was necessary to obliterate it.

Profitability Computations

A slave would give its owner a stream of income. That income was the value of the product that the slave produced for the owner minus the cost of the slave's maintenance. For example, a slave could help the owner increase his cotton production by, say, three bales of cotton. Let's say that those bales could be sold in the open market for 10 cents a pound, or $50 a bale. That would mean that the total revenues of the plantation owner would go up by $150 if he hired

Cotton Firm by Edgar Dégas. (Musée des Beaux Arts)

this additional slave. We can't accept that as the first year's *net* revenues on the slave purchase because we have to subtract out the cost of maintaining the slave, say $25 per year. That meant that the net profits to the owner from having the slave would be $125 per year. Now we would have to stretch this over the expected lifetime of the slave. Let's add all this up and properly account for the fact that some of it occurred in later years. Having done this, assume our answer for the current value of the future streams of net profit from hiring the additional slave would be equal to $1250. $1250, then, would be the maximum price that a slave owner would pay for an additional slave.

This is indeed how the price of slaves was determined in the open slave market. It was, hence, a function mainly of the price of cotton and the productivity of slaves. Ignoring the latter, we find that the price of cotton was, for the most part, either stable or rising. Slave owners anticipated that the price of cotton would continue to be high for many years in the future. So on the eve of the Civil War, they were far from pessimistic about the profitability of slavery.

Cotton Prices Not Falling

Look at Figure VI–1. Here we show the price of raw cotton in cents per pound, corrected for general changes in the price level. It grew from 7.4 cents in 1840 all the way up to 12.4 cents in 1850, then fell again during the first few years of that decade, but started to rise again in 1857. There is no question that any drop in the price of cotton was viewed as temporary by plantation owners. They therefore anticipated continuing high revenues from having slaves on their plantation. The price of slaves reflected the slave owners' anticipations of future prices for cotton. The price of slaves in the upper South, for example, was only $521 during the period 1830 to 1835. But by 1856 it had risen to over $1200. In the lower South in 1860, a prime slave could have fetched $1800. We present in Table VI–2 the various prices of slaves as five-year averages.

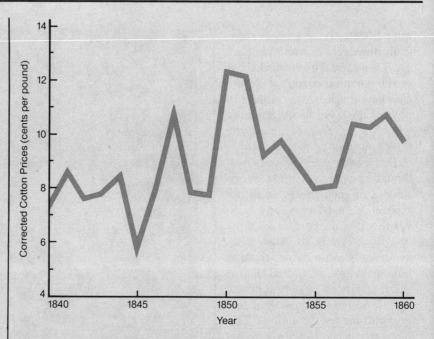

FIGURE VI-1 CORRECTED PRICE OF RAW COTTON

The real price of raw cotton grew gradually from 1840 to 1860, reaching a high in 1850 at 12.4 cents per pound. There was no indication that the value of the output that slaves produced was going to fall. (*Source:* Fogel and Engerman, *op cit.,* Table 1, p. 316.)

Slaves a Profitable Investment

What did all this have to do with the profitability of slavery? Well, it's very simple. A correct investigation of the data shows us that the average rate of return on slaves was as high as or higher than on any other capital investment that was available to Southerners during that period. In the lower South, for example, it was 12 percent during the period 1830–1835, rising to a peak of over 18 percent by the 1840s, then falling to about 10 percent on the eve

TABLE VI-2

SLAVE PRICES IN THE UPPER AND LOWER SOUTH

PERIOD	UPPER SOUTH PRICE	LOWER SOUTH PRICE
1830–1835	$ 521	$ 948
1836–1840	957	
1841–1845	529	722
1846–1850	709	926
1851–1855	935	1240
1856–1860	1294	1658

There was a gradual increase in the price of slaves for the period from 1830 to the Civil War, reaching a peak, just prior to the Civil War, in the lower South of $1658. (*Source:* R. Evans, Jr., "The Economics of American Negro Slavery," *Aspects of Labor Economics,* Princeton, N.J.: Princeton University Press, 1962, p. 216) of the Civil War. This was at least as high as rates of return that prevailed elsewhere in the economy. Remember that we assumed that people would respond to changing relative rates of return. So long as the rate of return to slavery was as good as or better than the rates of return that existed in other capital investments, we would expect that the institution of slavery would continue. And that is exactly what happened.

Slavery Viable, but Maybe Not

Slavery was indeed profitable and, at least in the short run, clearly viable. A slave was economically viable when his price covered his reproduction costs. This was certainly so if slavery was still profitable and could be so even if it weren't. However, we must mention some salient facts that could counter this position. At that time, new competition in the world cotton market from India and Egypt was appearing. Moreover, there were the beginnings of a worldwide emancipation movement that was certain to reach the United States sooner or later. Perhaps slavery would have died out of its own accord at some time in the late nineteenth century, but the Civil War was necessary to abruptly terminate the existence of this institution considered by all those except its beneficiaries as an outrage in a nation of free men.

Definitions of New Terms

CAPITAL INVESTMENT: investment in a productive asset—that is, an asset which will yield a stream of income in the future. The purchase of a slave was a capital investment.

Questions for Thought and Discussion

1. Why do you think it was possible to obtain slaves from Africa?
2. Do you think an economic analysis of slave ownership is inaccurate? If so, what type of analysis would you suggest, and does it lead to different conclusions about the profitability and viability of slavery?
3. Why would the value of a slave depend on the price of cotton? Does the value of other people's labor services depend on the market price of the product they make?

Secession and the Workings of the War Economy

7

By 1860 THE cotton kingdom encompassed perhaps 400,000 square miles. By that time the South was importing only 17 percent of the West's total exports. Incomes in the South were rising at a faster rate than the national average. Slavery continued to be a profitable and viable institution. The South consisted of a fairly homogeneous group of free people with very few immigrants, except perhaps for a few Germans, French, and Scotch-Irish. It seems clear in retrospect that secession after the election of President Lincoln was not an irrational thing for the South to do. Slaveholders were extremely sanguine on the eve of the Civil War. It appeared that they anticipated a continuation of their social order and also a new era of increased prosperity. The South seceded out of economic strength, not weakness.

THE OUTBREAK OF WAR

The outbreak of war brought with it the usual problems of obtaining manpower, paying for that manpower, ammunition, and all the items necessary to kill. The North had a more difficult job than the South because it was attacking; the South was merely defending its home territory. That is, the military goal of the South was much more modest than that of the North: All it had to do was obtain a draw or stalemate. Compare, for example, the ability of the relatively small 13 colonies to obtain their independence from England.

WHAT HAPPENED IN THE SOUTH?

At one time or another, almost one million soldiers served in the Confederate Army. At the height of the war, there were perhaps over one-half million engaged in combat. This represented an impressive 50 percent of the white male population between the ages of 15 and 50. As can be expected, the economy suffered from a scarcity of food, clothing, and war materials. The North had quickly set up a foreign blockade—a disaster for the South since it had engaged in extensive trade with the East and with foreign ports. At the beginning of the war, only one-tenth of the total value of manufactured products used in the South were made in the South. Self-sufficiency would indeed be difficult; trade was important. Despite these and myriad other problems, the Southern economy supported a large army for four years of extremely difficult fighting.

Shifting Productive Capacities

Among the South's greatest problems was the shifting of productive resources out of cotton—which was no longer a useful industry because the output could not be traded for needed manufactured goods and foodstuffs—into providing increased foodstuffs and supplies for the armies, as well as other manufactured goods for the civilian population. To this end, cotton production was cut back sharply in 1862. The government didn't need to enforce this cutback. After all, the Southern cotton growers were not going to continue increasing production if they could not sell it. They quickly shifted their capital into areas where relative rates of return were higher. Reduction of the crop continued: In 1863, it was well below 1 million bales, as compared to 4 million a few years earlier, and in the following years the output was halved again. Tobacco production also was reduced, again because the surplus over what was consumed in the South could not be sold in foreign

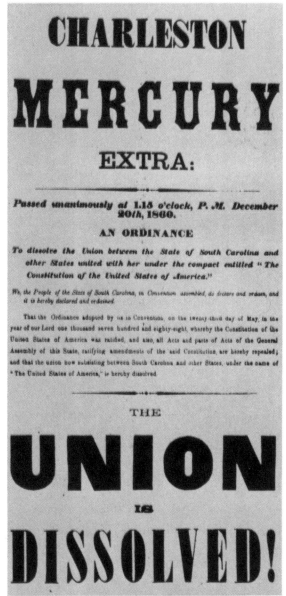

South Carolina greeted secession with jubilation. Charleston, one observer noted, "was wild with excitement . . . church bells mingling with salvos of artillery. . . . Old men ran shouting down the street. . . . The whole heart of the people had spoken." But a lonely Unionist said sourly, "South Carolina is too small for a republic and too big for a lunatic asylum."

trade. Entrepreneurs made a valiant effort to produce substitutes for the manufactured goods that the South had previously imported. A noteworthy achievement was the development of homespun cloth.

Urbanization

The rise in the manufacturing industry in the South dramatically increased urbanization. Before the Civil War, the South had remained a very rural sector of the United States, with only one major city, New Orleans. After the war started, Charleston, Atlanta, Richmond, and Wilmington all became increasingly crowded, for there industrial and administrative employment were available. Southerners were seeking out areas where they could earn the most income, and that no longer was on the farm.

WERE THE SOUTHERN FORCES DEFEATED FROM WITHIN?

Many observers of the rout of the Confederacy maintain that government policies of inflationary finance and improper foreign trade caused the downfall of the South during the Civil War. We will find that the evidence in support of this view is not overwhelming.

Trade Policies

The Confederacy did make a number of mistakes in trade policy, at least in retrospect. The Northern blockade really didn't take effect until 1863 and 1864, so before that time—that is, during the first two years of the war—the South could have continued exporting cotton to obtain needed munitions, manufactured items, and foodstuffs. However, the Confederate government discouraged any export during this period, so out of a 4-million-bale crop from '61 to '62, only 13,000 bales were reported to have left the South. The government was so sure that "Cotton was King" that by withholding it from the North and foreign countries (especially Britain) the South hoped to obtain support for the Confederacy by all the industrialists who would be hurt. Obviously, the South would have been better off had they exported as much cotton as possible in order to obtain supplies for the army and the civilian population.

The Southern government also had a strict ban on cotton trading through the lines with the North. In addition to the Cotton King argument, there were moral reasons why this was not to be done. It is easy to see in retrospect, however, that the South would have been better off trading because it would have obtained the materials that it needed to fight the war. Anyway, the cotton that was sent to Cuba and Bermuda was re-exported to New England. It is interesting to note, moreover, that there was quite a bit of illegal trading with the North as the needs of the Southern economy became more and more pressing.

Inflationary Finance

The government, of course, had to somehow obtain part of the civilian output for use in fighting the war. Foreigners were unwilling to lend very large sums to the Confederacy and, certainly after the Northern blockade on trading came into effect, there were very few import duties that could be used to support the war effort. The South did obtain a certain amount of federal government property and that of Union citizens when the war broke out. The most noteworthy is the Harpers Ferry arsenal and the naval shipyard at Norfolk. There was a certain amount of confiscation of privately produced goods in addition to internal taxes and loans. But that wasn't enough, accounting for perhaps less than one-half of the total outlays of the Confederate government during the war. These outlays were then valued at about $3 billion. How was the rest made up? By what we call **inflationary finance.** That is, the Confederacy issued large amounts of paper notes, or printed money. We see in Figure 7-1 that an index of commodity prices in the South rose from 100 in January 1861 to 9210 in April 1865. An index of the stock of money grew from 100 in January of 1861 to 2000 in April of 1865. We note here a not-atypical situation in what is called a **hyperinflation**—that is, a dramatic, overwhelming increase in the price level over a short period of time. As prices begin to rise very fast, consumers start anticipating this rise: They realize that the dollar bills—in this case, Confederate notes—that they are holding in their wallets are going to lose their purchasing power because of inflation. That means that it becomes more expensive to hold cash. What do these people attempt to do? They attempt to get rid of these pieces of paper because the cost of holding them is going up. As they attempt to get rid of them, they bid up prices even faster than they would do otherwise. During these periods, some people think there is a scarcity of money when, in fact, it's just the other way around. The reason that prices are going up so fast is because there is *too much* money around.

The Confederacy also faced a problem not encountered by most countries during hyperinflations: Toward the end of the war, it was assumed that Confederate notes would have a zero ex-

FIGURE 7-1

INFLATION IN THE CONFEDERACY

The rate of inflation was not very great in the beginning, but by the end of the Civil War the value of a Confederate dollar had depreciated to about 1 percent of its original value. (*Source:* E. M. Lerner, "Money, Prices, and Wages in the Confederacy, 1861-65," *Journal of Political Economy*, volume 63, February 1955, p. 29.)

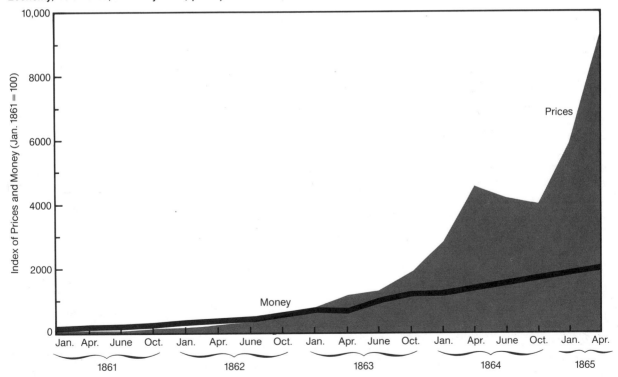

High Street, Richmond, Virginia, during the Civil War. (Historical Pictures Service, Chicago)

change value if there was a Union victory. And that was true. How much do you think a Confederate dollar note would be worth if it were known that in several months it could be exchanged for nothing? That is the main reason that the inflation reached astronomical proportions in 1865, and even as early as April of 1864.

It is not clear that this type of inflationary finance actually hindered the Confederate effort. We have evidence of other hyperinflations in other economies that did not really stop the growth in real output. For example, in post-World War I Germany, the hyperinflation did not slow down the growth in real incomes until it became impossible to use money for transactions, with a full wheelbarrow of bills required just to get a loaf of bread. Barter commenced and, as we all know, if one has to spend half of his day trying to exchange two pots for a pair of shoes, that doesn't leave much time for work. Barter leads to a reduction in real income as opposed to what is the case when money is used. It appears that in the South also there was some resort to barter, especially in the few months before the Union victory.

THE COLLAPSE

Valiant as the Confederate forces were, their ultimate collapse had to occur given the steady drain upon Southern resources at that time by the fighting needs, away from what we will call economically productive employments. This is not the only thing that happened, as everyone well knows. The physical base on which the Southern economy rested was slowly but surely whittled away by the Union. Union forces were continuously making inroads into the western and coastal fronts of the South. By 1861 there were almost no Confederate forces in Missouri; Kentucky and West Virginia were held for the Union. One of the big disasters of the war was the loss of New Orleans to federal amphibious forces in the spring of 1862. During that same year, western Tennessee was captured. This event closed off much of the South's access to the Mississippi. Many of the ports that could have been used to good end during the war were unavailable, such as Savannah and Jacksonville. Then in 1863 the Union conquered the entire Mississippi. The Confederacy was cut in two. In 1864 Sherman marched through Georgia breaking up the Confederacy into fourths. Atlanta fell. This continuous loss of territory could not allow for a Confederate military stalemate, which is all that was desired. We now turn to what happened in the North.

THE FEDERAL WAR ECONOMY

The outbreak of the Civil War meant immediate losses to Northern merchants, as all of the $300 million in debts owed by Southerners were never to be repaid. Most of the cotton textile factories soon became idle. In 1861 over 6000 business failures were reported by Dun, a forerunner of Dun and Bradstreet Reports. Banks started to fail; for example, 80 percent of the 110 banks in Illinois closed their doors. But by 1863 there was a minor war boom going on in the Northern states.

Military Manpower

About 15 percent of the labor force was involved in the Union effort. There had to be some way to get all these men into the army. By 1863 the North saw fit to pass the Enrollment Bill. However, this system of drafts was slightly different from our recently defunct system of conscription and is worthy of comment. It allowed those men who were drafted to buy someone to go in their stead. Thus, even though the method of conscription was somewhat arbitrary, the final determination of who would go to war was quite a bit more flexible. What do you think happened? Obviously, those whose civilian incomes were relatively high found it useful and, indeed, advantageous to hire people whose civilian incomes were relatively low to enroll as replacements.

This makes economic sense, even though it may not seem equitable. Those whose incomes are high will suffer a greater dollar cost if they are drafted than those whose incomes are low.

Also, from society's economic point of view, it is more efficient to allow high-income earners to pay low-income earners to fight the war, because income is generally a reflection of a person's productivity in society. That means that if high-income people are left to do their jobs and low-income people fight the war, the total output of the economy will be higher than otherwise. This is what is meant by economic efficiency—it has no normative connotation or value judgment attached to it. An efficient situation from an economic point of view is merely one in which the economic value obtained from the resources at hand is as high as possible. When we move from an inefficient to an efficient situation, we generally increase total output. But, of course, this "efficiency" is always defined relative to the existing endowments of wealth.

Increases in Northern Manufacturing

While the Northern generals were showing their ineptness during the first few years of the war, industrialists were showing how well they could adapt to increased chances of profits. Philadelphia saw 58 new plants built in 1862, 57 in 1863, and 65 in 1864. Within two years of the start of the war, four new cannon factories were built. The Colt arms plant in Hartford, Connecticut, went into production with a highly automated and efficient system. Northern mills were making shoes with innovative machinery such as new sewing machines. It is easy, however, to overrate the amount of increase in Northern manufacturing during this period, for many areas of industrialization activity, such as railroad expansion, came to a screeching halt. This offset the increased production elsewhere.

Financing the Northern Effort

With the declaration of war, in 1861, there was an immediate financial panic as banks suspended specie payments, and, as we mentioned above, business failures were common. The federal treasury was almost empty; federal credit was at a low point, as the government itself suspended specie payment. The Union had to finance the war somehow, and it did it by increased loans, taxation, and paper money.

Loans. With respect to the first form of war finance, J. Cooke, a Philadelphia banker, floated many loans for the government. He popularized bond issues by emphasizing the advantages of the investment and the patriotic duty of the citizens of the North. Over $2 billion were raised in this manner. Cooke's fee was 1 percent on sales up to $10 million and three-eighths of 1 percent on sales that exceeded that figure. He made a mint.

Taxes. The North probably used taxation to raise funds more than did the South. Excise taxes were raised in 1862 and extended to numerous goods and services. They produced almost $300 million. The Morrill Tariff, passed in 1861, raised another $300 million. And then there was the income tax, which produced about $55 million.

Money Creation. And as in the South, large amounts of paper money were created. Almost half a billion dollars in United States notes, otherwise called **Greenbacks,** were issued. These bills were not backed by gold or silver; they were merely promises on the part of the government to redeem them. Their value fluctuated wildly in terms of gold. By 1864 the rate of exchange was one Greenback for 40 cents of gold. It wasn't until 1879 that specie payment was resumed when Greenbacks were made convertible into gold or silver on a dollar-per-dollar rate of exchange.

THE EFFECTS ON INCOME DURING THE WAR

While it is necessarily true that some manufacturing occurred during the war that would not have occurred otherwise, it is not as obvious that total output in the North—and certainly not in the South—was any greater during the Civil War than it was before, or than it would have been without the war. There are no good data for that particular period, for the censuses were taken in ten-year intervals. However, New York and Massachusetts did take censuses for 1865, and these show that in both states there were declines in real output between 1860 and 1865, and also between 1855 and 1865. It appears that these two key manufacturing states, which accounted for over one-third of total manufacturing value added in 1860 and a little over 30 percent in 1870, did not have what one would call a rapidly expanding manufacturing sector during the war years.

Whenever there was a financial panic, the streets of every financial district filled with worried money-men. (Museum of the City of New York)

Little Capital Investment

Estimates of residential construction during this period indicate that after the war there was twice as much residential building as during the war. To further strengthen the case against the war years being a period of investment boom, one could look at the sales of McCormick reapers used in the gathering of wheat. The sales pattern showed a boom after the war, not during it. And there was certainly not a large surge in what we normally call war industries. Generally, the Civil War was not one of intensive capital investment. For example, the iron needed for the small-arms production during the war was only 1 percent of total U.S. iron output during the four years starting in 1861—one small factory could have done that. At the same time, the iron used in laying railroad track was *decreased* by seven times this figure. Another often-cited war industry was the manufacturing of boots for servicemen. However, at the same time that more boots were needed for federal soldiers, fewer boots were sold to the South. For example, in Massachusetts employment in the boot and shoe industry fell from almost 80,000 to 55,000 during the Civil War. Output fell from 45 million pairs to 32 million.

TABLE 7–1

THE EFFECT OF THE CIVIL WAR ON THE SOUTH

	OUTSIDE THE SOUTH	SOUTH
1860	$ 74.8	$77.7
1870	81.5	47.6
1880	105.8	61.5

Here we present commodity output per capita by region from 1860 to 1888 in 1879 prices. The South, even after 15 years of recovery from the Civil War, still had a per capita commodity output which was less than before the start of the Civil War. (*Source:* R. A. Esterlin, "Regional Income Trends, 1840–1950," in *American Economic History*, S. Harris, ed., New York: McGraw-Hill, 1961, pp. 525–547.)

Little Growth

The picture we find in the North during the Civil War was not unequivocally one of tremendous growth. We are used to thinking of wars, such as World War I and World War II, as being accompanied by large increases in output. However, these modern wars started out in periods of economic recession or depression, and they also involved much more extensive production facilities than were necessary for the premodern Civil War. Moreover, there is no doubt that the South suffered a tremendous decrease in real output during this period.

RECOVERY IN THE SOUTH

The Southern economy recovered relatively faster in manufacturing than in agriculture. By 1870, manufacturing production approached the prewar level and transportation and railroads were also recovering. It is obvious why manufacturing could recover faster than agriculture. The whole makeup of the agricultural society had been altered by the Emancipation Proclamation, while in manufacturing, there had been predominantly a free white labor force before the war anyway.

There is no doubt that in the postwar years the South was burdened by large material and human losses, as well as by an incalculable amount of social disorganization caused by the unquestionably changed status of slaves. Although the full cost of the war can, of course, not be seen in the statistics, we nonetheless present Table 7–1, which shows the commodity output per capita by region from 1860 to 1880. Whereas outside the South, per capita income increased almost 9 percent, Southern per capita output in 1870 was only about 60 percent of what it had been in 1860. The South was hurt badly and took many years to recover. But the question remains whether the sum total of the war's effects on the economy was to cause higher growth than would have occurred in its absence. That probing question is taken up next.

Definitions of New Terms

INFLATIONARY FINANCE: the issuance of large amounts of money to help finance government expenditures, usually during wartime.

HYPERINFLATION: a consistent rise in the price level that attains astronomical rates, such as a 1000 percent increase a month!

GREENBACKS: United States Bank notes that were not backed by gold or silver; they got their name from their color.

Chapter Summary

1. The Civil War caused great disruption in the South since it had been mainly a rural, agricultural society without the immediate ability to produce war goods.
2. In the South the war brought about urbanization that would not otherwise have occurred for many years.
3. The Southern government restricted trade even before the Northern blockade of its ports, severely limiting the possibility of obtaining needed war materials in exchange for export goods, such as cotton.
4. The Confederate government resorted to large amounts of inflationary finance by issuing many Confederate notes. As must be expected, the price index rose dramatically; toward the end of the Confederacy, a hyperinflation was experienced.
5. The Northern military effort was much less pervasive; nonetheless, 15 percent of the labor force was involved. At that time, draftees were able to pay someone else to go in their place, thus allowing for a more efficient though not necessarily more equitable military manpower-procurement system.
6. The federal government also resorted to inflationary finance by issuing large amounts of Greenbacks, whose value fell to 40 cents in terms of gold by 1864.
7. The war reduced residential construction in the North, as well as railroad extensions.

Questions for Thought and Discussion

1. Do you think that the South could have at least reached a stalemate if its trade policies had allowed for extensive importation of war materials in exchange for Southern export goods?
2. What do you think the Emancipation Proclamation did to the wealth of plantation owners with large numbers of slaves?
3. Inflationary finance has been called a tax. If you agree, who pays the tax and how? (Hint: What happens to the purchasing power of the dollars you hold during an inflation?)
4. During a hyperinflation when does it become no longer worthwhile to use money as a medium of exchange; that is, when does it become more advantageous to resort to barter?

STATE HISTORICAL SOCIETY OF WISCONSIN

THE MAN AND HIS REAPER

Cyrus Hall McCormick (1809–1884)

Inventor, Manufacturer, Philanthropist

THE YEAR was 1851, the place was London's Crystal Palace, where the Great Industrial Exhibition was being held. The American participants were sad. Many American exhibitors had backed down at the last minute so that numerous stalls stood unused. And besides a huge quantity of native products on exhibition—tobacco, preserved peaches, and Indian corn—there wasn't much in the way of manufactured products. But then a man on a horse-drawn contraption slowly worked his way to a wheat field at Tip-Tree Farm in Essex. What he did was unbelievable. He harvested the field in a time that no one believed possible: Grain was gathered from 74 yards in 74 seconds, which meant that McCormick's mechanical reaper would clear 20 acres a day. The *Times* (London) declared, "[McCormick's] reaping machine has carried conviction to the heart of the British agriculturist." McCormick's invention had indeed done that. It had already begun to change farming in the United States.

McCormick was born on a farm in Rockbridge County, Virginia. His formal education was limited. It wasn't until the age of 22 that his inventive spirit allowed itself to blossom. He invented and took out a patent for a hillside plow of quite original design. During this same year his father attempted for the twentieth unsuccessful time to perfect a reaping machine and finally abandoned the project; Cyrus decided to take it on. Within a very short period, starting from scratch and avoiding the mistakes his dad made, young Cyrus had a successful invention. The principles contained in his earliest reaper have proved essential to reaping machinery down to the present time. Actually, McCormick's patent, taken out in 1834, was preceded by one entered by Cincinnati's Obed Hussey. For some unknown reason, Hussey moved his plant to Baltimore while McCormick went to Chicago, where he would be closest to the grain country. It was in Chicago that McCormick built his fortune. Here he pioneered installment sales geared to the farmer's own seasons and made it a practice not to sue for overdue payment. Soon McCormick's output rose to 1000 reapers a year, and his name became synonymous with the product.

By 1860 Cyrus McCormick was a millionaire, but the best was yet to come. During the Civil War, farm machinery sales took off like a rocket.

For you'll remember that in the North up to 15 percent of the labor force was involved in the war effort. Young men were taken off the farm. Lincoln's Secretary of War, Edwin M. Stanton, was moved to say in 1861, "Without McCormick's invention, I feel the North could not win." The mechanical reaper was in part responsible for the development of the large-scale farming which we find throughout this nation.

By 1902 the McCormick farm machinery business had sales of $75 million. In that year, through the successful services of J. P. Morgan and company, the McCormick firm and three of the other top industrial firms in the farm machinery business joined hands into what became the International Harvester Company, accounting for 85 percent of the machinery used by America's 10 million farmers.

By the turn of the century the reaper originally invented by McCormick permitted one man to harvest as much grain as scores of men in 1840. Food costs were consequently dramatically lowered, benefiting everybody; Cyrus McCormick got rich by performing a useful social purpose.

ISSUE VII DID THE CIVIL WAR STIMULATE GROWTH?

What Happened to the Economy?

The War and Government Legislation

Perhaps because of faulty data, or perhaps because of the general notion that war is good for the economy, early students of the Civil War were convinced that it spurred economic growth and had a lot to do with America's subsequent era of industrialization. You should have gotten some inkling of what actually happened during the war period itself in the last chapter. From that it would logically follow that the Civil War did not itself stimulate further growth since it is questionable whether even during the war years it stimulated growth. But this would be too facile a view of the potential impact of the Civil War on future U.S. economic development. For during the war period, several innovative pieces of government legislation were passed that in theory—and perhaps in practice—could have influenced the future course of the economy. Before we deal specifically with tariffs, the National Banking Act, the Homestead Act, as well as railroad subsidies, we first want to look at what happened to the economy in the years following the war.

The North and the South after the War

Little need be said about what happened to the South after the war. In the last chapter we presented some statistics showing the drop in per capita income that the South suffered for many postwar years to come. Much of its productive capacity had been wiped out; it also had to reorganize its entire agricultural system and contend with the social disorganization from a freed slave population. In the North, of course, there was no such problem, except for the more than 300,000 lost lives, for the destruction was insignificant.

Because of the large issue of Greenbacks during the war period, by 1864 the price index rose to two times its pre-1860 level. Since many people associate inflation with periods of prosperity (even though this association is not guaranteed), they would naturally assume that there must have been prosperity during the war, at least in the North. There is also the notion that during the war the North had a large body of manufacturing lords who obtained excessive profits by selling shoddy merchandise to the government. In fact, very few manufacturers made a killing during the war. Some prominent people—for example, J. Cooke, mentioned in the last chapter—did in fact make millions, but there weren't very many of them.

What Do the Statistics Show?

The growth rate of output from 1859 to 1869 was the lowest it had been in many years. In fact, if we examine the long-term trends, we see that total commodity output rose at an average annual rate of 4.6 percent between 1840 and 1860, dropping to an average annual rate of 4.4 percent between 1870 and 1900. With respect to industrialization, the shift out of agriculture into manufacturing was as rapid during the two decades before the war as it was during the two decades after the war. If we look at how much manufacturing contributed to the increases in output, we find that while value added in manufacturing grew at about 7.0 percent per annum from 1840 to 1860, it grew at only 6 percent per annum from 1870 to 1900. Of the total commodity output from 1860 to 1870, its growth rate was only 2 percent, the lowest rate during any decade in the entire nineteenth century. There was also a relatively large decline in the productivity of labor in the manufacturing sector from 1860 to 1870.

Rather than being a decade of tremendously increased production and industrialization, the Civil War and Reconstruction years marked a departure from the general output, productivity, and income trends that had existed prior to it. At least in part, this shouldn't be surprising when you realize that out of a labor force of 7.5 million, 1 million men were involved in the fighting. This is a reduction of about 15 percent. How could the economy have experienced an industrial renaissance with that kind of depletion of the ranks of the working force?

Government Expenditures

There is also the idea that large amounts of government expenditures caused a rapid increase in the manufacturing sector, especially in the North. This, however, was not true. Government expenditures went mainly for bounties, salaries, and food—especially beef—and a few unsophisticated weapons. (After all, we didn't use tanks during the Civil War.) In any event, the total amount of Northern government expenditures during the Civil War repre-

sented a minor part of total output. And, to top it all off, these expenditures were generally substitutes for what the private sector would have spent anyway. In other words, the private sector did not spend all of its income because the government obtained part of it through loans, increased excise taxes, an income tax, and also taxation by inflation. These foregone expenditures in the private sector were merely made up by the government.

The Business Atmosphere

It is true that business was booming after the first few disorganized months of the war. However, good business does not necessarily imply economic development. Many profits may be derived merely from speculation, and this is just a transfer from one sector of the economy to another sector. Also, with all the good business that there was, there was just as much bad business in some sectors. In fact, there was more bad business than good in the Northern cotton textile industry because it was brought to its knees after the blockade of imports from the South. Numerous mills closed down and others were forced into the production of wool which, as can be expected, grew as an industry to replace the cotton textiles that could no longer be spun. However, there were costs involved in shifting over, and these

costs contributed to the reduced productivity in that sector. Moreover, even during the Civil War there were in the North severe pockets of unemployment. To be sure, the conscription at that time did ameliorate to some extent this problem of unemployment, but not completely.

Again, it must be stressed that even though the above facts and figures give a quite compelling picture of nondevelopment during and after the Civil War, this does not categorically answer the question of whether or not the Civil War stimulated growth, for we must also look at the legislation that was passed during that time. One of the most significant pieces was the National Banking Act.

Enactment of the National Banking Act

Prior to federal legislation in 1863 and 1864 which established a national banking system, the banking atmosphere was one of almost unbridled freedom throughout all of the states. In this era of free banking, just about anybody could charter a bank in just about any state. The main intent—at least that which was aired in public—of the National Banking Act was to establish a national system that would unify all of the banks in the entire United States. However, the original legislation which provided for the chartering of national banks was based on the free banking charters of that day—in almost all respects. The several exceptions made all the difference in the world. The result was *not* a national banking system and in general *not* the creation of a national institution which would foster further development by greatly expanding credit markets and credit availability.

Congress Wanted More Money

In the first place, Congress really enacted the banking legislation in order to increase the government's borrowing power during the war. It did this by requiring all national banks to invest a portion of their capital in government bonds. And the capital which was necessary to open a national bank was, it turned out, substantially higher than most banks actually had, especially in the rural areas. What did this mean? Simply that national banks did not in fact become established as the one and only institution for banking throughout the United States. In the agricultural areas of the country, the average capital of nonnational banks was less than the *minimum* required to open a national bank or to be transformed into a national bank. This was to hinder the growth of rural banks. The consequence was higher rural interest rates in the South and West.

No National System Created

Even by 1900 there were still almost 9000 nonnational banks as opposed to about 4000 national ones. Obviously, the Civil War legislation did not give the United States a single, unified banking system. We might tentatively conclude that there was actually a restraint in the number of banks that were started after enactment of the legislation as compared to what would have happened had it never been passed.

A Unified Reserve System

On the plus side of the national banking legislation was the fact that the country's banks were linked together through a reserve system which provided a legally sanctioned formal mechanism for transferring funds between banks. This tended to promote an efficient allocation of loanable funds throughout the country. In other words, it was easier for funds to go to areas where they could yield the highest social product—that is, to areas where the rate of return would be highest. This generally meant the transfer of bank funds from agricultural to industrial uses, which helped funnel credit to areas which required large amounts of capital, such as railroad investment and large-scale industry.

In any event, we cannot at this time decipher the evidence enough to answer with any certainty the question about the true effects of the national banking system legislation passed during the Civil War on the future course of development in the United States.

Giving Away Free Land

In 1862 the Union Congress passed the Homestead Act. This provided that 160 acres of land which was hitherto owned by the federal government could be acquired by a settler if he agreed to live on it or cultivate it for at least five consecutive years. What effect did this magnanimous act have on the distribution of land holdings in the United States and, consequently, on the development of our open spaces? It turns out that the amount of land put into cultivation after the Civil War attributable to homesteading was less than 20 percent. The rest was either purchased from federal, state, or local governments, or was land grants given to railroads. But the numbers alone do not speak of what actually could have happened.

Many historians maintain that the Homestead Act caused a reduced growth of national product during this period because it caused famers to use inefficient amounts of capital and labor on what turned out to be too small a tract of land. Remember that the Homestead Act provided for only 160 acres. But, indeed, could this have caused grave misallocations? Yes, but only for a short period of time. After all, whoever took care of the land for five years could sell it thereafter. So, by allowing only 160-acre grants, the government perhaps induced a short-run misallocation of resources into homestead properties, but not a long-run misallocation. One thing is clear, however: By not selling that land, the government did not obtain revenues. That meant that taxpayers in general were worse off. There was a redistribution of wealth away from taxpayers in general to those who obtained the free homestead land. What effects this might have had on growth are quite unknown by scholars in the field.

Land grants to railroads were just mentioned as one possible way of disposing of land in the public domain. Other railroad subsidies were given out during this period, and again we must ask the question: Did this piece of government intervention in the marketplace during the Civil War increase our rate of growth?

Helping out the Railroads

Remember that during the war itself there was almost a total stop to the construction of railroad mileage. But there were some notable exceptions. The federal gov-

ernment had established a policy of subsidizing the railroads by giving them land grants for their rights-of-way. Five railroad systems accounted for 75 percent of all of these subsidies: the Central Pacific; Union Pacific; Atchison, Topeka and Santa Fe; Northern Pacific; and the Texas and Pacific railroad systems. The Union Pacific Railroad, which obtained land grants by the Acts of 1862 and 1864, did indeed turn out to be, according to a reinterpretation of the data, a good deal. That is, the **social rate of return** on that investment was relatively high. So the government subsidies were indeed justified from a social point of view. However, the increase in national income made possible by the Union Pacific was only 0.01 of 1 percent. Not a very large number, is it? Similar computations have been made for the Central Pacific Railroad with similar results. Although all of these numbers certainly leave some room for doubt, nonetheless, it does not appear that legislation during the Civil War allowing more subsidies to the railroads provided a great impetus to the growth of output in the United States.

Protective Tariffs

There is a theory that has been hanging around in economics for at least two hundred years. It's

called the **infant industry argument.** Supposedly, if certain industries are to be able to start up and become technologically efficient so that they can eventually compete in the world market, they must be "protected" in their infancy. That is, a tariff wall must be erected around that infant industry. The tariff wall causes the price of imports to go up high enough so that the less efficient "baby" American producer can compete. Eventually, though (goes the argument), technology will be developed in the infant so it will become a full-grown, sassy young adult. The tariff walls can then be lowered. Even if the argument were strictly correct—which it isn't unless we add some assumptions—we find that in the history of protective tariffs for infant industries, when the infant has grown up the tariffs are generally not taken off. Nonetheless, the argument is often used when discussing the economic impact of legislation during the Civil War.

It should be remembered that the two decades prior to the Civil War saw the rise of manufacturing and economic growth under a low-tariff policy. The Republicans, however, came into power in 1861 committed to making sure that there were higher duties to "protect" American manufacturers. Since there were no Southern Congressmen to fight them, they raised the tariff even before Lincoln took office. Then, using the excuse that they needed to raise more war revenues, they raised the tariff even higher. By 1867 the average duty on all imports reached a whopping 47 percent. It wasn't clear at that time which industries benefited and who was hurt.

Distortions Caused

What is clear is that in almost all cases a tariff causes a distortion and a misallocation of resources. After all, the way we obtain the highest economic value from the scarce resources we have is by using them where they have the highest comparative advantage. If other countries can produce goods at a lower price than we can, we should take advantage of that if we want to maximize economic welfare (although certain industries may be hurt in the short run). On the other side of the coin, we end up producing those goods which other nations do not have a comparative advantage in. We export the latter and import the former. That's what free trade is all about, and that's why so many economists are against setting up tariff walls around nations.

Exceptions to the Rule

There are some exceptions to this rule, particularly in the case where a country is effectively a monopolist in the purchasing of a particular product. That might be true, for example, in modern-day America, where we consume a large fraction of the total world output of coffee and bananas. In such a case, it might be advisable for *overall* economic welfare to impose a tariff, but it has nothing to do with protecting domestic industry—we don't even grow coffee or bananas. In any event, these exceptions are not numerous.

Even though the tariff was raised substantially during the Civil War, it is not at all obvious that the Northern people benefited and that economic growth in general was increased. No doubt some of the manufacturers benefited; and no doubt the economy at large suffered.

This is just another instance where there is no clear-cut evidence to show that legislative actions during the Civil War helped promote the growth of the United States.

Definitions of New Terms

SOCIAL RATE OF RETURN: the rate of return on an investment that takes account of not only the benefits to the private investor but also any other benefits that society obtains.

INFANT INDUSTRY ARGUMENT: the argument used in support of high tariffs; presumably an industry, if protected by a high tariff, can improve its technology and efficiency so much that later on when it is full-grown, the tariff can be removed, but it will still be able to compete in the world market with other full-grown competitors.

Questions for Thought and Discussion

1. Why do many people believe all wars are good for the economy?
2. What effect on the rest of the economy could an increase in railroad track mileage have had during this wartime period?
3. If a tariff is put on a particular good, what happens to the domestic price of that good? Who benefits and who loses?
4. What arguments could be used to support the contention that the Civil War did cause an increase in the growth rate of the economy?

Half a Century of Peace

8

ONCE THE Civil War was ended, the nation got back to its primary economic task—raising its standard of living. It did so with increasing vigor, as the railroads expanded far into the West, as investment banking became super-big business, as the health standards of the population rose, as the educational attainment of the workingman steadily increased. For businessmen, the period from 1865 to 1890 has been called the epoch of unbridled freedom. Fortunes were made. Wealth was accumulated. This was the era of large trusts and monopolies which necessitated passage of our first antitrust act in 1890. This was also an era of tremendous increase in the communications capacity of the nation. The harnessing of electricity for communications by Samuel F. B. Morse was eventually to be seen as only a beginning. Thomas Edison and Alexander Bell continued Morse's pioneering work to turn the nation into one big telephone network. Even before the start of the First World War, another great achievement had been heralded by the introduction of the first Model T in 1908. Mass-production techniques had become available for a mass market. For indeed, native population growth was continuing and immigration was also reaching unprecedented heights.

INCREASES IN LIVING STANDARDS

While we have seen that per capita income was increasing rather steadily through the 1840s and '50s, the Civil War brought an abrupt halt. It took a while for the South to recover from the devastating effects of all the material capital destroyed and men killed. In fact, it took a while for the North, too, because naturally there were casualties on both sides—a total of more than 600,000 men died, reducing

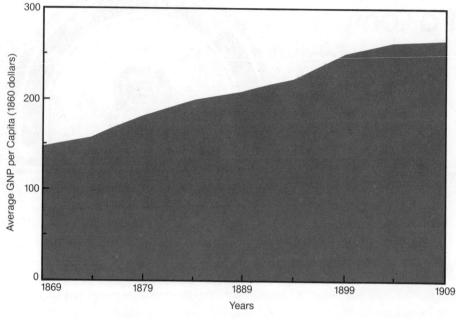

FIGURE 8–1

RISING STANDARDS OF LIVING

We see that from the start of the period, 1869, to the end, 1908, the average annual GNP per capita in 1860 dollars rose from 147 to 268. (*Source:* R. E. Gallman, "Gross National Product in the United States, 1834–1909," in National Bureau of Economic Research, *Output, Employment, and Productivity in the United States after 1800,* New York: Columbia University Press, 1966, p. 30.) pp. 17-18

the nation's labor force at that time by more than 5 percent. Nonetheless, for the half century following the Civil War, the standard of living per capita in the United States grew at an average rate of about 2 percent per year. By World War I it was roughly three times its level at the end of hostilities in 1865. This can be easily seen in Figure 8–1. This is, of course, not the end of the story. There were large amounts of immigration during that period, and population grew at a fairly rapid rate. Hence, total output expanded even more than per capita income. Its average rate of growth was around 4 percent a year. The eightfold increase in total output is shown in Figure 8–2.

THE GROWING AMERICAN CITIZENRY AND THE GROWING AMERICAN TERRITORY

During this half century between the two wars there were expansions, both in the number of

The Quay of Dublin, 1854. (Courtesy of The New York Historical Society)

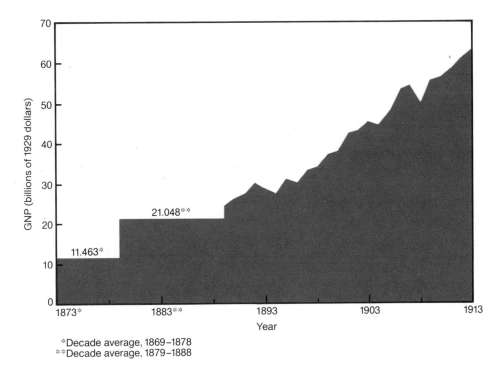

*Decade average, 1869–1878
**Decade average, 1879–1888

FIGURE 8–2   **GROWTH IN TOTAL OUTPUT**

The average growth rate of total output was around 4 percent during this period. There was an eightfold increase from the end of the Civil War until the start of World War I. (*Source:* J. W. Kendrick, "Productivity Trends in the United States," National Bureau of Economic Research, Princeton, N.J.: Princeton University Press, 1961.)

people who worked and played in the United States, and in the territory in which they were able to work and play. Population grew at an average rate of over 2 percent a year, rising from 36 million at the end of the Civil War to over 100 million by the beginning of World War I. By the end of the period, however, the growth rate of the population was slower than at the beginning.

Why Population Grew

Population grew for two reasons: (1) because of a large influx of immigrants, and (2) because the birth rate exceeded the death rate. The second reason contributed far more to population growth than the first.

Immigration. However, immigration was important. We can see how many thousands of immigrants landed on our shores during this period by looking at Figure 8–3. The gold areas in that figure represent business depressions. It is not merely coincidental that decreases in net immigration coincided with business depressions. After all, one of the main reasons that people desire to expend the energy and all the other costs involved in migrating to another country is for increased real standards of living. When business recessions and depressions in the United States reduced the possibility of finding employment, there was less economic incentive for immigration, and consequently there was less of it.

Fertility. It is perhaps less easy to explain why the fertility of the native population decreased toward the end of this period. But if we look a little bit into the economics of the matter, we can find at least a partial explanation. Urbanization increased during this period as more and more people moved off the farm and into the city. When this happened, children no longer were as much of a productive asset as they had been on the farm, where they could start working from very early ages. Rather than being an investment in

productive capacity, child-bearing created for the city dweller an item that we will call a **consumption good.** That is, it yielded mainly pleasure; it could not generate as much future net income for the producers of it, the parents. Hence, children were a less valuable asset in the city. Also, in the city, twentieth-century women had greater opportunities to work outside the household. Hence, if they were forced to stay home to raise children they bore a cost—lost wages—that they had not previously borne while on the farm. This was an additional incentive to limit the number of children per family.

IMPROVING THE LAND

Turning now to the increased amount of inhabited land, we note that we had acquired tremendous

FIGURE 8-3   **IMMIGRATION INTO THE UNITED STATES**

Here we see net immigration into the United States—arrivals minus departures—from the end of the Civil War to the start of World War I. The gold areas represent business depressions. Usually net immigration was low during these periods. (*Source:* Simon Kuznets and E. Rubin, *Immigration and the Foreign Born,* New York: National Bureau of Economic Research, 1954, p. 95.)

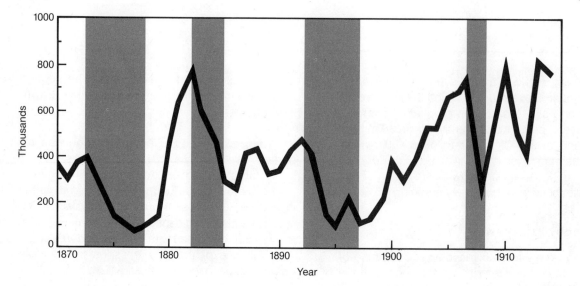

additional acreage in territories before the Civil War: The Republic of Texas joined the states in 1845; the Oregon Territory became ours in 1846; the Mexican Secession gave us even more land in the West and Southwest two years later. These additional lands gave us 70 percent more territory. But land per se is useless. Only when it is *improved* can it increase the productive capacity of the nation. Unimproved, it might be nice to look at, but it is generally not useful, particularly for a nation that was striving for increased standards of living for every inhabitant. Hence, at the end of the Civil War, this 70 percent increase in the national domain was virtually uninhabited. During the next 50 years, however, the "frontier" was finally eradicated. There were no longer large areas in the United States which had no population. This large availability of uninhabited land throughout the period, land that could be cultivated generally for the raising of crops and livestock, had allowed Americans to forestall any detrimental effects that diminishing returns might have.

Remember back in Issue III when we talked about the Malthusian doctrine. As soon as all available arable land was used up in European societies, the specter of diminishing returns came to haunt the population. In the absence of technological change, the additional output that an additional worker could obtain on a fixed amount of land had to fall. In the United States, this was not the case because as old lands became more populated and used up, new ones could be cultivated. Later on, of course, when all good lands were already in production, we countered diminishing returns by increases in our technology. That is, we were able to increase the productivity of farm workers.

One of the main reasons that land was in fact not used up sooner in the United States was the scarcity of transportation. During earlier periods in this nation land was not economically accessible for farmers. That is why the frontier existed. It was only with the expansion of the railroad network that farming moved westward to the fertile new lands in Nebraska, Kansas, Texas, Oklahoma, the Dakotas, and the Far West.

THE GOLDEN AGE OF THE IRON HORSE

At the beginning of the Civil War, there were perhaps 30,000 miles of railroad track in all of the United States. But by the end of the nineteenth century, the railroad system was almost as completely developed as it would ever be. There were over 200,000 miles of track, and most of it was standard gauge width, quite unlike the unintegrated system that existed in 1860. Moreover, whereas in 1860 there were hardly any bridges, in 1900 they dotted the landscape. Locomotives increased in power and grew in number; freight cars multiplied by 20 in only 40 years. And the capacity of each car increased 300 percent; hence, the rolling car capacity of the railroads had jumped by a multiple of 50 at the end of the decade. Employment on the railroads was also up, growing from 100,000 to 1 million men. Whereas in 1860 1 percent of the labor force engaged in railroad employment, three times that proportion were involved in it by the turn of the century. Passenger miles and ton freight miles increased immensely—500 percent and 6000 percent, respectively. The railroad had become a freight carrier. But because of other means of traveling the role of the passenger train was relatively diminishing. By the year 1910, the railroad reached its peak of influence on the American economy.

High Finance and Rate Wars

The 1880s saw a wave of competitive construction in the railroad industry. Each system found itself in competition over certain routes with other systems. We found *eleven* lines going from New York to the Midwest!

The monetary debt of all the railroad systems combined started to exceed that of the entire United States government. In floating much of this debt, numerous shady deals seemed to get lots of shady characters tons of money. For these were the days of the Vanderbilts, the Fisks, and the Goulds. There were some pretty outrageous schemes used to obtain control of various railroads to form monopolies. Cornelius Vanderbilt, for example, was busy during and after the Civil War buying all the small lines he could get his hands on. He controlled the lines running from New York City to Albany. Then he started buying New York Central stock in 1865. Not content with the rate at which he was acquiring that company, he came up with a scheme to cause the price of Central stock to drop. Part of this scheme involved stopping his trains short of a bridge at Albany, thus forcing the Central's passengers to cross by themselves to make the connection (even in the rain). There were other things he did which we don't have to go into now; the end result of Vanderbilt's shenanigans was the capitulation of the Central Railroad and the combination of the Central line with Vanderbilt's Hudson line, with Vanderbilt, of course, as president.

There were also scandals with the construction of the railroads to the West, the most famous involving Credit Mobilier, an ephemeral construction company. It was rumored that the Mobilier made direct profits for building the Union Pacific at between $33 and $50 million.

Rate Wars and Price Fixing

This was the era of rate fixing and rate wars, which seemed to alternate with each other. It's not hard to figure out why. After all, think about how a railroad is built. It contains lots of massive locomotives, expensive cars, and thousands of miles of track. In other words, the **fixed** or **sunk costs** for a railroad are tremendous. And, moreover, just as the name implies, *sunk costs are forever sunk;* they have no bearing on the decision that a firm

or business has to make about *future* prices and outputs, for nothing can be done about sunk costs once they are incurred. For railroads, this meant that in order to compete for freight two lines would be willing to lower their prices until they barely covered the out-of-pocket costs that were incurred for running the lines. These out-of-pocket costs, which seemed to vary with the rate of use or production, are called, as you might have guessed, **variable costs.** So as long as the railroad line covered its variable costs, it would be willing to lower its price in order to compete for business that it could take away from other lines.

The railroad lines had an obvious incentive to get together to fix rates so that they would *not* compete, and could therefore avoid *price* competition. All parties to an agreement could feel they would be better off. However, the incentive for cheating on such agreements is tremendous, particularly if one is not caught. If one railroad cheated on a rate-fixing agreement, it could obtain lots of business, thereby increasing its profits, since the other railroads would not lower their prices if they were still abiding by the agreement. There were continuous pools and internal regulating committees for railroads, but none of them seemed to work; none of them seemed to insure a continuous system of rate fixing. This was the time, then, of secret rebates. This was also the time of **price discrimination.** Most railroads ended up charging more for short hauls than for long hauls because there was generally no competition in short-haul routes. It was only in the long-haul routes that more than one railroad would build competing lines.

Finally, in 1887 the Interstate Commerce Act created the Interstate Commerce Commission and with it a set of rules to create ''fair'' business practices by railroads. In reality, however, many economists and historians believe that the ICC was created at the behest of the railroad lines so that they could have government supervision of their rate fixing.

PUBLISHED BY CURRIER & IVES   Copyright 1876 by Currier & Ives, N.Y.   125 NASSAU ST NEW YORK

THE PROGRESS OF THE CENTURY.
THE LIGHTNING STEAM PRESS.   THE ELECTRIC TELEGRAPH.   THE LOCOMOTIVE.   THE STEAMBOAT.

(The Granger Collection)

OTHER AREAS OF CHANGE IN THE ECONOMY

There were so many things happening during this half century that it is difficult to know where to begin and where to end in this short chapter. However, what we clearly can talk about are the additional factors which contributed to increasing incomes in the United States. We first mentioned increasing population and the expansion in territory that was soon to be improved and used for agriculture. The railroad was also an obvious vehicle for economic growth, the extent of which we will examine in the following issue. Furthermore, increases in the productivity of the labor force cannot be underrated. That is, in the nineteenth century the American investment in education grew by leaps and bounds.

Education

We sometimes call the investment in education an investment in human capital because any investment, strictly speaking, will create the possibility of increased production in the future. That is exactly what education does, whether it be formal or informal. Formal education is, of course, what you are doing right now—going to a formally organized school. But informal education is important also. This involves on-the-job training—gaining more experience by observing what is happening around oneself.

The American nation has always had high literacy rates. In 1870, almost 90 percent of all adult white Americans could read and write. By the beginning of the First World War, this figure had risen to 96 percent. The black population, while having only a 20 percent literacy rate in 1870, increased it phenomenally to 70 percent by 1910. The total resource cost devoted to education in 1860 was 1.4 percent of GNP; by 1900 this proportion had doubled. This figure includes not only the direct but the indirect costs of education. The direct costs are quite obvious: books, tuition, and things like that. The indirect costs are perhaps less so. Can you guess what the largest indirect cost is? Well, think about it this way. When you go to school, you don't work. When you don't work, you don't earn income. Therefore, going to school involves giving up the *opportunity* to make current income. Hence, one of the greatest indirect costs of going to school is the forgone income that could have been earned had a person remained in the labor force. Economists like to call this **opportunity cost.**

Investment in Health

Investing in education was not the only way to raise the productivity of the labor force and of the population at large. Investment in health was another way, and a most important one in the nineteenth century. Compared to today, health standards in those times were abysmal, although they were probably superior to what existed in other countries in the world. There were numerous epidemics: Yellow fever, smallpox, typhoid, diphtheria, typhus, and cholera were common. There were also such things as dysentery, malaria, and the "grippe." Tuberculosis was rampant. Today we know why those things occur, but at the end of the Civil War, medicine could hardly be called a science. During that half century, there were very few improvements in medical care per se; in fact, one was generally better off by not going to a doctor. There were only two serious diseases

which responded to the black bag of the MD: Malaria could be treated by applications of quinine, and smallpox prevented by a vaccination.

It was, rather, the discovery of the need to improve sewage disposal and treatment and to provide pure water that accounts in large part for the vast improvement in health standards at that time. The discoveries of Louis Pasteur and the subsequent pasteurization of milk contributed much. A falling death rate was sure to result, and indeed it did—in 1915 it was about 60 percent of its 1870 level. But more important economically, better health conditions allowed workers to be more productive, to be absent from work less, and to feel generally more like pursuing their individual endeavors.

MONEY PROBLEMS

All was not a bed of roses throughout this period. There were many problem times and problem areas. One of the most recurrent was that of inflation and deflation. Looking at Figure 8–4, we see that the period after the Civil War was generally one of a drop in price levels, oftentimes called deflation. Notice, however, that when we compare the price index changes apparent in Figure 8–4 with average GNP per capita in Figure 8–1, there is a slight negative correlation. In other words, falling prices—deflation—did not spell depression.

Reduced Supply of Greenbacks

There was, however, a distinct relationship between changes in the price level and changes in the stock of money during that period. Right after the Civil War, the federal government deliberately reduced the quantity of Greenbacks in circulation in order to get their price up to where a dollar in Greenback was worth a dollar in gold in exchange, which finally happened in 1879. We note that during this period there was a cry for more Greenbacks, not fewer, particularly by the Greenback Labor Party, which associated a rising price level with a higher price of products and, hence, higher incomes and a higher standard of living.

On a Gold Standard

After the year 1878, we were on a *de facto* gold standard. That is, gold served as a medium of exchange and also was the backing for reserves in the banking system. Hence, the entire money stock was tied to the production of gold, which did not increase rapidly enough to keep up with the nation's transactions' need for money, and hence the nation experienced deflation for three decades. It was only after discoveries of gold in South Africa and the Yukon, plus development of the relatively inexpensive cyanide reduction process, which allowed the gold stock—and,

hence, the money stock—to increase faster than the increased rate of output in the economy, that the deflation was stopped. Notice that in the latter period under study, we finally saw a rise in prices.

STRUCTURAL CHANGES

To finish this chapter, and as a lead into the next one, we note that there was a distinct change in the structure of the economy. Looking at Table 8–1, we see that the percentage of output attributable to agricultural production fell from 53 percent in 1870 to 33 percent by the end of the century (though there was still an *absolute* increase in farm output). The opposite was the case for manufacturing, whereas in the areas of mining and construction combined there was no change. We

---

FIGURE 8–4 **A PERIOD OF DEFLATION**

Prices rose during the Civil War but followed a long-run trend downward to a trough before the turn of the century, and then moved slightly upward until World War I. (*Source:* Bureau of Labor Statistics.)

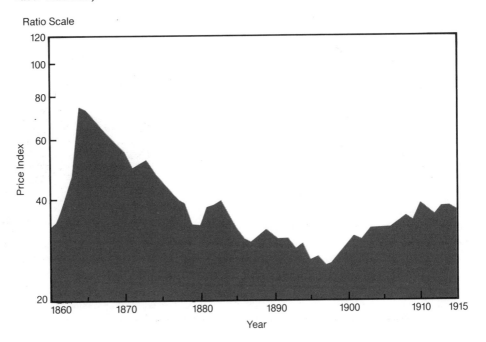

TABLE 8–1

THE CHANGING COMPOSITION OF OUTPUT

YEAR	AGRICULTURE	MANUFACTURING	MINING AND CONSTRUCTION
1869	53	33	14
1874	46	39	14
1879	49	37	14
1884	41	44	15
1889	37	48	15
1894	32	53	15
1899	33	53	14

At the beginning of the period, agriculture accounted for 53 percent of total output, whereas manufacturing, only a third. These proportions reversed themselves by the turn of the century. (*Source:* R. E. Galman, "Commodity Output, 1839–1899," in *Trends in the American Economy in the Nineteenth Century,* National Bureau of Economic Research, Princeton, N.J.: Princeton University Press, 1960, p. 26.)

had become a manufacturing instead of an agrarian economy. At the same time, the percentage distribution of the labor force was changing accordingly. In farming, fishing, and mining there was more than half the working population in 1870, but barely a third by 1910. This trend was to continue even until today, when a little more than 4 percent of our population is in these fields. What happened, of course, was that the labor force became more active in the manufacturing, trade, and construction sectors.

There was also a distinct movement to the West. This was understandable since migration usually responds to economic opportunity. People moved to the West because that's where the opportunity was. They moved in an attempt to improve their economic standard of living. Because we had such a highly mobile population, we found people moving as soon as the economic opportunity warranted it.

The era after the Civil War was indeed a period of tremendous change in the American economy. It was an era of transformation, and that, in more detail, is the subject of our next chapter. But before we go on, let's reexamine the great railroad debate in the following historical issue.

Main Street, Deadwood, South Dakota, in the 1880s. When the rains came, the mud became almost knee deep. (Western History Department, Denver Public Library)

Definitions of New Terms

CONSUMPTION GOOD: a good which yields utility in the current period, but not in future periods. Consumption goods are such things as food, movies, and trips. To be contrasted with an investment or capital good, which yields a stream of services or utility in the *future*.

FIXED OR SUNK COSTS: costs which are incurred once and for all and cannot be altered. Fixed costs are not dependent on the rate of use of an asset. For example, a car you buy will depreciate to some extent every year even if you don't use it at all. This type of depreciation is unavoidable and would be considered a fixed cost.

VARIABLE COSTS: costs which vary with the use of an asset. For example, gasoline would be a variable cost in using your car: The more you drive it, the more gasoline you have to buy.

PRICE DISCRIMINATION: charging some people higher prices than other people when these higher prices do not reflect higher costs. Price discrimination is usually illegal, although often practiced. (Every time you go to a movie and pay a student price, you are the beneficiary of price discrimination.)

OPPORTUNITY COST: the alternative cost of doing something. Opportunity costs can be explicit, as in the case of a clearly marked price of a good or service, or implicit, as in the case of a value of a person's leisure time.

Chapter Summary

1. During the half century following the Civil War, the standard of living per capita in the United States grew at an average annual rate of about 2 percent. However, this growth was not steady; there were numerous ups and downs in business activity.

2. Population grew rapidly during this period, not only because the birth rate exceeded the death rate, but because of a large influx of immigrants. Immigrants came more during periods of business prosperity than they did during periods of business recession. That indicates most likely that they came seeking greater economic opportunities than existed in their own countries. This is just another demonstration that resources—here the resource is labor—flow to areas where they yield the highest rate of return.

3. The specter of diminishing returns for agricultural production was at least partially forestalled by the availability of new fertile lands.

4. Railroad mileage increased tremendously during this period, as did the number of passengers moved and the amount of freight carried. Railroads, however, caused headlines because of scandals involving their financing. Moreover, rate wars and price fixing were apparently rampant during this era.

5. Railroads had relatively tremendous fixed or sunk costs with all of the track and locomotive equipment they had to purchase in order to go into business. Their variable costs were relatively small.

6. During this period, investment in human capital (here, formal education) progressed, increasing the literacy rate of whites to 96 percent and of blacks to 70 percent on the eve of the First World War.

7. An important concept in economics is that of opportunity cost, which measures the actual opportunity forgone by any action.
8. We also invested in our health by improving sewage disposal, treating water, pasteurizing milk, and so on. Better health conditions allowed workers to be more productive and to be absent less from work, as well as making life generally more agreeable and health and longevity a more certain prospect.
9. During this period, we experienced falling prices, or a deflation. However, this deflation was not associated with business contractions; rather, there was a slight negative correlation between average gross national product per capita and price index changes.
10. The structure of the economy changed; we became more manufacturing oriented and less an agrarian society, although in absolute terms agricultural output increased steadily.

Questions for Thought and Discussion

1. Do you think children are an investment good or a consumption good today?
2. What is the opportunity cost of your reading this book?
3. Why is it profitable to engage in price discrimination if you can get away with it?
4. Today we spend a larger percentage of our income on health care than we did before World War I. What do you think explains this increase in relative spending on health?
5. If you were the owner of a large number of Greenbacks when specie resumption at par value was announced, would your wealth go up or down? Would you want to spend more or less?

THE GRANGER COLLECTION

THE RUTHLESS BUSINESSMAN, PAR EXCELLENCE

Jay Gould (1836–1892)

Railroads and Gold Manipulations

THAT ONE man caused what Wall Street called Black Friday on September 24, 1869, sounds impossible, doesn't it? But it actually happened, and that one man was Jay Gould, who with the help of his flamboyant sidekick, Jim Fisk, cornered the market in gold, sold out, and watched it fall. Gold was a very precious commodity after the Civil War, for the issuance of Greenbacks, which could not be redeemed at par in specie, brought great speculation in all precious metals. However, the growth of confidence in the government, improvement in the U.S. trade balance, and perhaps the postwar prosperity brought the price of gold down again in terms of Greenbacks. $131 in Greenbacks bought $100 of gold by 1869. Gould bought $7 million worth, sending the price up to $140. Since Jim Fisk seemed to have similar ideas they banded together and started to buy all the gold they could with as much money as

they were able to get out of a Tammany Hall controlled bank called the Tenth National. At the same time, however, they were worried about the $80 million in gold that the U.S. Treasury held, part of which could be thrown on the market at any time, thus causing them great financial loss.

To forestall that day, Gould befriended the man who had married President Ulysses Grant's middle-aged sister. To make sure this man used his influence correctly, Gould bought him $2 million in gold bonds on margin, so if the price of gold continued to rise, Grant's brother-in-law could reap sizable profits. When Major Dan Butterfield was named Assistant U.S. Treasurer at New York, he, too, suddenly had somewhere around $2 million in gold bonds in his account, purchased, of course, by Gould.

By September of that year, Gould and Fisk really did have a corner on the entire gold market, when the price of gold was at $141 in Greenbacks for $100 in gold. When Gould got wind that the President was going to force the Treasury to unload its holdings of yellow metal, he quietly started selling out, as did all of his associates, while simultaneously acting and talking like a bull. The price of gold went up to $150, then $164.

Finally the President ordered the Treasury to sell $5 million in gold immediately. In 15 minutes the price fell 25 points. Gould and Fisk were already in their headquarters guarded by police and their own thugs. Gould alone made $11 million. But, kindheartedly, he announced his regret over the Black Friday panic. And the Assistant Treasurer, General Butterfield, sanctimoniously pointed out that only speculators had lost money.

No one had ever dreamed that little Jason Gould, who was born in Roxbury, New York, the son of poor hill farmers, would become a great American financier. He first started working for a blacksmith, then as a clerk in a county store.

Here we see Jay Gould's "private bowling alley." His assets (in millions of dollars) are listed on the chalkboard. (The Granger Collection)

He learned the rudiments of surveying and obtained enough education to write before his twentieth birthday the *History of Delaware County and Border Wars of New York*. Before he was 21, he had $5000 in capital, with which he joined hands with a New York politician and opened a large tannery in northern Pennsylvania. He abandoned the tannery, became a leather merchant, and finally found where he had a comparative advantage—speculating in small railroads.

His notoriety became immense during his battle with Cornelius Vanderbilt over the Erie Railroad. While they were attempting to bring the price of Erie stock down, Fisk and Gould found a printing press in the cellars of the Erie offices and turned out phony stock certificates. Eventually, they did get control of the Erie, the stock of which they successfully "watered."* The money he made on the Erie and other speculative ruthless adventures was Gould's starting capital to corner the gold market. The public scandal was so great that Gould was finally ejected from his control of the Erie on March 10, 1872. At that time his fortune was estimated to exceed $25 million. What did he do?

He went to greener pastures. He took over the Union Pacific Railroad, became its director, and remained in virtual control until 1878, while at the same time buying control of the Kansas Pacific. Then in 1879 he bought control of the Denver Pacific, Central Pacific, and Missouri Pacific. In another seemingly unscrupulous deal with the Union Pacific and the Kansas Pacific, he made a stock deal which supposedly netted him $10 million. Gould was the epitome of the ruthless American businessman, with no outside diversions except books and gardening. He apparently had few friends, but some observers point out that he was a warm and kindly family man. He died of tuberculosis at age 57 with an estate of $70 million.

*The term "watering" comes from the practice of salting cattle just before they go on route to market and not allowing them to drink until just before being weighed.

ISSUE VIII   LIFE WITHOUT THE RAILROAD

The Iron Horse

Forging a National Economy

For decades historians have hailed the expansion of the railroad as a major factor in the transformation of the American economy. Indeed, some have gone so far as to single out the railroad as *the* cause of increased and sustained economic growth in the United States in the nineteenth and twentieth centuries. And if that isn't enough, the railroad is held responsible for everybody's ability to "Go West, young man."

The improvements in transportation in the pre- and post-Civil War era were extremely important for forging a national economy. Several kinds of favorable influences that transportation had on the economy can be singled out. The importance of lower transportation costs per se allowed new lands to be cultivated and allowed the market to grow in size. Remember that specialization is determined by how large the market is. The larger the market, the more specialization, and generally the higher real incomes will be.

Moreover, total expenditures in the U.S. transportation network, and especially in railroads, were very large relative to the capital invested in other areas. The increased demand for labor, particularly in the beginning, was brought about by the very labor-intensive construction of both railroads and canals. On the other hand, because we imported rails from England free of duty, little manufacturing of them was done in America. This was to change later on.

Secondary Effects, Too

Transportation improvements also had secondary effects. For example, they caused the expansion of existing capacity to supply the larger market that was made available by canals and railroads. After the Civil War, the sheer magnitude of railroad investment and activity made it one of the most prominent features in our economy. As we mentioned in the previous chapter, the debt of the railroads exceeded that of the entire United States, and the total capital stock of the railroads was almost 15 percent of that of the entire economy by 1900. To at least some extent, the railroad set the tempo of American life during the half century after the Civil War.

Opening up the West

The most prominent feature of railroad expansion after the War Between the States was the fairly rapid attempt at opening up the West to transcontinental passenger and freight service. Between 1865 and 1878 30,000 miles were laid just for transcontinental lines. There was additionally some filling in of the networks during that period. A second boom came between 1878 and 1882, almost all of it devoted to construction west of the Mississippi River, especially in Texas.

This is not to say, of course, that railroad expansion grew steadily. There were drops of as much as 50 percent in railroad investment in a one- or two-year period. This, of course, had destabilizing effects on the entire economy.

Other Effects of the Railroad

The extensive network of railroads created a large demand for skilled technicians; this demand was met. This perhaps represented an additional impetus to industrialization because these skilled technicians were scattered throughout the United States and would be available during the period to go into other lines of work in industries where their skills could be used. By 1900, 3 percent of the total labor force was in railroads. This is almost equiva-

AN AMERICAN RAILWAY SCENE, AT HORNELLSVILLE, ERIE RAILWAY.
THE GREAT TRUNK LINE AND UNITED STATES MAIL ROUTE between New York City and the Western States and Territories, renowned for its Beautiful Scenery, its substantial road bed, DOUBLE-TRACKED with steel rail, and its well appointed Passenger trains, equipped with the celebrated Pullman Hotel, Drawing Room and Sleeping Coaches.

lent to the percentage of farmers there are in the United States today.

The railroad also allowed more regional specialization within the United States itself. We can be fairly certain that the railroad played a pioneering role in the development of the Great Plains because that area depended for its development on a low-cost transportation system to provide the necessary inputs to raise livestock and to ship products back to market. The railroads also created numerous towns, such as Des Moines, which would not have been important otherwise because they did not lie on natural transportation links such as large bodies of interconnected waterways. Most important, though, the railroad created a national market. This allowed certain types of activity to be concentrated in big cities where **economies of scale** could be realized. Economies of scale occur when, say, a doubling of the capital and labor used by a firm results in *more* than a doubling of output. Only by large-scale production techniques can economies of scale generally be obtained. In other words, there has to be a large enough market for one to cater to in order to take advantage of this economic fact of life. The railroad allowed for this large-scale market by interconnecting cities and states throughout the country.

Reexamining the Data

To be sure, the railroad was extremely important in the development of the United States' economy. Absolute facts and figures, however, don't tell the true story. We have to look at *relative* facts and figures. That is, was the railroad important relative to the rest of the economy, or relative to the totals involved?

Consumption of Iron

Take the railroad's consumption of iron, long considered one of the major impetuses to economic growth in the nineteenth century. Numerous historians have stated that the railroad was "by far the biggest user of iron in the 1850s." A cursory inspection of some of the data indicates that by the start of the Civil War, the iron horse used up one-half of the annual iron production in the United States for laying tracks. However, looking particularly at the demand for pig iron to make rails between the years 1840 and 1860, for example, we find that it consumed only about 5 percent of the total iron output in the United States. This was chiefly because by 1860 60 percent of domestic rail production involved re-using previously worn-out rails—that is, rerolling them into new ones. Obviously there was an increase in the rerolling industry, but there was no increase in the demand for the product of blast furnaces.

If we take into account the other uses of iron in the railroad industry, such as for engines and things like that, this figure rises to an average of 17 percent of the total U.S. production during the twenty-year period just mentioned. How important was this figure? Well, if we compare it to other uses of iron, not very important. Some historians have stated that the initial leap in iron production between 1845 and 1849 was due to "nails not rails" because the domestic production of iron in nails exceeded that of rails by a factor of two in 1849.

Coal

The railroads' use of coal was negligible before the Civil War. Charcoal was the major fuel in making the rails and in engines in the period before the Civil War. The amount of wood used to feed the hungry iron horses and to lay the ties for the tracks previous to the Civil War was about one-half of one percent of all lumber production.

The demand for different goods by the railroad industry may have been important, but certainly not as much as we previously thought. This, of course, does not tell the full story, for we have to compare what happened with the railroads with what would have happened without them. If it can be shown that transportation, for example, would have been in a much worse state without railroads, then indeed there is a case to be made that life without the iron horse would have been quite a bit more constrained and expensive.

What Could Have Happened

It is unrealistic to assume that without railroads no transportation networks would have been built. After all, roads and waterways had been developing for some time before the railroad came into being. The canal system, for example, could have been extended to take advantage of the demand for improved transportation during the period between the Civil War and World War I. By some ingenious calculations, one can come up with the actual savings accounted for by having a railroad system rather than relying on an extension of the canal system. The difference between the two is called the **social savings.** If the social savings turn out to be large, then the railroads were important to increasing the standard of living in the United States. But if they turn out to be insignificant, then in fact an alternative transportation network of canals, rivers, and roads would have allowed a similar (though certainly not the same) development in the United States. One such study of this problem came up with the social savings attributable to the railroads of less than 5 percent of gross national product in 1890.* In other words,

*Robert W. Fogel, *Railroads and American Economic Growth: Essays in Econometric History,* Baltimore, Md.: Johns Hopkins Press, 1964.

had the railroads never existed and an alternative transportation network been used instead, annual gross national product would have been only about 5 percent less. Now this may seem small, but it could add up. So even if this estimate were to be believed completely, the railroads did have a small but important effect on the growth of the American economy, but not as important as many historians had thought previously.

The author of the study concluded that "despite its dramatically rapid and massive growth over a period of a half century, despite its eventual ubiquity in inland transportation, despite its devouring appetite for capital, . . . the railroad did not make an overwhelming contribution to the production potential of the economy" (page 235). And, further, "no *single* innovation was vital for economic growth during the nineteenth century." Of course, this should not come as a surprise. Growth in general has been steady with trends continuing through long periods of time, both in this country and in most other developed countries in the world.

A Final Comment

There are lots of important caveats in a study of an entire transportation system. No matter how impressive and detailed the analysis, there will always be areas where research was not carried out. For example, in assessing the impact of railroads, we must remember that they did go a lot faster than barges and canals. This is taken account of when assessing the social savings to railroads by looking at the higher costs of inventories of goods. Inventories would have to have been kept because replacements could not have been obtained as fast with the waterway system as they were with a railroad system.

Improved Health Conditions

However, one important aspect of rapid transportation was left out in this calculation: The ability of fresh fruit, vegetables, and meats to be brought to the cities during all seasons may seem trivial, but it probably accounted for many improvements in health and general well-being of city dwellers. This may have meant an increased demand for an urban living environment that would not have existed had railroads not been built and canals been used in their stead. We have no idea how to quantify this effect, but it could be important.

A Transcontinental Canal?

Moreover, if we look carefully at an alternative canal system, we note immediately that it would have required gargantuan amounts of water. In many cases, it is not obvious that enough water was available. And, additionally, it certainly would have been a long time before California would have developed without the railroad. People who now live in Los Angeles might think they would have been better off, but the fact remains.

Definitions of New Terms

ECONOMIES OF SCALE: reduction in the average per unit cost of producing something due to producing on a larger scale. Strictly speaking, economies of scale occur when an increase in *all* inputs leads to a more than proportionate increase in output.

SOCIAL SAVINGS: the reduction in costs to the whole society by using one specific economic enterprise over another one. In the case of railroads, we compute the social savings by comparing the costs of transportation without the railroads and the costs of transportation with the railroads.

Questions for Thought and Discussion

1. Depict the nation during this period without the railroad. Do you think you would have been better or worse off?
2. When do you think Los Angeles would have developed smog if the railroad had never existed? In other words, how long would it have taken for the city to develop?
3. Did the railroad have anything to do with the extermination of buffalo?
4. Do you think there has ever been a single innovation that was vital for economic growth at any period in the history of the United States?

Changes in the Structure of the Nation

9

THE HALF CENTURY after the Civil War was a period not only of rapid economic growth and of large increases in population and westward movement, but also of tremendous structural change—that is, change in the basic makeup of the entire U.S. economy. We were able to allude only briefly to some of these changes in the last chapter. It is time now to deal with them more seriously. Between the Civil War and the Great War was a period of the rise of cities, with all the accompanying gains and costs; a period of increasing industrial power and concentration; and finally, a period of massive changes in the agricultural sector, both good and bad. While these trends may have gotten their foothold in the era under study, they continue even into the present, and we are still faced with finding solutions to the multitude of complex problems brought about by modern society. We'll wait until the last pages of this book to talk about today. For the moment, let's talk about yesterday and the rise of the urban population.

URBANIZATION

Figure 9–1 speaks for itself. At the end of the Civil War decade, about one-fourth of the population lived in cities of 2500 or more. Fifty years later, almost one-half the entire population was crowded into cities. In fact, by the end of World War I there were more city dwellers than country folks. Of course, this doesn't mean that everybody lived in big cities. In fact, it wasn't until more recently that the population concentrated itself in what we consider the major cities in the nation. Back in 1870, for example, out of the 663 extant cities, almost 500 had a population of less than 10,000. This proportion was to fall somewhat, but not drastically, even by 1910, when 1665 cities of the extant 2262 still had populations of less than 10,000. Before we get into the problems that the city dweller of yore faced, let's see if we can figure out why cities exist in the first place.

Why Cities Exist

It's not just coincidental that many major cities are located near areas of significant mineral deposits or natural resources, or in areas that can be easily serviced by natural transportation networks. In other words (particularly in the past), there were many *natural* reasons why cities would develop where they did, because they could be focal points for commerce and, in some cases, extractive industry. Also, concentration of industry within a fairly constrained area allows for decreased costs of production. This is because there are many interactions between firms; if the firms are spread out, they have to engage in extensive long-distance communication and transportation in order to trade among themselves. When they concentrate in one environment, they save on many of these costs. Furthermore, a concentration of production will generally lead, at least in the beginning, to what we have called economies of scale. That is, firms which can obtain sufficient demand for increasing their rates of production will find that their average per-unit costs fall. This may be due to internal or external factors. Internal

factors are often associated with the techniques of **mass production,** although this is not strictly what economies of scale mean. The latter are associated with the reduced costs of doing business in a city as opposed to being spread out.

And last, the concentration of people and resources in the city allows for more efficient provision of such public services as fire and police protection, potable water, improved sewer systems, and the like. (On the other hand, certain services like sewers aren't needed for a widely dispersed population.)

Note that a prerequisite for the rise in city populations is a rise in agricultural productivity, a subject we will treat later on in this chapter. Only if the agricultural population can increase output sufficiently to feed city dwellers can cities exist. That means that there must be technological progress on the farm, and that's exactly what happened. Additionally, there is a feedback from the cities themselves that causes a growth in productivity throughout the economy, for increased concentration of economic activities allows for increased specialization.

We would expect that cities would have risen because income was rising—and it was. But it turns out that people's demand for agricultural goods—foodstuffs—does not grow as fast as their income. That is, the income elasticity of the demand for food is relatively small. Income elasticity

---

FIGURE 9–1

THE FLIGHT TO THE CITIES

At the end of the decade of the Civil War, only a quarter of the population lived in cities. Half a century later, almost half of all Americans crowded into urban environments. (*Source:* U.S. Bureau of the Census.)

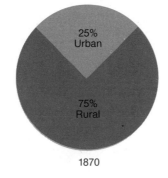

1870

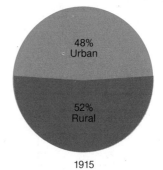

1915

is, then, obviously, higher for nonagricultural products, and these products are most cheaply produced in the city, not the country.

A Hierarchy of Cities

Prior to the Civil War, most cities were retail trade centers. It was only after the war that many of them became oriented toward manufacturing. As manufacturing grew from barely one-third of commodity output in 1860 to over one-half in 1900, we would expect certain concentrations to occur in very physically constrained areas, and indeed they did.

There is a good reason why cities were more commercial than manufacturing centers prior to 1860 and even afterward. Many cities were to remain mere trading centers for as long as the horse and buggy was the primary means of transportation. After all, folks in the countryside weren't about to drive their horses long distances merely to obtain some nails and whisky. Moreover, these little centers of rural population were not large

enough to support the more specialized economic outputs that could be provided in larger cities. A regular hierarchy of cities grew up that remains with us even today. It looks like the following:

City Size	What Happens
2500 to 10,000	Mainly trading centers; the reduction in costs are enough to get people to drive their horses in from the countryside; total demand not high enough for the provision of specialized services. Remember, specialization is determined by the size of the market.
10,000 to 50,000	Still mainly trading centers, but provision of certain specialized services, such as stock brokers and the like.

(Courtesy Chicago Historical Society)

| 50,000 and more | Still commercial trading, plus increasing specialized services: stock brokers, insurance salesmen, more specialized doctors, etc. |
| The Really Big Ones | Commercial trading, many specialized services, operas, orchestras, brain surgeons, multitudinous delights of the palate, etc. |

This was indeed the era of the big ones: New York, Chicago, Philadelphia, Boston—they all had their special characteristics and their special brands of vice and social disamenities: tuberculosis, slum housing, crimes, pollution, and corruption. In 1890, the top ten cities were also the big manufacturing centers. They accounted for more than 40 percent of all manufacturing output. They were additionally the focal points of commerce, finance, and communications.

Value of Land

For all the bad effects that cities had, they certainly provided ample rewards to thousands of businessmen who had located in them. We have very good evidence of how much businessmen actually valued being located in the center of a big city. For example, in Chicago, from 1873 to 1910 the value of inner-city property rose by more than 700 percent. Land was immensely valuable in the crowded centers of crowded cities.

A STRUGGLE FOR LIFE

Urbanization may have allowed for more profitable business opportunities; it may have resulted in economies of scale; it may have resulted in increased specialization and higher real living standards for the nation at large; but it also meant, particularly at the beginning of the period we are talking about, increased mortality and morbidity among the urban populations. In 1860, it was far

The growth of cities: Chicago at the turn of the century and an immigrant family doing garment piecework in their New York City tenement home, ca. 1900.

(The Granger Collection)

safer to live on the farm than to move to the city: The death rate per 1000 in the countryside was about 20, as compared to about 30 in the large city. What did people die of in the city? Mainly communicable diseases: diphtheria, tuberculosis, and the like. They drank foul water from wells that were polluted by improper and unsafe sewage systems, and hence contracted typhoid and dysentery. They were unable to obtain as much fresh food as people who lived in rural areas, so their diet was not as healthful.

This was all to change toward the turn of the century. Rising real incomes enabled people to demand better health conditions. For example, they were willing to pay for better diets, causing decreased morbidity. They were also willing to buy more spacious housing. They demanded and got purification of their water, improved sewage disposal, regular garbage collection, and swamp drainage. So in spite of the numerous unhealthful aspects of congested urban living, people had obtained distinct improvements in health in the city by the eve of the First World War. There still remained numerous problems for the urban dweller, as there are today. We conclude this section by asking: Why, then, live in the city?

The answer is quite obvious: The benefits from living in the city outweigh the costs. The costs we have already gone into, but not all of the benefits for the individuals concerned. The most obvious benefit from living in the city in this interwar period was higher income: Uncorrected for the higher skill level of the workers in cities, real wages for them were twice those of the countryside. Also, and perhaps no less important, there were many more things to do in the city, just as there are today. Farm life must have been quite dreary in the good old days compared to the numerous possibilities for diversified life styles in New York, Chicago, Philadelphia, Boston, San Francisco, and, to a lesser degree, in places like Spokane, Sacramento, and Atlanta. That didn't mean that life wasn't changing on the farm, as we shall soon see it was.

The Agriculture Building at the World's Columbian Exposition, Chicago, 1893. The city pays tribute to mechanized agriculture. (Courtesy Chicago Historical Society)

AGRICULTURAL TRANSFORMATION —THE AGE OF TECHNOLOGY

Remember that way back when, almost 90 percent of the population was engaged in agricultural activities. By 1860 this figure had fallen to 60 percent, by 1880 50 percent, and by 1900 38 percent. In spite of this percentage decline of the agricultural labor force, there were tremendous gains in total output. Acreage and productivity per worker increased, as did, in absolute numbers, the population engaged in this activity. So this period was still one of *absolute* growth in the farming sector.

By the end of the nineteenth century, there was little frontier left. The amount of land in cultivation doubled after the Civil War. The expansion in agricultural output was not as rapid as in industry, but it grew faster than before the Civil War.

Three McCormick combines, more refined versions of the mechanical reaper, are seen in a Midwest wheat field. The reaper was to make large scale farming the only profitable way of producing the nation's grains. (State Historical Society of Wisconsin)

Two different factors accounted for this expansion, the most obvious being the physical extension of cultivated land. But also important was increased productivity. Although change in productivity was less rapid than in the manufacturing sector, it accounted for perhaps 40 percent of the increase in farm output. This was the age of the mechanical reaper, the horse-drawn cultivator, and the improved harrow. We saw, therefore, a rapid rise in the agricultural implement industry. The fortunes of Cyrus McCormick can attest to that.

There was also a change in the relative importance of the crops that were grown. Corn, oats, and wheat output skyrocketed. Dairy production increased—this was to be expected because real incomes were rising, and the income elasticity of demand for such items as milk was fairly high. Since the increased demand for dairy products increased profitability, more resources flowed into this industry. And the production of livestock expanded proportionately with the population rise. We see at the end of the nineteenth century a much greater diversification in agricultural production than before the Civil War. There was also a shift in location.

Illinois, Wisconsin, Iowa, and Indiana changed from wheat-producing to corn-producing states. In contrast, the wheat production moved on to Minnesota, the Dakotas, and Kansas. The Great Plains had been opened up by the railroad, and they were to become the breadbasket of America.

This was also a period of agricultural disarray and distress. In the following issue, we investigate whether or not farmers really were worse off during this period of industrialization. But for the moment, we can present the facts as seen by the agrarian movement.

THE AGRARIAN MOVEMENT

A movement flourished in the 1870s and the end of the '80s which coincided with two periods of falling prices. In addition to the Populists there were several groups, the main ones being the Grangers and the Farmer Alliances. These two groups were very different. The Grange Society originally was a social organization. Some Granges tried to eliminate the middleman to make higher profits for the producer. Grangers also got some state laws passed in the 1870s to regulate railroads. Further, they had important educational and social functions, although we can be fairly certain that economic well-being was the main goal. The Grangers attempted cooperative mass marketing to eliminate profits for distributors. They

The Grange Awakening the Sleepers. This newspaper cartoon of 1873, inspired by the Vanderbilt system of secret rebates, shows the farmer trying to rouse the country to the railroad menace. (The Granger Collection)

were organized most effectively in the farming states of the Upper Mississippi Valley.

In contrast to the Granger movement was the Alliance movement. Farmers tried to get alliances together, but it just wouldn't work. After all, the farming population was not that homogeneous, so no national movement came about. Instead, the farmer Alliances gave their support to the Populist Party.

The election of McKinley, increased prosperity, the Spanish War, and a number of other factors eventually led to the downfall of the agrarian movement.

Other Complaints

Besides falling prices, agrarian discontent was based on hatred of capitalist creditors whom the western farmers thought were gouging them with usurious interest rates. Another complaint was discrimination in railroad rates that were not consistent with the differences in costs for different types of railroad transportation. There was a hatred for the common practice of charging more for short hauls than for long hauls.

Inelastic Demand

One of the basic problems that farmers were to face was that people's food demands are generally quite unresponsive to changes in price. We noted this in Chapter 3 when we talked about what the colonists did to their tobacco crops in order to get higher prices—they burned them in 1639. Economists say that the demand for most foodstuffs is price inelastic. Therefore, if farmers have large crops, the only way they can sell them is to drastically reduce the price. This is a dilemma that the agrarian movement never succeeded in solving until it obtained favorable legislation during the Great Depression. But more on that in Chapter 11. Now we turn to the last major topic of this chapter, the era of business consolidation.

MONOPOLY CAPITALISM

The structure of American business was changing throughout this period. There was a shift away from **proprietorships** and **partnerships** to a form of business organization called the **corporation.** The corporation wasn't really new, but it became most popular during this period for several reasons. A corporation is a legal entity owned by stockholders, who usually all have limited liability; that is, the most they can lose is the value of their stocks. They cannot be assessed any further liability in case the corporation goes bankrupt. Another appealing aspect of the corporation is that it is essentially eternal: The death of shareholders does not terminate the legal existence of the corporation, whereas it does for proprietorships and partnerships. A corporation has another advantage, its enhanced ability to obtain large amounts of initial capital and large additional amounts for expansion. For a corporation can sell shares in itself, and it can float large amounts of debt capital. This is generally more difficult for partnerships and proprietorships to do because of their uncertain longevity. It was especially important for corporations to be able to raise large amounts of capital during this period of industrial expansion because, as never before, it was an era of large-scale manufacturing.

Steel was certainly one of the most preeminent of the industries that required large amounts of capital. The Bessemer and open hearth processes for making steel allowed the rapid development of this industry. Moreover, these two processes are most efficient when used to produce large amounts of steel. It is not hard to imagine, then, that large companies were soon to spring up in this industry, the most famous being the one founded by Andrew Carnegie in 1872. Eventually his properties were consolidated with others by J. P. Morgan. Here we had the first billion dollar company in the world—United States Steel.

The petroleum industry also saw rapid development. Everybody knows that John D. Rockefeller made his fortune providing such petroleum products as kerosene for heating and manufacturing. In the twentieth century the automobile became a most conspicuous consumer of Rockefeller's oil. Henry Ford's application of assembly-line mass-production techniques using interchangeable parts to produce the Model T gave a tremendous boost to this industry. By 1919, annual automobile sales were a billion dollar affair.

All of this rapid industrialization was merely an extension of what had occurred in England, and was similar to what was occurring in France and other European countries. This was the era of America's industrial revolution. Along with this industrial revolution was a scientific revolution and the beginning of a technological elite, or technocracy. M.I.T. was founded. Engineers were universally recognized as necessary and desirable in an industrial society. The age of Taylorism was upon us: Time and motion stu-

Henry Ford seems proud of his first automobile, 1896. (The Granger Collection)

dies became faddish. It was realized that industry could profit through advances in scientific knowledge, and it did. It was also realized that higher profits could be made by creating monopolies, and that is why we call this the age of monopoly capitalism.

THE GROWTH OF BUSINESS CONSOLIDATION

In 1890 there were twelve important trusts or combinations with a total capital of $1 billion. By 1903 such combinations had a capital of $3 billion, and by 1904, $7.2 billion. This represented 40 percent of all American industry. One of the reasons businesses consolidated was to reap the benefits from economies of scale. When one is able to cater to a national market—which was the case during this period—why not take advantage of falling average per-unit costs by expanding production? And what easier way to expand production than to merge with similar companies?

There were basically two types of consolidations. One we call **vertical mergers,** and the other **horizontal.** No, it has nothing to do with geometry, but merely with what aspect of the production process is acquired by merger.

Vertical Integration

When firms vertically integrate by merger, the various production processes are brought under one name; for example, a coal mine is consolidated with an electric utility plant. Mergers of this type were not so feared in those days; rather, the other kind was.

Horizontal Integration

In horizontal integration one company buys up similar companies, the most famous example being Rockefeller's Standard Oil, which acquired or forced many competitors into the Standard Oil Trust.

People got so afraid of the possibility that giant companies would take over the country that Congress finally passed the Sherman Antitrust Act in 1890. However, we find that the Sherman Antitrust Act actually contributed to a wave of consolidations which peaked between 1897 and 1903. This is because one way to get around the illegality of conspiring in restraint of trade was to merge. Mergers at that time were not against the law, even if they resulted in reduced competitiveness in an industry. Even though Standard Oil and American Tobacco were prosecuted under the Sherman Antitrust Act in 1910 and 1911, this was generally a period of a government hands-off policy. As Jefferson once said, the best government is "that government which governs least." And, as many Congressmen, Senators, and Presidents could attest to, it seemed best to leave business alone. Did this hands-off policy diminish the welfare of the working man, both on the farm and in the city? Let's see in our next issue.

Definitions of New Terms

MASS PRODUCTION: production technique involving many units of a product. Mass-production techniques are generally associated with a conveyor belt and large factories. When the techniques of mass production are used, the fixed or sunk costs are distributed to an ever-increasing number of units, thus reducing the average per-unit cost of production.

PROPRIETORSHIP: a single-owner business.

PARTNERSHIP: a business entity involving two or more individuals joined together for business purposes but who have not incorporated. Their liability is generally limited to their personal assets.

CORPORATION: a legal entity owned by stockholders in the company. Normally the stockholders are only liable for the amount of money they have invested in that company.

VERTICAL MERGERS OR INTEGRATION: the joining together of businesses which engage in the various stages of producing a final product. For example, the merging of a coal company with an electric utility would be a vertical merger.

HORIZONTAL INTEGRATION: the merging of businesses in the same activity, such as the merger of several gasoline companies, or several shoe manufacturing companies.

Chapter Summary

1. Between the Civil War and World War I there was a significant shift away from the farm to the city.
2. Cities allow for economies of scale in production and also for more efficient provision of such public services as fire and police protection and potable water.
3. Note that the growth of cities cannot occur without sufficient increases in agricultural output.
4. Health conditions in the city were not as good as in the country because of the greater probability of contracting a communicable disease in the city, chiefly because of fouled water and the inability to obtain fresh food. However, by the beginning of World War I this was to change.
5. As real incomes went up, city dwellers demanded purification of water, improved sewage disposal, swamp drainage, and regular garbage collection.
6. The shift of population to the city can be explained in economic terms: Higher income opportunities were available. Also, more numerous diversified life styles were possible in bigger cities.
7. Agricultural production increased absolutely, but the percentage of the population engaged in its production fell dramatically. This was possible because of improved productivity in that sector—horse-drawn cultivators were improved, the harrow was improved, as was the mechanical reaper.
8. The agrarian movement in the 1870s and '80s coincided with periods of falling agricultural prices.
9. Farmers face a relatively price inelastic demand for their food products; therefore, if farmers have large crops, the only way they can sell them is to drastically reduce the price.
10. This was the period of so-called monopoly capitalism, during which we saw the growth of the large corporation as we know it today. Many firms merged into giant companies. Finally Congress passed the Sherman Antitrust Act in 1890 to counter this consolidation movement.

Questions for Thought and Discussion

1. Do you think there is a natural limit to how large a city can grow?
2. Why aren't people who live in small cities "allowed" to see live operas and symphony orchestras all the time?
3. If life in the city was so bad, at least at the beginning of the period under study, why did people continue to move there?
4. Does the reduction in the relative importance of agriculture mean it is no longer a sector worth studying?
5. We generally find that the price elasticity of demand for foodstuffs is relatively low. Can you think of other goods or services which also have price inelastic demand? Is it possible for all goods and services to have this demand characteristic? (Hint: What about scarcity?)

CARNEGIE CORPORATION OF NEW YORK

THE GREAT STEEL MAKER

Andrew Carnegie (1835–1919)

Industrialist and Scientific Philanthropist

"A MESSENGER boy of the name of Andrew Carnegie, employed by the O'Reily Telegraph Company, yesterday found a draft for the amount of $500. Like an honest little fellow, he promptly made known the facts, and deposited the paper in good hands where it awaits identification" (news clipping from the *Pittsburgh Dispatch,* November 2, 1849).

Five hundred dollars was indeed a lot of money for the son of a Scottish weaver—it represented ten years' wages. Later on in life, it would represent merely what could be earned every ten minutes of every day. The saga of Andrew Carnegie has indeed inspired at least one or two generations of schoolboys. At age 12 the young immigrant worked in a cotton mill for $1.20 a week. Then he moved into the telegraphy department of the Pennsylvania Railroad, where he quickly became the private secretary of its head. He started investing, first in a small oil company, and then in the Woodruff Palace Sleeping Car Company. Soon the young man was building railroad bridges, iron rails, and the like. Carnegie also made a small fortune in oil and took several trips to Europe selling railroad securities. His operations in bond selling, oil dealing, bridge building, and the like were so dashing and successful that conservative Pittsburgh businessmen regarded him as somewhat of a Young Turk. By 1873, however, Carnegie thought that steel was the new American industry. He began his famous policy which he described as "putting all my eggs in one basket and then watching the basket." He was then a mere 38 years old. His business life for the next three decades was to some extent a microcosm of the industrial history of the United States for the same period. During this time he was a staunch advocate of a tariff when it was for an infant industry, but he considered it a wicked device "when used merely to swell the profits of an established business." Even before he retired he advocated the removal of tariff duties on imported steel. (As well he might, since his firms could produce at lower cost than the British!)

Industrialist Andrew Carnegie rose to power in the steel industry during the period after the Civil War that has been characterized as one of uninhibited exploitation and cutthroat competition. Even Calvinist attitudes were insufficient to excuse what was happening. Carnegie found his philosophical underpinnings in the English writer Herbert Spencer, who applied the fundamental principles of Darwinian evolution to society. His thesis was that of social Darwinism—in the struggle for existence among men, survival went to the fittest, whether it be in business or economics. And the fittest had to become the wealthiest. When Carnegie read Spencer, he found an idol. The industrialist said that when he read Spencer's *First Principles* in 1862, "light came as in a flood and all was clear." Carnegie and other businessmen of the day used Spencer as an argument against government intervention and also against the rise of unions. It should be noted, however, that there's many a slip 'twixt cup and lip. During this period big business in conjunction with the government was active in attempting to throttle free competition.

In 1868 the steel maker wrote a memo to himself: "Thirty-three and an income of $50,000 per annum! Beyond this never earn—make no effort to increase fortune, but spend the surplus each year for benevolent purposes. Cast aside business forever, except for others." He didn't follow his advice until he was 66, but then he engaged in what he called scientific philanthropy. The major projects worth giving money to were universities, free libraries, hospitals, and parks, in that order, in addition to swimming baths and churches, which ranked low on his list.

Carnegie retired after the sale of his steel company to the new United States Steel Company in 1901. Of the $250 million he got, he left a $5 million pension and benefit fund for his trustworthy employees. He didn't stop giving from that moment on. Over $60 million of his money went into almost 3000 free public libraries around the world. The size of Carnegie's gift depended on the town's population; it averaged $2 per person. (This formula left some small towns with an uneconomical library which had to be closed down; nobody ever thought of pooling the funds for regional libraries.)

Giving away money seemed to be as hard as making it. "Pity the poor millionaire, for the way of the philanthropist is hard," he wrote to a newspaper in 1913. After working for ten years at giving away $350 million, he realized that no one man could do such a big job; the Carnegie Corporation in New York started with an endowment of $125 million. It was the first modern philanthropic foundation administered by trustees who were skilled in their different areas. Carnegie chose only trustees who had been good businessmen.

He died in 1919 after fulfilling his personal pledge of giving away just about everything he had accumulated.

ISSUE IX
DID THE LITTLE MAN GET WIPED OUT BY INDUSTRIALIZATION?

The Plight of Workers

Getting Put Down

The era between the Civil War and World War I has often been labeled the American industrial revolution. While it may not have been a revolution, industrialization occurred at such a rapid pace that there is little doubt about its importance during this period. However, many social commentators and historians have labeled this the era of *monopoly capitalism,* during which the little guy—the factory worker and the farmer—suffered greatly, thereby enriching the coffers of the money-hungry entrepreneurs who exploited everybody and everything in sight to further their own ends. There is little question about the sordidness in the slums and factory lives of many workers in America. There is little question that numerous farmers suffered from falling prices and discriminatory railroad rates. There is little question that many people lived an existence which, by modern-day standards, was almost unthinkable.

Making Correct Comparisons

But herein lies the problem: We cannot properly apply today's standards to the kind of life that existed before World War I. We must compare, as we have stated before in this book, the real with the real. What was actually happening to workers and farmers during this period? Were they becoming worse off than they had been used to or than they could have expected to become? Was it a large percentage of the population that was feeling the pinch of industrialization? Was this really the era of Robber Barons who used up industrial workers as if they were expendable pieces of machinery? The best way we can test many of these assertions for validity is to examine the most accurate facts we have about aggregates—that is, what happened to groups in the population as a whole? What happened to farmers? What happened to workers? Let's treat agrarian discontent first, and then go on to see what the Robber Barons actually did to the little guy in industry.

The Plight of the Poor Farmer

Farmers were convinced that the big industrialists and railroad magnates of their time were responsible for their "bad times." Remember, we talked about one of the planks of the agrarian movement, to stop falling prices. Farmers were convinced that the price of manufactured goods was rising relative to the price of agricultural goods. As John F. Kennedy once said, the "farmer is the only man who sells everything at wholesale, buys everything at retail, and pays transportation both ways." While it is true that farm prices were falling during this period, so, too, were the prices of manufactured goods. In fact, it looks as if the average **terms of trade**—that is, the relative amounts of goods and services that the farmer could buy with a unit of his crop—stayed about the same overall between 1865 and 1900. The farmer also had very little ground to complain about his decreased profits. After all, productivity was not increasing as fast in agriculture as it was in manufacturing.

The Credit Question

Farmers were convinced they were being ripped off by large creditors from the East. They complained about the high interest rates they had to pay, and particularly about the conditions under which they were allowed to obtain credit. This is indeed strange. It is true that they were worse off because of the falling price level that they had not (at least in the beginning) expected.

However, after a while, everybody expected prices to fall, and the price of credit, like all other prices, fell accordingly. In any event, since most mortgages held by farmers were of relatively short duration—three or four years— they could not have been hurt for very long (unless they were foreclosed). And at the same time, the largest debtor group in the nation was the railroads, not the farmer, so the unexpected falling price level affected the profitability of the railroad and, additionally, manufacturers as much as or more than it did farmers.

Farmers were forced to go into debt because after the Civil War you couldn't be a farmer without being a capitalist. You had to buy equipment—reapers, planters, harrows, and the like. You also had to buy chemical fertilizers and large amounts of land and sometimes irrigation facilities.

It is quite true that credit was somewhat limited, particularly in the Western and Southern agricultural regions. We stated, however, in Issue VII that one of the reasons for the restriction in credit was the National Banking Act, since it prevented the growth of smaller banks in less-populated regions and allowed those which did exist to have a monopoly on money lending. In this instance, the farmers did have a legitimate gripe. But consider also that farmers just weren't very good credit risks at that time. A tre-mendous number of mortgage companies failed during this period because of all the poor credit risks they had taken with farmers. On average, it doesn't appear that many Eastern bankers were able to make a killing by exploiting poor Western farmers.

Railroad Rates

The farmers were rightly concerned and annoyed about discriminatory railroad rates that they were charged. But it's not clear that a large percentage of farmers were really victimized by actual price discrimination against them. For example, rates west of the Mississippi were higher than those east of the Mississippi, but this was a function of the actual costs of providing railroad transportation in these two different regions. The real factor was that Western railroads had lower loading ratios. That is, because of major seasonal fluctuations in the demand for their services, their cars were not loaded as much as were those in the East. Essentially, then, during certain times of the year there had to be empty freight cars shipped from the East to the West to take account of seasonal peaks. This increased costs for railroads operating in the West, and you would expect them to charge a higher price. In fact, the rate of return to Western railroads was less than to Eastern ones. During the first few years of Western railroad expansion, there was hardly any business at all.

Conclusions?

What can we say, then? Not very much. The farmers had some legitimate complaints, and some illegitimate ones. Their discontent was obviously more clear-cut to them than to objective observers. Moreover, it's not obvious why one particular sector—be it farming, manufacturing, or what have you—should be guaranteed a favorable rate of return all the time. Many people have believed that the farmer is the backbone of America and that because of this there is an agrarian moral superiority that should be fostered by keeping farmers contented and in business. That is a value judgment which economics is incapable of assessing.

Blue-Collar Discontent

Along with agrarian discontent, there was blue-collar malaise. For many years the available statistics confirmed historians' suspicion that workers during the era of unbridled monopoly capitalism suffered losses in real wages—that is, their ability to sustain their standard of living fell during the period from the passage of the Sherman Antitrust Act until the First World War. However, we see

149

ISSUE IX   DID THE LITTLE MAN GET WIPED OUT BY INDUSTRIALIZATION?

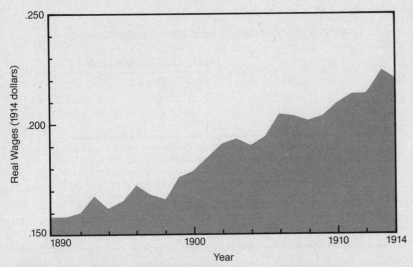

FIGURE IX-1 HOURLY EARNINGS IN MANUFACTURING

During the Robber Baron period from 1890 to the beginning of World War I, average hourly earnings in manufacturing in constant 1914 dollars rose from around 16 cents an hour to 22 cents, or an increase of over 30 percent during that period. (*Source*: A. Rees, *Real Wages in Manufacturing, 1890–1914*. Princeton, N.J.: Princeton University Press, 1961, p. 4.)

Some Real Costs

Don't get the impression, however, that the above discussion is meant to indicate that no problems were caused by industrialization. Many were. Progress always has a price. It is very difficult to obtain benefits without paying some costs, but that's the nature of the game. We have to decide whether the benefits are worth the costs. We can mention briefly some of the costs that were brought about by rapid industrialization in the nineteenth century.

Living Environment

One involved the living environment in which many industrial workers found themselves. Life in many factories was dismal. Life in the homes around the factories was perhaps despicable relative to the alternatives in the countryside. So there were numerous **external diseconomies** associated with the urban industrial complex which grew up during the age of industrialization. Moreover, workers were subjected to more severe and costly business cycles. You'll remember that when we were mainly an agrarian economy with lots of largely self-sufficient farms, the effects of bad business conditions on the vast majority of people were not as great as in our industrial economy. But by the end of the nineteenth century we started to experience periods of

in Figure IX-1, which displays the most recent estimates, that real wages of manufacturing workers during this quarter-century span rose considerably, being about 30 percent higher at the end of the period than at the start. It is also instructive to see what would have happened had monopoly capitalists been unable to extract any profits at all during this period.

Take a typical year, say 1901: Total corporate profits were somewhere in the neighborhood of $1.5 billion. If we make the ridiculous assumption that all of these profits could have been redistributed to everybody in the country, we find that the addition to per capita income would have been only about $15, or around a whopping 6 percent increase in actual per capita income of the time. It is hardly possible, then, to imagine that monopolistic entrepreneurs of the age were exploiting workers to a really severe degree. While a 6 percent increase in standard of living in any one year is not insignificant, it's not overwhelming. And moreover, it's hard to imagine that we could have obtained as high a rate of growth if we had attempted to redistribute all profits away from corporation shareholders. Why, then, would they have left any money in corporations?

more and more severe recession and depression. In fact, the recession/depression which began in 1893 was the second worst in the history of the United States. We see in Table IX–1 that the percentage of the labor force unemployed in depression years starting in 1876 was not insignificant.

Unemployment Trend up

If we want a complete picture of what happened to unemployment, Figure IX–2 shows that there has been a slight but noticeable upward trend in the average rates of unemployment from 1800 to the present. Unemployment in the past meant hardship for workers. Unemployment is all part and parcel of an industrialized society. You will never find unemployment among Indians who barely eke out a subsistence. They're always working at making sure they don't die. You will rarely find unemployment in any society where everybody is basically self-employed or a slave or serf. Again, though, we generally have to take the bad with the good. We can attempt, as we have by many government programs, to alleviate unemployment and its effects. We have not yet found the magic formula for stopping recessions, but that doesn't mean that as a highly developed industrial society we are worse off than we would be if we all went back to nature. The

TABLE IX–1

UNEMPLOYMENT DURING RECESSIONS AND DEPRESSIONS

YEAR	PERCENTAGE UNEMPLOYED
1876	12–14
1885	6–8
1894	18
1908	8

The unemployment rate during the recessions of the period under study was considerably higher than during the recessions and depressions in prior periods. In fact, the unemployment rate in 1894 is exceeded only by the periods during the Great Depression. (*Source:* S. Lebergott, *Manpower and Economic Growth,* New York: McGraw-Hill, 1964, pp. 187, 512, 522.)

FIGURE IX-2   THE LONG-TERM TREND IN UNEMPLOYMENT, 1880 TO 1960

If there is any long-term trend in unemployment, it is quite slight, as we can see in the above figure. However, the amount of unemployment during depressions has gotten worse over time. (*Source:* Lebergott, *op. cit.*)

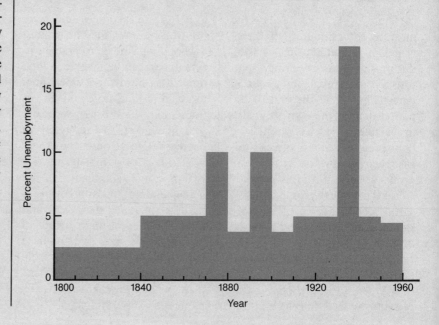

151

ISSUE IX   DID THE LITTLE MAN GET WIPED OUT BY INDUSTRIALIZATION?

situation was no different on the eve of World War I.

Lots of people had been hurt by the progress of the last half century, but even more had gained. If we take an aggregate or average view of the period, it would be difficult for us to categorically agree that the little guy was hurt by the industrial revolution.

Definitions of New Terms

TERMS OF TRADE: the terms on which a specific sector trades with another sector. In agriculture, for example, the terms of trade can be found out by seeing what a unit of agricultural product will buy in terms of units of manufactured products.

EXTERNAL DISECONOMIES: costs associated with an economic activity which are not taken account of by those who create these costs. In other words, external diseconomies are paid for by the public without any compensation made to them by the responsible parties.

Questions for Thought and Discussion

1. Do you think farmers were being cheated during the period under study? If so, are they still?
2. Is there other evidence we should be looking at to determine whether industrial workers were losing out during this period of monopoly capitalism?
3. Can you name some of the numerous external diseconomies which are associated with an urban industrial complex? Now can you name some of the external economies? How can we decrease the former and increase the latter?

Surviving the Great War

10

FRANZ FERDINAND IS assassinated in Sarajevo. War begins in Europe. The Great War was upon the world. The Central Powers of Germany and Austria-Hungary were fighting against the Allies—France, England, and Russia. The year was 1914 and America was in the throes of a recession. Unemployment had reached an uncomfortable one million the year before. From the very beginning, America attempted to stay out of the conflict. In fact, President Wilson used the slogan for his reelection that would soon be forgotten: "I kept this country out of war." The date was 1916. In April 1917 we declared war on the Central Powers. But we certainly didn't wait until that late date to start our war production. In fact, we started benefiting from the world at war as early as 1914. As a neutral, we were able to trade with both the Central Powers and the Allies. Our exports increased by leaps and bounds. The trade surplus for the years 1914 to 1916 was over $5.2 billion. Other countries made up for this deficit vis à vis the United States by shipping us gold and by borrowing from us. In some cases we never got repaid, particularly for the loans made to Germany. Nonetheless, most observers have concluded that our preparation for the war and entry into it pulled us out of a serious recession; by 1916 almost all unemployment had vanished.

World War I can be considered the first modern war—one that is fought with formidable weapons which require large amounts of capital and manpower. War had become expensive. While the Civil War cost the Union $3.5 billion, the Great War cost the United States alone $33.4 billion. This was a period of increased government expenditures and increased government powers. Government spending after the First World War was significantly higher than before. Federal revenues, for example, were only $750 million when we entered the war era, but rose to almost $5 billion after it. This trend has continued unabated up to the present: combined government revenues now exceed one-third the gross national product.

MANPOWER AND PRODUCTION

The war had to be fought with men. Although we did not use a large number of available manpower for the actual fighting, the total number of Americans who finally served during the conflict numbered almost 5 million—about 5 percent of the population. Add to this another 3 million needed for war production. It is true that during this time unemployment was down, but the civilian population was not necessarily better off. We expended a significant fraction of our output for the war effort and got little in immediate return —except, of course, the final victory for the Allied forces. This victory is not to be downgraded, but when we analyze what happened to the actual

standard of living during the war period, we must conclude that it fell. Industrial production didn't increase very much after an initial spurt when hostilities broke out in Europe. Industry produced about 1 percent more from 1916 to 1917, but in 1918 and 1919 it produced less than it had several years earlier. Since we were using up part of our real output for the war effort, fewer goods and services were available to the private sector, particularly since production did not significantly increase during the height of the hostilities.

It was not very difficult to get workers into war production industries because those industries generally paid higher wages. However, this led to very high turnover rates. That is, workers were quitting their jobs more than they normally

Victory drive parade in Washington, D.C., shortly after the United States entered World War I. (Wide World Photos)

did, because it was possible to obtain better jobs elsewhere. Generally, workers who quit jobs to go elsewhere increase the total productivity of the nation, because when a worker can make higher pay in another industry that usually means that he is more valuable doing a different job. The reason he is more valuable doing a different job is because his productivity is higher. Hence, the movement of workers from low-wage jobs to higher-wage jobs will lead to an increase in overall productivity for the economy. However, this increase did not occur during the war, apparently because there was too much labor turnover. That is, workers were moving so rapidly from one job to another that they never stayed long enough to pass the initial stage where their productivity was low due to the newness of the job.

WERE WE UNPREPARED?

It may seem that we were totally unprepared for the war effort because the President was relying on his ability to keep us out of the war in order

FIGURE 10–1   THE WAR INDUSTRIES BOARD

Here we see a simplified schematic of how the War Industries Board went about controlling the output of the economy.

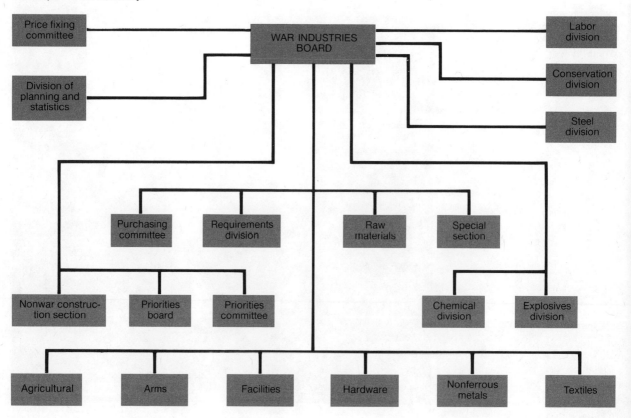

to be reelected. However, this is not a completely accurate view. The Naval Consulting Board had an Industrial Preparedness Committee as early as 1915. This became a full-fledged Committee on Industrial Preparedness in 1916. This organization was financed solely by private contributions, although it was officially an arm of the federal government. By late 1916 there was a new organization called the Council of National Defense. President Wilson said that the purpose of the CND was to organize "the whole industrial mechanism . . . in the most effective way." Even before we entered the war, the Council of National Defense set up a Munitions Standards Board, in February 1917. Eventually, the CND was to designate an entire system of food control, censorship of the press, and purchasing war supplies. Finally, a couple of months after we joined the side of the Allies, a War Industries Board was established to take control over the better part of the economy. We see in Figure 10–1 that it was a complicated but complete control mechanism which the rigors of war production and distribution brought upon the economy.

CONTROLS, CONTROLS, CONTROLS

It must be remembered that war always creates an atmosphere conducive to expansion of government powers. The Great War was no exception. In fact, we might view World War I as a period that was used to develop the administrative machinery that would set the stage for many of the government control mechanisms instituted during Roosevelt's New Deal at the nadir of the Great Depression, a topic we go into in the following chapter.

The War Industries Board took its job seriously. It soon became the coordinator and allocator of commodities and allowed the fixing of prices and the setting of priorities in production. Bernard Baruch became head of this great bureaucratic octopus in March 1918. Baruch was

an obvious candidate, for he had been an earlier supporter of our entry into the war and he had already presented a scheme for industrial war mobilization to the President in 1915, well before most people were convinced we were to enter the conflict. All of the leaders of the various departments in the control mechanism for war mobilization were, of course, big businessmen. And, as can be expected, they looked out for their own. For example, in the granting of war contracts, there was no competitive bidding. The big-businessmen-dominated War Industries Board handed out contracts as seemed appropriate to them, ignoring costs and efficiency in the process. This may be one of the reasons that productivity did not rise during our involvement in the war.

Price Fixing

Since wars have generally been associated with inflation, very early in the game the controllers desired to set up some sort of price-fixing mechanism in order that inflation would not take off. We will see below that given the nature of war financing used, inflation was inevitable. Nonetheless, the stage was set and so a Price-Fixing Committee of the War Industries Board was formed. Naturally, the public was told that the committee would set maximum prices so the consumer would not be hurt. However, what actually happened was that in many cases, a price was set so as to guarantee a "fair" or "reasonable" profit to all producers, even the high-cost, inefficient ones. What did this mean? Simply that the low-cost firms were allowed to make exceptionally high profits because it was the high-cost ones that actually set the prices. In a competitive system, this could not prevail, for the high-cost producers would be driven out of business. As can be expected, big business enthusiastically supported this type of price fixing. After all, there would be no market fluctuations to bother with, and profits for efficient producers could be kept high without fear that competitive forces would erode any excesses.

Price fixing in the agricultural sector was perhaps more blatant. The Food Administration was presided over by Herbert Hoover. Instead of direct control over food, the Administration used a vast network of licensing agreements. Every producer, warehouser, and distributor of food had to obtain a federal license from Hoover's Administration. Hoover used the licenses to good avail: He would only grant them if the licensees set prices to allow "a reasonable margin of profit." The goal, it would seem, was not lower prices, but rather stabilized noncompetitive prices. And in fact, the goal was met. Any competitor who tried to increase his profits above prewar levels by price cutting was threatened with loss of his license. And when there were direct price controls, a maximum was not set, but rather a *minimum*. For example, the Food Control Act of 1917 set a minimum price of $2 a bushel on the 1918 wheat crop. This figure was later upped by 26¢ in the summer of 1918.

Other Forms of Control

The government completely took over some industries. This happened with the railroads. At the beginning of the war, the railroads agreed to form a Railroads War Board and to cease competitive activities. However, the quest for higher profits soon won out over the railroad managers' patriotic promulgations. Price cutting became common and more and more overt forms of competition reared their ugly heads. Finally, President Wilson seized the railroads on December 28, 1917. Hence, we had a full monopoly by direct government operation. Many important railroad men were appointed to leading positions in the Railroad Administration. Soon there were numerous dicta for compulsory standardization of locomotive and equipment design, and the elimination of duplicate passenger and coal services. Additionally, no railroads were allowed to solicit business that they did not already have. All of this was done even before the Railroad Administration was legalized by the Federal Control Act of March 1918.

Wars seem to be associated with inflation, and World War I was no exception. And when the prices of things go up, especially food, people often express their disgust. (United Press International Photo)

WHERE IT ALL LED

The entire system of controls was more or less dismantled after the cessation of hostilities. However, the stage had been set for mixed collective action by which government and business joined together in a cooperative atmosphere. This cooperative atmosphere was to prevail under Franklin Delano Roosevelt's administration. We'll get to that in Chapter 11. Before we do, let's see how the war was financed.

FINANCING THE WAR

As can be seen in Figure 10–2, federal expenditures rose rapidly during the period under study. But federal expenditures do not come out of the

FIGURE 10-2

RISING GOVERNMENT EXPENDITURES

Before our engagement in World War I, federal government expenditures did not even hit $1 billion. However, by 1918 they were almost $13 billion, and reached a peak of $18.5 billion in 1919. (*Source:* U.S. Treasury.)

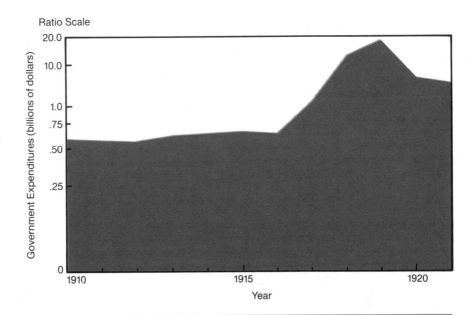

blue. Even the government faces a **budget constraint,** just as you or your friends or anybody does. We have to pay for what we buy (unless, of course, we steal it). The government is no exception. If its expenditures increase, it must somehow finance them. There are generally only three ways that the government can finance its expenditures: (1) taxation, (2) borrowing from the public, and (3) money creation. We will treat them individually because each is individually an extremely important aspect of government financing.

Taxation

Taxation is the most obvious manner in which the government can pay for its expenditures. When the government increases taxes, people have less take-home pay. Generally, their desired expenditures will then fall. That means that the government can obtain part of the nation's output that is no longer being purchased by the private sector. Almost none of the wars that we know of have been completely financed by taxation. The Great War was no exception. Congress continuously

increased tax rates in an effort to offset its increased expenditures. There was a change in the entire tax structure during the war: We started resorting to more direct taxes and a more progressive system. In 1916 the maximum personal income tax rate was raised from 7 percent to 15 percent, and the maximum corporation rate was raised to 14.5 percent. In 1917 there were increases in estate taxes and again in personal and corporate income taxes. The maximum rate went up on the personal taxes to 67 percent, and the normal corporation rate rose from 2 percent to 6 percent, with the maximum excess profits rate going up to 60 percent. This still wasn't enough, so the Revenue Act of 1918 (which was eventually passed in February 1919) increased the maximum personal rate to 77 percent, the normal corporation tax rate to 12 percent, and the maximum excess profits tax rate to 65 percent. Wars are always a good time to raise taxes because the public is less inclined to gripe, for that might indicate that they were unpatriotic. But we will see that it wasn't until World War II that tax rates really increased.

REMEMBER!
THE FLAG OF LIBERTY
SUPPORT IT!

BUY
U.S. Government Bonds
3rd. LIBERTY LOAN

Borrowing from the Private Sector

If the government runs a deficit—that is, spends more than it receives—it has the option of selling its bonds to the public. The government took full advantage of this option during World War I. In addition to its regular bond sales, which occur all the time in a dynamic economy, it instituted four Liberty Loan drives. And if that wasn't enough, there was one postwar drive, naturally called a Victory Loan. A total of $19.1 billion was raised in this manner. But, in fact, the government's increased bond sales were, and still are, a disguised form of increased taxes. After all, what happens when the government sells a bond? It obtains the price of the bond from an individual, a bank, or a corporation. In return it promises to pay interest for a certain number of years and then pay back the original price of the bond, called the principal. But how does the government pay the interest? Out of revenues. Where does it obtain revenues? From taxes. That means that when the government runs a deficit and makes up for it by selling bonds, it is increasing the future tax liabilities of the nation. Higher bond sales lead to higher future taxes. Of that there can be no question. Perhaps people can be fooled for a while by this method of government financing, but eventually the sad truth will become evident.

Just look at it this way: If the government financed all of its expenditures by selling bonds, it would have an increasing interest payment to make every year as it continued to sell more and more bonds to pay for increased expenditures and an increasing interest payment. Eventually the number of bonds it would have to sell would become tremendous, for the interest payments it owed would skyrocket into the heavens. There is no truth in the saying that bonds are cheaper than taxes: Bonds are taxes; they are just delayed into the future.

And of course you don't get anything for nothing. If you persuade someone to give up part of his income to buy bonds so that the government can increase its expenditures, that someone has to be paid a reward. And the reward is the interest rate, which we'll call a reward for waiting. So we have the option: Either pay taxes today to finance government expenditures, or pay higher taxes in the future to pay for those government expenditures.

Money Creation

The last method of government finance is money creation. It happened during the Revolutionary War when Continentals were printed. It happened during the Civil War when Confederate notes were issued, and so were Greenbacks. And it happened during World War I. But by World War I a more formalized machinery for money creation had already been established. It is sufficiently important in the history of U.S. economic development for us to make a little detour and investigate it.

A DIGRESSION—THE FEDERAL RESERVE SYSTEM

Remember that the National Banking System was established by legislation during the Civil War. But also remember its many weaknesses that we pointed out. It did not create a national system as originally intended. Moreover, its check clearance system seemed to be costly and inefficient. There were so many faults in the National Banking System that government officials felt the need to create a new central banking authority. So in 1913 the government passed the Federal Reserve Act. One of its duties was to create "an elastic currency." During the First World War, it made an elastic currency indeed, as we shall see. In any event, the Federal Reserve System was set up into twelve district banks, to one of which every member commercial bank would belong. In each of these district banks the member banks would be required to maintain a certain amount of reserves. That is, if the **reserve requirement** was, for example, 20 percent, a member bank which had a million dollars in checking account deposits and outstanding notes would have to keep $200,000 on reserve in its district's federal bank. The Federal Reserve banks were empowered to issue a new type of paper money called Federal Reserve notes. These were to be secured by **commercial paper** (the promissory notes of businessmen) and gold. The district banks were also empowered to lend reserves to member banks who requested them. Note, however, that this function was considered a privilege and not a right of the commercial banks. Finally, a more efficient and less costly check clearing system was instituted.

The Federal Reserve is governed by a Federal Reserve Board. Originally this was merely an administrative agency with little control over the system's operations. Today this is not the case. The Board of Governors of the Federal Reserve essentially runs the show. The various committees decide which monetary policies to pursue and how to effect them. This was not the case during World War I. The system was relatively passive; it felt obliged to give the United States Treasury its full support. This meant essentially that it was to pursue an easy money policy, that it was to allow a large amount of cash—demand deposits and currency—to enter the economy.

BACK TO MONEY CREATION

The formal mechanism for money creation was set within the Federal Reserve System. But how it happened is not as important as the fact that it did happen. The mechanism by which money was created during World War I is perhaps of special interest.

One of the easiest ways for the Fed to create money is to increase the reserves that member banks have. When member banks have more reserves, they can loan out more money. One of the ways that member banks can obtain reserves is to borrow them from the Federal Reserve Banks. What the Fed did during the war was to lower the interest rate charged and also to accept essentially anything in collateral for the loans they gave out to member banks at that lower interest rate. In this manner, reserves increased dramatically. This led to a rapid increase in the money supply in circulation.* For example, in 1917 money per capita was $22.50. In 1919, it had risen to $35 per person. Not surprisingly, the wholesale price index was up by 20 percent and the Consumer Price Index by 35 percent. We have already noted this relationship to massive in-

---

*The large increase in the money supply led to an increase in the demand for government securities, thus making it easier for the government to finance its war-induced purchases.

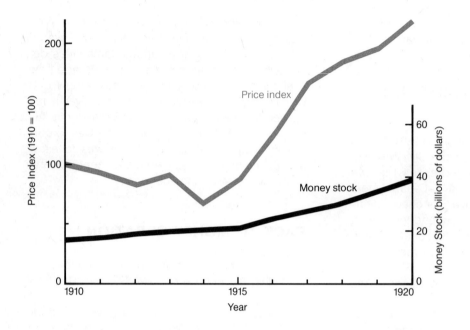

FIGURE 10–3

MONEY AND PRICES DURING WORLD WAR I

The money stock which grew very little from 1910 to 1914 soon started to rise at increasing rates. The price level was not far behind. (*Source:* Bureau of Labor Statistics.)

creases in the amount of money in circulation: Individuals find they have excess cash around; in an attempt to rid themselves of this excess cash, they spend. When people all together attempt to buy more than is produced, prices rise. This happened in Europe because of the gold and silver flows from the New World in the fifteenth and sixteenth centuries; this happened in the Revolution; this happened in the Confederacy and in the Union during the Civil War; and it happened again in World War I. Figure 10–3 shows increases in the stock of money and increases in the price index.

Generally it is thought that government expenditures financed by taxation and borrowing from the private sector are not inflationary because in both cases private purchasing power is reduced therein. If a person pays part of his income in taxes, desired expenditures are usually reduced. If an individual or a business firm decides to lend money to the government by buying a bond, then again individual purchasing power, or desire to spend in the private sector, will be reduced. Such is not the case when expenditures are financed by money creation. People who eventually receive this extra cash do not want to reduce expenditures. Indeed, they want to increase them. And that's exactly what happens. Notice that inflation is also another form of taxation, but a very special kind. If the price level rises, everybody who holds dollar bills in his wallet or in his checking account suffers. After all, if you have $100 in the bank and keep it there for a year while the price of everything goes up 10 percent, that $100 has lost 10 percent of its value. It has depreciated by 10 percent. In effect, then, you have paid a 10 percent tax on holding those dollars. There's no way to avoid this tax unless you get rid of all the dollars that you generally hold in your wallet or in your checking account. But that would be extremely inconvenient. So the government can be pretty sneaky about this type of tax. It's very easy to collect and it's very difficult to avoid. Latin American governments are experts at this way of obtaining resources for their use. In many countries in South America, rates of inflation range from 50 percent to 100 percent a year. That's a pretty high tax on the cash people down south might happen to hold.

HOW DID WE FARE?

We were an active participant in the war for only some 19 months. Our casualty rate wasn't high compared to that of the Civil War or the Second World War, but it was significant: 75,000 dead and 225,000 injured, a total of 300,000 casualties. We had put up an impressive productive effort. The weight of the metal fired in just one offensive in World War I was more than was used in the entire Civil War. And we produced it without enduring the hardships that were suffered throughout the European countries engaged in the war. While Americans knew what the word scarcity meant after World War I, they really hadn't paid the kind of price that Germany, France, England, Russia, and the other participants in the Old World had paid.

At the end of the Great War, America was indeed a modern industrialized nation. It was time for the Roaring Twenties, which were to come to a screeching halt with the beginning of the Great Depression. Before we turn to those dismal days, let's find out how World War I turned out to be the true emancipation of the black man.

Definitions of New Terms

BUDGET CONSTRAINT: the constraint that an individual, a government, or even the world has on its spending capacity. One is limited in how much he can spend by his budget constraint. So, too, is the government, except that it has the means of expanding its budget constraint by selling bonds and by creating money.

RESERVE REQUIREMENT: the reserves that commercial banks which are members of the Federal Reserve System must keep on account in their district Federal Reserve bank or in currency in their vaults. These reserves are expressed as a percentage of checking and savings account deposits outstanding.

COMMERCIAL PAPER: debt issued by individual corporations or by businessmen.

Chapter Summary

1. World War I used a significant part of our manpower resources, but not as much as during the Civil War. Workers were attracted into war production industries by higher wages; generally when workers move from a low-paying job to a high-paying job, their productivity (contribution to output) is greater in the latter.

2. During World War I, a large system of controls was instituted, headed by the War Industries Board. These controls resulted in numerous price-fixing arrangements.

3. As with all government expenditures, war efforts had to be financed, because even the federal government faces a budget constraint. Only part of the war effort was financed by taxation.

4. Almost all the rest of the war effort was financed by borrowing from the private sector. However, this borrowing was made easier by the large increases in the money supply.
5. The money supply is more or less controlled by the Federal Reserve authorities. During this time they were willing to take anything as collateral for loans of reserves to the member banks. This caused an increase in the money supply so that the demand for government securities (bonds) increased. That is why the government was able to sell enough bonds to finance the war deficit.
6. Generally, government expenditures financed by taxation and borrowing from the private sector are not considered inflationary because private purchasing power is reduced therein. However, excessive money creation is thought to usually result in inflation.

Questions for Thought and Discussion

1. Why didn't the government finance all of its expenditures by current taxation?
2. Why do you think war industries offered workers relatively higher wages?
3. What is a "fair" or "reasonable" profit?
4. Who benefits from *minimum* prices set by the government?
5. Do you keep part of your wealth in money (currency or checking deposits)? Why?

THE BETTMANN ARCHIVE, INC.

A WALL STREET WHIZ BECOMES WARTIME ECONOMIC CZAR

Bernard Mannes Baruch (1870–1965)
Financier and Economist for the Government

IN 1940 the National Defense Advisory Commission had a meeting with Bernard Baruch. The country was worried about the possibility of war. What to do in such an event was foremost in everyone's mind, at least everyone's in the government. Baruch urged the members of the NDAC to form industrial committees, establish priorities, and impose price controls, all under the centralized authority of a single agency. Such a recommendation from the former Wall Street whiz was not unexpected. After all, during World War I he had headed the War Industries Board, which controlled much of American economic life during the hostilities.

Baruch didn't start out as a government economist and advisor. He was the son of a well-known physician and writer on medical subjects, who lived in Camden, South Carolina. The Baruch family soon moved to New York, where Bernard eventually won his B.A. degree at the College of the City of New York. He then entered the brokerage house of A. A. Housman & Company. He spent literally hundreds of hours pouring over industrial and railroad manuals. In fact, his employer freely predicted his failure as a "customer's man." Failure he was not, however. Eventually he became a member of the firm and started negotiating some of the largest industrial mergers to occur in the United States. He soon had the esteem and confidence of Rockefeller, the Guggenheims, and a number of other financiers of the day. He was brought to the attention of President Wilson and this started him on his long career of government service.

In 1916 the President invited Baruch to sit on the Council of National Defense. He was made Commissioner of Raw Materials, Minerals and Metals. Finally he sold his membership in the New York Stock Exchange and never again returned to private business.

Baruch's penchant for assisting in producer organizations, which were later to result in numerous anticompetitive practices, started at the very beginning of his government career. In the raw materials field, he got cooperative committees of highly placed executives to assemble trade information and to facilitate the business-government partnership that Baruch was to be so fond of in the future.

When the Council of National Defense organized the War Industries Board on July 28, 1917, Baruch was named a member. During this time the operations of the various war agencies seemed to be little coordinated, at least in the eyes of President Wilson. There seemed to be a need for the creation of a "war cabinet" with autocratic powers, so the President made the War Industries Board independent, with Baruch as chairman. The Board was clothed with full power of enforcement for all of its rulings. Bernard Baruch became the industrial dictator of wartime America. The operations of the board affected practically every phase of the nation's economic life. Price fixing seemed to be a major occupation. Accordingly, the prices of aluminum, cement, copper, cotton, cotton linters, hides, leather, hemp, lumber, platinum, sand, gravel, crushed stone, steel wool, and zinc were fixed.

There was also a distinct desire to reduce "wasteful" duplication. Hence, the Board under Baruch's iron hand regulated the style and color of clothes, reduced the number of types of such items as paints, farm implements, tires, furnaces, refrigerators, sofas, metal beds, and spring wagons. The War Industries Board also waged a campaign to eliminate "unnecessary" delivery service. At one extreme, the War Industries Board's activities were thought to simplify and standardize manufacturing methods to the end of saving labor, materials, and costs. However, many critics of Baruch's methods pointed out that he was helping stifle competitive forces within the nation's economy.

Baruch's organizational methods were simple: When he wanted an industry to do something, he commandeered the industry's heads to Washington jobs. He paid little attention to precedent, and never allowed his mind to be lost in the mazes of organization charts. Nor did he allow his purposes to be thwarted by government "red tape." When he had a goal, he proceeded by the shortest possible route.

For all of Baruch's efforts on the War Industries Board, President Wilson gave him the Distinguished Service Medal.

After the war the President got a firm "no" when he asked Baruch to become Secretary of the Treasury. Instead, the President was able to get him on the commission to attend the peace conference in Paris, where the former financier became the sole American member of the economic drafting committee. His work has been severely criticized, for he single-handedly wrote many of the sections which outraged certain domestic observers. For example, he specified that all alien property taken over by the United States during the war should remain under the control of Congress.

Then Baruch went into semiretirement, devoting himself to the study of what he called "practical" economic questions, both national and international. He wrote reports on the defects in the business side of farming and suggested remedies. He advised the American Farm Bureau Federation and attempted to get the financial world interested in the business troubles of American farmers.

Although retired from the world of Wall Street that he knew so well, Baruch nonetheless kept his keen insights: he began liquidating all his stocks as early as 1928 and putting the proceeds into gold. He died a very rich man.

ISSUE X — WAS WORLD WAR I THE REAL EMANCIPATION?

Huh! de wurl' ain't flat
An' de wurl' ain't roun'
Jes' one long strip
Hangin' up an' down.
Since Norf is up,
An' Souf is down,
An' Hebben is up,
I'm upward boun'.*

Freeing the Slaves

Abraham Lincoln signed the Emancipation Proclamation on September 22, 1862. It stated:

That on the 1st day of January, A.D. 1863, all persons held as slaves within any State or designated part of a State the people whereof shall then be in rebellion against the United States shall be then, thenceforward, and forever free; and the executive government of the United States, including the military and naval authority thereof, will recognize and maintain the freedom of such persons and will do no act or acts to repress such persons, or any of them, in any efforts they may make for their actual freedom.

We all know by now that just because legislation goes into effect, the world doesn't necessarily turn upside down (or rightside up). While legislation obviously can have an immediate impact,

*Lucy Ariel Williams, "Northboun'," *The Negro Caravan,* edited by Sterling A. Brown. New York: Random House, 1969, p. 377.

it generally takes time for the full effect to be felt. Although the black man was freed during the Civil War, his true emancipation certainly was not obvious during the next five decades, for blacks generally remained in the South and generally were not exceedingly well treated. Even in 1915 there were still lynchings: 54 blacks found their deaths at the end of a rope in that year.**

Moving out of the South

There had been some migration of blacks from the South to the North ever since the Civil War. However, until the beginning of World War I it was only a trickle. Starting in 1916, there was a mass exodus of blacks to Northern cities unprecedented in the history of the nation. And the entire geographical distribution of this minority group in the United States completely changed. Whereas in 1900 77 percent of blacks were

**So, too, did 13 whites.

living in rural areas, the trend toward urbanization picked up so rapidly that barely a half a century later 60 percent were urban. Almost all of the migration to the North during World War I was a movement to cities. In fact, the 1920 Census revealed that almost three-fourths of northern blacks were found in the ten industrial centers of the nation, such as New York, Chicago, St. Louis, Pittsburgh, and Kansas City. If we look at the makeup of blacks within these different cities, we find that by the Great Depression more than 50 percent of those in New York, Chicago, Philadelphia, Washington, Detroit, Memphis, St. Louis, Cleveland, and Pittsburgh had been born in some other state. Detroit, for example, had more blacks from Georgia than did Augusta or Macon. Chicago had as many Mississippi-born blacks as the entire black population in Vicksburg, Meridian, Greenville, and Natchez.

Why Did It All Happen?

Why did it take 50 years for blacks to start a massive migration to the Northland? Was it merely fortuitous that the start of World War I signaled the start of black migration? Perhaps, but another explanation may be more plausible. It involves two aspects of the war: the increased demand for workers and the decreased immigration from the Old World. Additionally, at this time the boll weevil was ruining cotton cultivation, making it less profitable for rural blacks. In Table X-1 we see the percent of reduction from full yield per acre of cotton due to the boll weevil. It started out as only 1.3 percent in 1911, but it grew to 13.4 percent in 1916 and increased dramatically until the middle of the Roaring Twenties.

We have already talked about why people migrate. The basic reason is not hard to figure out. A person will migrate to another country or location generally for economic reasons. While there were many social and political reasons why blacks would want to go to the North, as there were many such reasons for Germans and Swedes and Italians and Scots to want to come to America, the overriding reason was economic: to achieve a higher standard of living. In the period just before our entry into World War I, blacks were making 10 to 15 cents an hour in the South. Soon they started hearing stories about northern employers willing to pay 30 or even 40 cents an hour.

A decision to migrate, on purely economic grounds, will include not only the potential gain in income, but also any costs involved in migration.

Costs of Migration

The most obvious cost of migration is transportation. By World War I, the transportation costs were drastically reduced because the railroad had essentially linked all parts of the nation together. The potential black migrant would have to look at the price of a railroad ticket as the most immediate cost he must endure. In fact, he would have to come up with the price of a ticket in order to even attempt to make a move. After that is the cost of searching for a job once he arrives in another city. The job-search cost can be high if, in fact, the migrant is out of work for a long time. During this period, migrants presumably felt that job-search costs would be minimal since they expected to find work immediately upon arrival.

Another cost to consider is the cost of setting up a new household in a different city, and dismantling the one already created in the would-be migrant's current city. The costs here are not only economic but also psychic—losing old friends and trying to make new ones, leaving relatives, and so on. All of these costs of migration are incurred at the very beginning, so they loom larger in the would-be migrant's mind than the potential benefits of higher wages that he will obtain once he gets work in

TABLE X-1 BOLL WEEVIL DESTRUCTION

YEAR	PERCENT OF REDUCTION IN FULL YIELD PER ACRE OF COTTON DUE TO BOLL WEEVIL
1911	1.3
1912	3.3
1913	6.7
1914	5.9
1915	9.9
1916	13.4
1917	9.3
1918	5.8
1919	13.2
1920	19.9
1921	31.0
1922	24.2
1923	19.5
1924	8.0
1925	4.1

The percentage of reduction in full yield per acre of cotton due to the mischievous boll weevil rose dramatically during World War I and a few years thereafter, reducing the profitability of cotton growing for rural blacks (and whites). (*Source:* U.S. Department of Agriculture, Statistical Bulletin No. 99, Table 52, p. 67.)

another city. In the economic decision, then, the expected or anticipated stream of *differences* in wages (because that's really what one has to look at), must be compared with the anticipated migration costs that are incurred almost immediately, but which are generally of a once-and-for-all nature.

Labor Raids

There was a very good reason for many blacks to believe that they could obtain instant work in the North at higher wages, for the South was filled with Northern labor contractors. The South was becoming increasingly upset at what they called labor raids of Southern blacks for Northern jobs. In fact, various state and local governments in the South attempted to prevent the raids by passing ordinances which allowed the fining and imprisonment of anybody convicted of "enticing" a laborer to leave the city for another place of employment. Other states placed heavy license taxes on emigration agents. The demand for labor was high enough in the North, however, that it still paid four licensed agents to cough up $1000 each in Birmingham in order to "entice" blacks to come North.

The Effects of Immigration Laws

Even though the North had been expanding its industrial economy for many years, our liberal immigration laws had made it rare to need to go South to obtain workers. We see in Figure X–1 that immigration into the United States sometimes reached as many as 1.28 million foreigners landing on our shores a year. During the first 14 years of the twentieth century, over 12 million immigrants found their way to the United States. This all came to a screeching halt, though, as we became more involved in the war and more xenophobic. In 1915, less than a third of the 1914 number of immigrants arrived. In 1916, only a fourth, and by 1918, only 110,618 foreigners landed in the United States, while 94,585 left. The flow of relatively cheap foreign workers was stopped. But by 1915, the North needed labor. Northern industry was expanding to meet the demands of a war-torn older continent, and eventually we were to enter that struggle and increase the demands for war production even more.

New Meaning for the Black Franchise

It is generally considered that by 1914 Negroes were completely disfranchised in the South. Even

FIGURE X–1   IMMIGRATION INTO THE UNITED STATES

The number of immigrants reaching our shores from all countries sometimes almost reached 1.3 million per year, as in 1907. However, we started restrictive immigration policies in 1917 when we passed the literacy test and then started a quota system in 1921: Immigration was curtailed drastically. (*Source: Historical Statistics,* p. 56.)

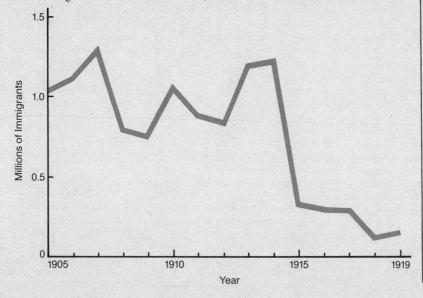

the handful of black voters who remained were considered such a challenge that in South Carolina, the General Assembly voted in January 1914 to repeal the Fifteenth Amendment to the United States Constitution! But in the North blacks could vote and even hold office. Civil rights for blacks in the national political arena made a great leap forward during this period of massive migration. The large numbers of blacks who came into Northern cities were potential voters. Politicians had to take greater cognizance of this increasingly important subsection of the population. By 1915 the first black was elected to Chicago's City Council, Oscar dePriest. Blacks were registering and voting in the largest numbers since the turn of the century, and by 1921 the New Jersey House of Representatives had a black President, Assemblyman Walter G. Alexander. Later on, the Democratic Party in New York State made an attempt to win the black vote by taking a strong position against the Ku Klux Klan.

According to students of black history, the migration caused by our entry into World War I, the increased demand for more labor, and the shutting off of immigration from abroad are responsible for laying the groundwork for equal rights for the black man. "In the very process of being transplanted, the Negro was becoming transformed."*

*Alain Locke, "The New Negro," *The Negro Caravan*, p. 950.

Questions for Thought and Discussion

1. Can you think of noneconomic reasons why blacks wanted to leave the South during this period?
2. Why would some Southerners try to prevent Northern labor agents from operating in the South?
3. Why do you think the United States passed such restrictive immigration laws in the early twentieth century?

The Great Depression Leads to a New Deal

11

W E CAME OUT of the Great War victorious. After a brief but sharp recession at the beginning of the 1920s, the economy set itself on a course of increasing prosperity. The real growth rate in the twenties was about 3 percent per year, leading to an increase in real GNP of 62 percent over what it was in 1914. The economy did not appear to be overly strained in the year the stock market crashed, 1929—3.2 percent of the labor force was unemployed, prices were not rising. In short, the nation did not appear to be living beyond its means in the Roaring Twenties. But some very definite changes had occurred in the consumption pattern of American citizens. We turned our paychecks over to the retailers of numerous consumer durables—radios, refrigerators, stoves, and above all, automobiles. Over 3 million new automobiles were purchased a year. By 1929, there were over 26 million cars on the road. People started using these cars to good avail; longer and more extensive vacations were becoming a part of the American way of life.

SOME AFTEREFFECTS OF THE FIRST WORLD WAR

In the last chapter we saw that the war atmosphere prompted a fairly broad extension of government power throughout the economy. We have seen that generally after past wars this extension of government power was quickly curtailed. However, there were certain sentiments which remained after the Great War and, indeed, which materialized into actual government intervention in the market economy.

One of the key figures responsible for the extension of government powers during the Roaring Twenties was none other than Herbert Hoover, who later became president. Remember that he was in charge of the Food Administration during the First World War. After the war, he became Relief Administrator in Europe. On returning to the United States, he was appointed Secretary of Commerce by President Harding. Immediately upon his appointment, he set out to "reconstruct America." During the recession of '20–'21, Hoover repeatedly presented his views on how public works could be used to stabilize employment during depressions. Keeping close to the food problem, with which he had been so familiar during World War I, Hoover helped write the act of August 1921 which expanded the funds allotted to the still-existing War Finance Corporation. This act permitted the WFC to lend directly to farmers' cooperatives.

Not satisfied, Hoover attempted to create a federal Farm Board which would support farm prices by creating a federal corporation for stabilization. This corporation was to purchase farm products and to lend money to cooperatives. We will see below that when Hoover became president, he continued his policy of fostering government stabilization policies in order to help the American people during the Depression, which was getting worse by the day.

THE GREAT STOCK MARKET CRASH

Toward the end of the Roaring Twenties, the stock market was taking a turn for the better. Stock market prices were rising at astounding rates. The barber, the janitor, the butler, and the ditch digger had money in the stock market and were making money on their money. And those who couldn't afford to pay for the stocks they wanted to buy were allowed to buy on margin. That is, they only had to put up a certain percentage of the total price; their brokerage company would furnish the rest. Of course, they paid interest on this loan—but what did they care? Their stocks were going up so fast that they still made tons of money.

Look at Figure 11–1. Here we plot what happened from the beginning of the 1920s to the depths of the Depression. By 1929 stock prices were already one and a half times what they had been a mere three or four years earlier. Trading was increasing every day. Something had to give, and it did. In October of '29, investors started to get jittery. There were continuous reports that economic activity was falling off. There were threats of a recession. Of course, nobody at that time ever conceived of the Great Depression that would follow.

On October 1, average share prices fell $5 to $10. On October 3, the same thing occurred again. The next day was no better. Prices kept declining, although the number of shares traded was actually relatively small. Toward the end of the month, when disaster seemed near, business and political leaders tried to intervene in order to stop the precipitous decline. However, on Monday, October 28, 1929, there was a nationwide stampede to unload stocks. In the last hour of trading, over 3 million shares were traded. In just one day the value of all stocks fell by $14 billion! The next day was even worse. Blue Monday and Black Tuesday had arrived. Although stock prices rallied for the first few months in 1930, that was the last major rally that a nation of investors was

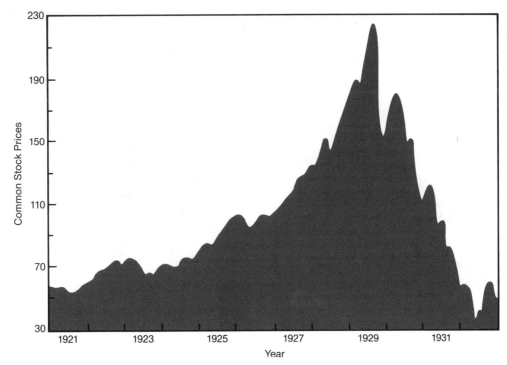

FIGURE 11-1   THE STOCK MARKET GOES UP AND DOWN

The Roaring Twenties saw common stock prices rise almost 500 percent before the Crash in 1929. By 1931, they were right back where they started in 1921. (*Source:* Standard Statistics Index of Prices of 421 Common Stocks, Monthly Averages, 1926 = 100.)

to see for many years to come. By the summer of 1932 the value of stocks had fallen by 83 percent from their September 1929 prices!

THE REST OF THE ECONOMY FOLLOWS

It was not long before the entire nation was well into a serious recession. Of course, no one imagined that this recession would become the greatest depression in the history of the United States— nay, in the history of the modern world. In fact, at the time, the great American economist, Irving Fisher, who was also a leader in the Temperance movement, went around giving speeches to Ro-

tarians and similar groups. He proclaimed that the economic troubles of the United States were bound to be short-lived because Prohibition had made the American worker more productive!

Real output started to fall continuously, a phenomenon that rarely occurs in a growing economy. Notice that we are talking about real *total* output, not output per capita. That meant that real output per capita was falling even more rapidly. Look at Figure 11–2. By 1933 actual output was at least 35 percent below the productive capacity of the nation at that time. In fact, the total output lost during this Great Depression was a little over $350 billion measured in 1929 prices. What that means is incredible: If we hadn't had the Great Depression, we could have built,

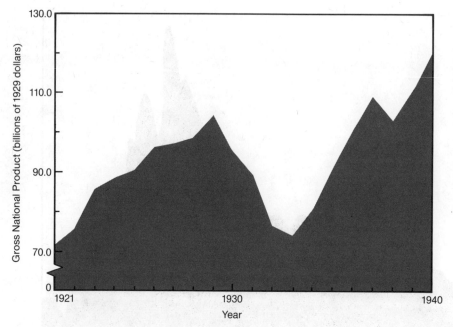

FIGURE 11–2

**REAL GROSS NATIONAL
PRODUCT TAKES A BEATING**

Measured in 1929 prices, gross
national product grew from the
beginning of the 1920s until
the end of the decade. Then it
fell precipitously, not starting to
rise again until 1934. In 1938 it
was about the same as it had
been ten years before. Of
course, per capita real GNP fell
even more. (*Source:* J. W.
Kendrick, *Productivity Trends
in the United States, op. cit.,*
and Office of Business
Economics.)

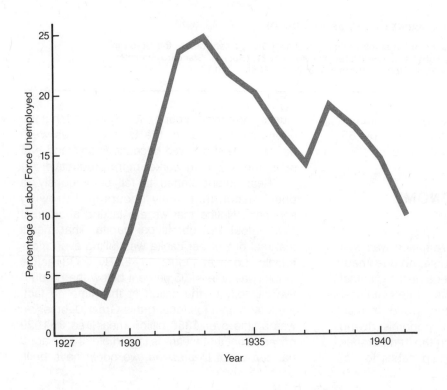

FIGURE 11–3

**THE DEPRESSION SEES
MASSIVE UNEMPLOYMENT**

Unemployment rose to 24.9
percent of the civilian labor force
during the depths of the
Depression in 1933. Even by the
end of the decade it was still at
14.6 percent. (*Source: Economic
Report of the President.*)

for example, another 700,000 schools, each costing a half a million dollars, or another 36 million homes, each costing $10,000. That's an awful lot of output to lose. And remember, once it's lost, you never recover it. Lost output is like lost time: It can never be regained.

The Employment Situation

The employment situation got increasingly bleaker. As can be seen in Figure 11–3, by 1933 fully one-fourth of the entire labor force was walking the streets. That means that 1 out of every 4 adult members of society who wanted to work could not find a job. And unemployment stayed high for many, many years. The Great Depression was not a short-term event. From 1930 through 1940, an average of 10 million people were out of work, and that's in a labor force that was approximately one-half of ours today, so today's equivalent would be a decade during which an average of 20 million workers are out of work. The actual labor force may have been understated, thus understating the amount of unemployment. There was a consistent "no jobs for married women" policy throughout the entire 1930s. In other words, married women were denied jobs in favor of men. Additionally, many men moved their families into rural areas or onto squatters' land. Instead of looking for a job in the city, they attempted to scrape out a bare existence in the countryside.

This unemployment is so incredible as to boggle the modern mind, for we are not used to numbers that large when measuring economic distress. Now the entire nation becomes alarmed when the unemployment rate reaches 6 percent. Nobody today can even conceive of a 25 percent rate of unemployment, but that's what occurred during the depths of the Depression.

The Banking System

By March of 1933 there was a virtual collapse of the entire commercial banking system in the United States. When Roosevelt became president, he closed every single bank in existence and declared a temporary moratorium on debts. Between the years 1929 and 1932 more than 5000 banks—one out of every five—had failed and their customers' deposits vanished. Personal savings fell as income fell. By 1932 people were *dissaving* almost three-fourths of a billion dollars, whereas in 1929 they had saved over $4 billion. Not only did banks fail, but so did thousands upon thousands of other financial intermediaries—loan companies and credit unions and the like.

And Farmers, Too

Farmers hadn't been faring well ever since the end of World War I. After all, fewer exports were called for as European nations tried to go it on their own. They had neither the inclination nor the wherewithal to purchase American foodstuffs. Moreover, European nations set up numerous protective tariffs to make sure that their farmers would have a competitive advantage over Americans. Then the recession of '20–'21 hit. Farmers felt this as people bought less food. Agricultural real incomes didn't really rise very much during the 1920s; farmers were considered one of the few groups that missed out during these years of prosperity. When the Depression hit, farm incomes went into a tremendous slide. By 1932, the net income of farm operators was barely 30 percent of what it had been in 1929.

This doesn't mean, however, that total farm output was lower. It was in fact about 3 percent higher. What had happened, of course, was that farm prices had plummeted. Prices received by farmers in 1932 were a little over 40 percent of what they had received in 1929. This is as could be expected. The demand for food is relatively price inelastic. Farmers tried to counter their lower and lower incomes during the early years of the Depression by increasing their output. But they could get rid of these increasing surpluses of foodstuffs only by lowering prices even more, for it takes a tremendous reduction in the price of corn or wheat to get consumers to buy much more corn or wheat. That's always the case when one is dealing with a product whose demand is relatively price insensitive.

Farmers became delinquent in paying their taxes and their debts. In 1929 alone there were almost 20 forced farm sales per every 1000 farms because of failure to pay taxes or debts. This figure had risen by 100 percent in 1932. Even this figure understates what actually happened, because as the Depression wore on, local tax officials became more and more tolerant of farmers who didn't pay their taxes. And it usually didn't do much good to force a farm sale. Who would buy the farm, and at what price?

The Rest of the World

If it was any consolation, we weren't much worse off than the rest of the world. By 1932, the world's

"Bindlestiffs" is the term that was applied to roving farm workers who owned no car and carried their gear on their backs. (Wide World Photos)

total number of unemployed measured at least 30 million. The international monetary system got increasingly confused. The value of gross trade in the world was falling daily. Nineteen thirty-one was a year of international crisis never again to be matched. It began in May 1931 after the failure of the Credit Anstalt, which was the most important bank in Austria. Its failure made all the other Austrian banks uneasy. Foreign creditors rushed to the country to take out all their loans. Then Hungary suffered the same problem. Next was Germany. And the crisis finally hit the center of the international monetary world—London. No country seemed able to maintain the price that its currency was valued at in terms of gold. No country seemed strong; no currency did either. By the time President Roosevelt was inaugurated, the international economy was in as large a shambles as America's.

WHY DID IT HAPPEN?

Why did what would otherwise have been a normal recession turn into the greatest depression in the history of modern man? The debate still continues. There are numerous theories, but we have time to treat only two major ones here. We have already obliquely referred to some general notions that people had about the Depression. One notion was that Americans were living beyond their means. But there is very little evidence to show that; the productive capacity of the nation was not particularly strained in 1929. Others believe that the failure of the agricultural sector to prosper led to the ultimate demise of the rest of the country. But we find little evidence that such a small part of a big economy could bring on a great depression. Perhaps it could cause a recession, but nothing of the magnitude of what happened. That leaves us with the two major and, in some sense, competing theories of why it all happened.

The first theory is associated with the great Lord John Maynard Keynes, father of the Keynesian Revolution. The second is associated with Professor Milton Friedman, currently of the University of Chicago. We treat the two in order of their appearance in the history of economic thought.

THE KEYNESIAN EXPLANATION

In 1936, when we were still in the Depression, a rather remarkable book appeared, *The General Theory of Employment, Interest and Money.* It was written by John Maynard Keynes, a respected and eminent economist who lived and worked in England. In his book Keynes introduced the possibility that unemployment would exist for a long period of time. That is, he introduced the possibility (hitherto unthought of) that unemployment on a large scale would not correct itself by natural forces within the economy. He pointed out that what was necessary to keep full employment was *effective* aggregate demand. He also pointed out that one of the key drivers in the economy was investment. And to provide for investment there had to be saving. In other words, consumers would have to be willing to save part of their income in order for investors to have resources for investment. But, noted Keynes, there might be times when there is not enough effective investment demand to use up all of the private sector's savings. When this occurs, there would be unemployment. For saving as such is only useful when it is put back into the economy. And it is put back into the active economy only when investors use it to build houses or machines or buildings.

Proponents of the Keynesian theory of how income and employment are determined point out that during the 1920s the public engaged in an abnormally high level of saving. By the Keynesian theory this was dangerous because unless that saving were put back into the economy by investment, there would result a drop in aggregate demand. Unemployment would occur. In fact, however, during the twenties there was a very high

rate of net investment. But this would eventually mean a reduction in the rate of investment as the stock of private capital reached excessively high levels. When this occurs, the expected profitability of future investment probably falls. And hence, businessmen feel less desire to increase investment. Unless consumers decrease saving accordingly, the desired level of saving will exceed the desired level of investment. Reduced demand on the part of the entire public will result and so, too, will unemployment. A recession begins and, in fact, a recession without appropriate government action can lead into a depression, according to this theory. The government must step in to increase effective aggregate demand by appropriate monetary and fiscal policies. We will deal with them later.

Basically, then, we can use this Keynesian theory to state that the Great Depression occurred because of a *collapse in the desire for new capital formation on the part of businessmen.* That is, there was a *collapse in the propensity to invest.* Investment fell behind saving, reducing output, and thereby causing unemployment. This theory corresponds nicely with the available statistics. We see in Figure 11–4 that net investment fell precipitously in the years following the stock market crash. However, the reduction in net investment could have been triggered by something else. At least that is what the other major theory contends.

MILTON FRIEDMAN AND THE MONEY SUPPLY

While not denying the possibility that investment decisions by businessmen relative to saving decisions by individuals are an important determinant of how the economy moves, the proponents of **monetarism,** led by Professor Milton Friedman, place considerably more emphasis on what happens to the amount of money in circulation. While our sketch of their theory is simplified, perhaps even oversimplified, we can point out its most

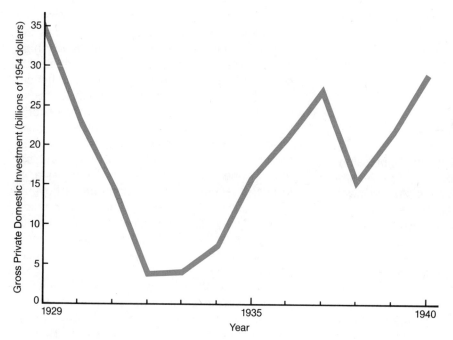

FIGURE 11-4

THE COLLAPSE IN THE PROPENSITY TO INVEST

Here we see plotted real (constant 1954 dollars) gross private domestic investment. From 1929 to 1932 it fell from $35 billion to a mere $4 billion. Even by 1940 it hadn't reached its 1929 peak. (*Source:* Office of Business Economics.)

obvious aspects and apply it to what happened during the Great Depression.

Monetarists believe that what happens in the short run in the economy can be determined by how the Federal Reserve System alters the amount of money in circulation. Money, you must remember, is comprised of currency which you carry in your wallets and hold in your checking account balances. As we pointed out in the last chapter, the Federal Reserve System was established before our entrance into World War I. It was chartered to establish an elastic currency. According to the monetarists, during the Great Depression it did just the opposite. Now, why should the amount of money in circulation be important?

The monetarist theory states that people have a certain desire for money because it facilitates transactions. That is, to live in a world without money would be quite costly indeed, for we would have to resort to barter. Therefore, people keep money in their checking accounts and in their wallets in order to facilitate transactions and to have a temporary store of purchasing power. It seems fairly obvious that if the number of transactions goes up, the amount of money desired by the public would increase. In other words, there should be some relationship between the level of income and the level of money desired by the public. And, indeed, according to the monetarists, this relationship not only exists but is fairly stable. Therefore, if the Federal Reserve System increases the total number of dollars floating around and transactions do not increase, some people will find that they have excess money. In order to get rid of these excess money balances, these people will attempt to spend it, or buy bonds. The only way they can get rid of their cash balances is by spending more than they receive. This will lead to, among other things, an increase in the amount of goods and services demanded. Hence, if we are at full employment, this will lead to a rise in prices—inflation. If we are not at full employment, it will lead to, at least in part, a rise in output, or real income.

Now, taking the opposite tack, if the Federal Reserve System, sometimes called the monetary authority, decides to *decrease* the amount of money in circulation, then some individuals and businesses will find they have less money than they desire, which is, as we have noted, a function of how much income they make. The only way they can add to their desired money balances is by spending *less* than they receive. But when lots of people spend less than they receive, the total demand in the economy for goods and services will fall. Either prices will fall or output will fall. In any case, money income will be decreased.

What Happened During the Depression

Now, using this very simplified version of monetarist theory, we can see what happened during the Depression. Although the Federal Reserve made lots of overt attempts to stimulate the economy, the statistics presented in Figure 11–5 show that the money supply in circulation actually decreased by a third from the start of the recession to the depths of the Depression. According to the theory presented above, this could only mean one thing: a reduction in the total demand for goods and services, and hence a reduction in output and employment. The monetarists maintain that what would have been just another recession turned into the Great Depression because of the contractionary efforts that the Federal Reserve engaged in during this period. Whether or not the Federal Reserve was aware of what was happening is irrelevant. As we can see in Figure 11–5, the money supply decreased instead of increasing. The monetary authorities dealt a crippling blow to an already weak economy and hence, we got a depression.

Possible Reverse Causation

At this point we should mention the possibility of the reverse causal link between the money supply and income. We find that as incomes fall,

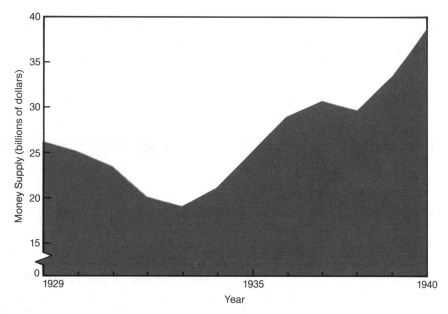

FIGURE 11–5

THE PRECIPITOUS DROP IN THE MONEY SUPPLY

By 1933 the money supply had fallen by one-third its 1929 level. It again fell in 1938. (*Source:* Board of Governors of the Federal Reserve System.)

banks are less inclined to loan out money. Hence, not all of the reduction in the money supply is necessarily to be blamed on the Fed. In fact, some observers maintain that the Fed has the power to pull on the string but it can't push it. Banks at this time were very unwilling to loan out any of the increased reserves they got. But, of course, that might just mean that the Fed would have had to increase reserves even more to reverse the decline in the money supply during this period.

ATTEMPTING TO PULL US OUT—THE NEW DEAL

There are lots of myths concerning what happened before the election of President Roosevelt and what happened after. In the main, many observers contend that Hoover was a complete laissez-faire president who was unwilling to attempt any government intervention to pull the nation's ever-declining economy out of a deepening recession. On the other hand, there has been extensive belief that President Roosevelt took Keynesian analysis to heart and attempted, by every means necessary, to stimulate the economy through federal programs designed to increase aggregate demand. Both of these common notions are misleading. We have already made reference to the interventionist attitude that Hoover had exhibited during the First World War. This attitude was to continue during his stay as Secretary of Commerce and, more importantly, during his first three years as President of the United States of America.

HOOVER, THE GOVERNMENT ADVOCATE

Hoover was both a mobilizer and an economic planner during World War I. During the '20s he was a persistent advocate of government-business partnership in stabilizing industry. In fact, Hoover campaigned for reelection in 1932 on a platform of past government intervention into the private business affairs of the nation. He said, ''We might have done nothing. That would have been utter ruin. Instead, we met the situation with proposals to private business and to Congress of the most gigantic proportion of economic defense and counterattack ever evolved in the history of the Republic.''

He wasn't exaggerating that much, for as soon as the stock market crashed in 1929, he started putting his program into operation. He called a series of White House conferences with the leading financiers and industrialists of the day. He got them to pledge, for example, that they would not reduce wage rates and that they would, indeed, expand their investments. His theory was that the way to prevent recession was to maintain the purchasing power of the working man. How better to do that than by not reducing his wages?

Keeping Wages up

What Hoover ignored during this period was that if prices are falling and the wages workers receive stay the same, then the *real* wages that they receive are rising. Just like any other good or service, the demand for labor is negatively related to its price. If the price—the real wage rate—goes up, a lower quantity will be demanded. If there is unemployment, an explicit program to keep real wages up will lead not to more employment, but rather to more *un*employment. And that is exactly what happened. It was only in 1932, after several years of extremely severe depression and extensive unemployment, that nominal wages began to fall.

Hoover had been quite active in trying to prevent that decline and, indeed, was outraged by the United States Steel Corporation's first attempt at lowering wages in the fall of '31. Overall, real wages actually rose from 1929 to 1933. In an economy that is growing this is what we expect.

For example, in the last chapter this is what we saw for the period 1890 to 1914. But on the other hand, in an economy that is declining we would not expect this. It could only lead to a decrease in the number of workers demanded because just like the demand for everything else, the demand for workers falls as the price rises, other things being the same.

Expansion of Public Works

In December of 1929 Hoover proposed to expand public works by some $600 million. In 1931 Hoover was instrumental in pushing through the Employment Stabilization Act, which established an Employment Stabilization Board. This board expanded public works during the Depression and was allocated $150 million to do so. Hoover was not content to stop there. He instituted the start of the Boulder, Grand Coulee, and Central California dams, and also signed a treaty with Canada in order to build the St. Lawrence Seaway. Hoover was the first president to actively engage in creating large amounts of public works.

Finally, in January of 1932 Hoover created the Reconstruction Finance Corporation. It was modeled after the old World War I War Finance Corporation, which extended emergency loans to business. The Treasury furnished the RFC with half a billion dollars, and it was allowed to issue bonds up to another $1.5 billion.

Also, even prior to the Depression, Hoover had a Federal Farm Board which was ready to take action as soon as the Depression arrived. Its first big operation was to cartelize wheat farmers into cooperative marketing units in order to withhold wheat stocks, thereby causing a rise in prices. But this didn't work too well. Persuasion was not adequate to keep wheat farmers voluntarily from producing more wheat. Then the Grain Stabilization Corporation was set up. It was supposed to purchase enough wheat to prevent the price of wheat from falling. However, opposing economic forces were too great.

Shacks of unemployed at the Seattle waterfront in 1933. The village was called "Hooverville." Was Hoover to blame? (Wide World Photos)

A Change of Heart

Finally, in the last year of Hoover's administration, he started rethinking what he had been doing. Many leaders of the day had encouraged him to continue his efforts to increase the scope of government intervention in the marketplace and increase the amount of cartelization among industry leaders. He declined, and this is where he got the label of being a laissez-faire president. Although the label seems to be somewhat out of line with what actually happened during Hoover's administration, Franklin Roosevelt was nonetheless able to capitalize on it and become president for the remainder of his life.

THE FIRST HUNDRED DAYS

Roosevelt's sweep into office allowed him to push through Congress a massive and extraordinary amount of legislation in the first 100 days of his administration. We do not have the space here to go into the details of every single program that America's thirty-second president instituted. We can, however, look at the major ones he started.

It must be noted that Roosevelt did not enter the presidency with the idea that government deficit spending was a necessary stimulus to economic recovery. In fact, it was only later in his administration that he appears to have believed deficit spending was indeed the way to prosperity for an economy in a gravely depressed state. We find in many of the utterances of the President that he was convinced that a balanced federal budget should be maintained. Nonetheless, he wanted to start numerous programs to get the country back on the road to recovery.

Using Hoover's Ideas

Many of Roosevelt's ideas were merely extensions of Hoover's. Roosevelt felt that it was necessary to increase workers' wages in order to simulta-

neously increase purchasing power in the economy and reduce "cutthroat" competition. Therefore, he was convinced that a new system of cooperation among workers, businessmen, and the government was necessary. Hence, the National Industrial Recovery Act was passed and the National Recovery Administration was formed. Its basic purpose was to allow collusion among businessmen to prevent price cutting. Those businessmen who joined in the national recovery effort were allowed to post the Blue Eagle emblem to identify themselves.

For labor, the National Industrial Recovery Act (Section 7a) allowed for collective bargaining by employees. This was a great impetus to the union movement, which had started many years before. In fact, it is important enough for us to treat it in the next issue.

From the very beginning, a considerable portion of the population was against the National Recovery Administration and its obvious monopolizing tendencies. Finally, on May 27, 1935, the Supreme Court, in the Schechter case, declared that the NIRA was unconstitutional. Mr. Schechter was allowed to continue to sell sick chickens, for that was the original complaint against him by the NRA.

Farm Programs

Remember that the Federal Farm Board had already been set up with an appropriation of half a billion dollars to be used to stabilize the prices of the three major commodities in the program: wheat, cotton, and wool. The Farm Board soon ran out of money, though, in attempting to keep the price of these commodities high. The major replacement for the Farm Board was brought about by the Agricultural Adjustment Act of 1933. It established within the Department of Agriculture the Agricultural Adjustment Administration (AAA). Its stated goal was to keep the prices of farm products up. One of its methods was to control the production of farm products, for which it got some help by the Bankhead Cotton Control Act, passed in 1934, as well as the Curr-Smith Tobacco Control Act. Both of these acts levied fines on farmers who produced in excess of their quotas. Many farmers who signed agreements to limit their production were given benefit payments from the government. From the very beginning there were scandals over the programs of the AAA. One was entitled:

"The Murder of Six Million Little Pigs"

What happened was that a survey at that time showed young pigs to be extremely numerous, indicating that in the near future there would be such a large quantity of pork supplied that prices would have to plummet in order to sell it all. (Remember the law of demand.) So the Farm Bureau, the National Corn Hog Committee, and the Farmers Union recommended that 6 million pigs be killed. They were, and the baby pork was bought by the Federal Surplus Relief Corporation. In another incident, people were enraged that the AAA got farmers to plow under 11 million acres of already growing cotton.

At this time, the Commodity Credit Corporation was formed. It was allowed to make what are called **nonrecourse loans** to farmers with cotton used as collateral. In other words, the farmers would pay the CCC cotton in exchange for a stipulated price that was above the market price. Farmers never had to repay the loan, but if they decided to, they could get their cotton back. The CCC is still with us.

Effects of Price Supports

Finally, the original AAA was declared unconstitutional in 1936. Undaunted, Roosevelt got the AAA of 1938 passed. It contained a soil conservation program, production allotments, CCC nonrecourse loans, payments to farmers who kept their production within quotas, and federal purchase of so-called surpluses. All of these programs had essentially been in effect earlier, but the AAA of '38 made them slightly more flexible. These pro-

grams were destined to have perverse effects on the farming sector of the economy from their very inception. After all, if a farmer is paid a price support, then the benefits he receives are directly proportional to the amount of production he has. The bigger the farmer, the bigger the payment from the government. What happens is that the richest farmers get the most money from the U.S. Treasury and the poorest get the least. In 1973, for example, it was estimated that the top 7 percent of farmers were receiving 42 percent of the benefits under the various farm subsidy programs. Additionally, consumers were paying prices considerably in excess of what they would have paid without a farm program.

OTHER PROGRAMS: RELIEF AND SOCIAL SECURITY

Numerous other programs were instituted during the New Deal. Many of them were aimed at providing employment for the down and out. There were the CCC and the NYA and the CWA and the WPA.* None of these programs lasted, but they did provide jobs for a certain number of lucky persons during the Depression years. One program that did last was Social Security.

Social Security

The Social Security Act was signed by Roosevelt on August 14, 1935. It was to provide one of the most important social insurance programs in the history of the United States and is still with us today. The major aspects of it were unemployment and old age insurance plus survivors' benefits. It started out small, enabling the federal government to provide grants to states to help them meet their old age assistance programs. There were also grants for aid to dependent children and to the blind.

*Civilian Conservation Corps, National Youth Administration, Civil Works Administration, Works Progress Administration.

The Social Security Act levied a basic payroll tax on payrolls of all employers, which was initially 1 percent but rose to 3 percent after 1937. While it is not clear how effective the Social Security provisions were during the early years of its undertaking, today we have ample evidence that Social Security is indeed one of the most pervasive aspects of government intervention in individual decision making. Everybody pays Social Security no matter how poor he is. In fact, one starts paying Social Security the minute he starts making any money at all. The basic rate in 1973 was 5.85 percent for the employer and the employee alike, applied to the first $10,800 of earned income; these figures are scheduled to climb steadily in the future.

Don't be fooled into believing that the employer actually pays his fair share. Ultimately the employee pays for just about everything in a competitive labor market. The Social Security payment is merely a tax on labor income. Of course, it is redistributed to older, retired workers, but those who are paying in look at it as a pure payroll tax, because it reduces spendable income. It is not, strictly speaking, a guaranteed insurance program. Death benefits can be almost zero unless the deceased leaves a long-lived widow or minor children. Furthermore, Social Security payments are voted on by Congress. One can never be certain that the Congresses in the future will be as lenient as Congresses have been in the past. Nevertheless, it has remained as one of the major social insurance programs in existence today.

THE NEW DEAL SCOREBOARD

With all the hullabaloo about the first 100 days of Roosevelt's campaign of programs against the Depression, it is not at all clear that they had much effect on the important variable—aggregate demand. After all, we can't just look at what programs were instituted; we also have to look at how they were paid for and what other programs were dropped.

Look at Roosevelt's campaign. He lambasted Hoover for large budget deficits that had been marked up after the Crash of '29. In fact, Hoover's administration had the largest federal deficit in the history of the United States prior to Roosevelt's election. Once elected, Roosevelt told Congress that he did not want the country to be "wrecked on the rocks of loose fiscal policy." Apparently he took his warning seriously. Deficits during the Depression years were indeed small. In fact, in 1937 the total government budget, including federal, state, and local levels, was in surplus by $0.3 billion. During this time, taxes were repeatedly raised. The Revenue Act of 1932, passed during the depths of the Depression, brought the largest percentage increase of federal taxes in the history of the United States except for periods of war. It doubled total federal tax revenues if they are measured at full-employment national income.

Fiscal policies, then, were in fact extremely weak, and even perverse. At the same time that the federal government was increasing expenditures, local and state governments were decreasing them. If we measure the total of state, federal, and local fiscal policies, we find that they were truly expansive only in 1931 and 1936 as compared to what the government was doing prior to the Depression. And these two years were expansive only because of large veterans' payments, passed by Congress in both years—by the way, over the vigorous opposition of both Hoover and Roosevelt. In both 1933 and 1937, and, to a lesser degree, in 1938, fiscal policy was quite a bit less expansionary than in 1939.

Roosevelt's administration has often been characterized as expansionary. We have to look elsewhere, though, than the economic front to discover this. Perhaps it is the New Deal's psychological impact that must be studied. But that will be left for another book.

Definitions of New Terms

MONETARISM: a school of economic thought led by Milton Friedman of the University of Chicago. Monetarists believe that unexpected changes in the money supply cause fluctuations in real output and employment in the short run.

NONRECOURSE LOANS: loans which farmers obtain from the Commodity Credit Corporation in exchange for their crops as collateral. These loans never have to be repaid, but if they are not the CCC keeps the crops.

Chapter Summary

1. The stock market crashed in 1929. However, most students of the Great Depression believe this was only a symptom and not a cause of the business activity downturn.
2. The Depression years saw a decrease in total and per capita output with massive amounts of unemployment, sometimes reaching 25 percent of the labor market.
3. The banking system collapsed; when Roosevelt became president, he declared a banking moratorium.
4. Farmers were hurt just like everyone else: In 1932 their net income was 30 percent of its 1929 level.
5. There are two currently popular explanations of why the Depression was so bad. One involves the theories of John Maynard Keynes, and the other, the theories of monetarists, headed by Professor Milton Friedman of the University of Chicago.
6. Keynesian theory generally indicates that the Great Depression occurred because of a collapse in the desire for new capital formation on the part of businessmen; as investment fell behind saving, a reduction in output occurred, causing unemployment.
7. The monetarist explanation places key emphasis on the relatively large reductions in the money supply during the 1930s, for it fell by almost a third from 1929 to 1933, the biggest single reduction in modern times.
8. The New Deal was Roosevelt's attempt to pull us out of the Depression. It involved the National Industrial Recovery Act, which allowed for price fixing and the growth of labor unions. Additionally, there were programs aimed at keeping the price of farm products up and increasing federal relief.
9. At this time, Social Security legislation was passed which provided for survivors' benefits and unemployment and old age insurance.
10. The actual government fiscal record during the Depression was not as expansionary as previously thought. When federal, state, and local expenditures are combined, we find that taxes sometimes were greater than receipts.

Questions for Thought and Discussion

1. Even though the New Deal and other government actions were not expansionary from a fiscal point of view, do you think that their psychological impact was important in pulling us out of the Depression?

2. Why is Social Security considered not to be a true insurance program?
3. Why do you think that government officials wished to keep food prices high during the Depression? Who benefited and who lost?
4. Do you think another depression is possible in the United States today? Why?
5. Which theory of the causes of the Great Depression do you agree with, the Keynesian or the monetarist? Why?
6. Roosevelt was called a pragmatist. Do you agree?

THE INDUSTRIAL UNIONIST

John L. Lewis (1880–1969)

President, United Mine Workers, 1920–1960

"I HAVE never faltered or failed to present the cause or plead the case of the mine workers of this country. I have pleaded your case not in the wavering tones of a mendicant seeking alms, but in the thundering voice of the captain of a mighty host, demanding the rights to which free men are entitled."

These dramatic words from John L. Lewis were a combined program, epitaph, rallying call, and challenge to business management and presidents of the United States. During his forty years as president of the United Mine Workers and as the major spokesman for industrial unionism in an era of increasing consolidation between craft and industrial unions, Lewis ran the United Mine Workers with absolute control. He brought the union to prominence in the American Federation of Labor, formed the Congress of Industrial Organizations and broke with the AFL, then returned to the AFL and eventually forced the union to stand on its own for the twenty years before his death.

Industrial unionism received its greatest push during the early 1930s. The combined effects of the Depression and the increased numbers of unskilled and semiskilled workers in most American industries presented a serious challenge to the craft union doctrine of the AFL, founded by Samuel Gompers. It became evident to men like Lewis that it was no longer valid to base union solidarity and bargaining positions on skills irrespective of industry; he believed strongly that it was important instead to organize unions within specific industries, drawing the membership from as wide a basis within the industry as possible.

One of the major "advantages" of the tactic is the crippling effects of a strike within the industry. And through the late 1940s and into the early 1950s, Lewis led some of the most economically dangerous and emphatically effective strikes in American history.

Lewis was born to Welsh immigrant parents in Iowa in 1880. His father was a miner and a strong trade unionist. Along with some of his brothers, Lewis entered the mines at the age of 15, after leaving the only formal schooling he would receive. Six years later, he traveled in the western United States, working in various mines and learning about the mining industry. Lewis eventually became one of America's foremost experts on the coal mining industry, and almost all of his expertise was the result of his own reading and study. Upon returning to Iowa, he joined the UMW local and began extensive work in the union leadership.

He came to the attention of Samuel Gompers, and in 1911 was named a field agent of the American Federation of Labor. While traveling widely throughout the United States, he rose in the UMW ranks, becoming president of the union in 1920.

Lewis had his first of many confrontations with the federal government during World War I, while serving on the National Defense Council; in that position, he opposed government operation of the mines, a controversial question he was to take on again 25 years later.

The AFL convention in 1935 was torn by the economic troubles of the country and the internal disagreement between the trade and craft unions.

In a dramatic walkout, Lewis joined with several other trade unionists to form the Congress of Industrial Organizations, leaving the AFL to the craft unionists. The momentum behind Lewis' move resulted from several important gains for his union and for labor at large.

In 1933 he had obtained Section 7A of the National Industrial Recovery Act, which provided workers with almost complete freedom to choose representatives of their own choice for collective bargaining purposes; in addition to its effect on the total strength of the labor movement, the provision weakened the ability of the present union leadership to retain control.

He eventually organized four million workers into the CIO. The early years of the organization, of which the UMW was the core, were marked by violent strikes, one of which drew a "plague on both your houses," from Franklin Roosevelt. Up to that time, FDR had received Lewis' personal and organizational backing. "It ill behooves one who has supped at labor's table and who has been sheltered in labor's house to curse with equal fervor and fine impartiality both labor and its adversaries when they become locked in deadly embrace," declaimed Lewis. After that point Lewis and Roosevelt were on strained terms, culminating in Lewis' support for Wendell Wilkie for president in 1940.

Lewis resigned as president of the CIO in 1942 and pulled the UMW out of the organization. He returned to the AFL for a period of less than two years before taking the United Mine Workers down its own road. In 1955 the AFL and CIO merged without the participation of the man who had had a significant impact on the histories of both organizations.

Lewis' direction of the UMW was based on an "all the wagons in a circle" approach to confrontation with the government. "It is better to have half a million men working at good wages and high standards of living than to have a million working in poverty." (Lewis certainly knew that the law of demand applied to coal miners, too.)

Pounding Out Swords When We Need Plowshares

DEMANDS FOR A PERMANENT CIO

JOHN L. LEWIS

INTER-UNION WARFARE

PITTSBURGH CONVENTION

(Ross Lewis in *The Milwaukee Journal*)

His program to improve the wages and living conditions of his membership was based on his skillful ability to turn potential crises to his advantage. During the 1950s, increases in automation in mining were threatening to cut his membership; but automation was needed if coal was to remain competitive with oil and natural gas. He obtained a contract agreement which placed a royalty on mined coal, and the royalty was channeled into the union's pension fund, eventually boosting its value above $170 million.

Probably Lewis' most trying years were those of the Truman administration, as he attempted to lead strikes in both the soft and hard coal industries in the face of court injunctions. Truman seized the mines and had them worked by federal troops, but Lewis eventually received the settlement he wanted. He ran up more than $2.1 million in strike fines, and probably damaged the competitive position of the industry.

One of his major achievements was the 1952 Federal Mine Safety Act, the first of its kind in the United States. His dramatic appearance at the site of a mining disaster in 1951 provided a strong push for the act in Congress. Also during the 1950s he won extremely favorable settlements, including payment for underground travel time.

After his semiretirement in 1960 the UMW fell on hard times. Under the leadership of Tony Boyle the union suffered through a membership slowdown, and then was subject to a series of government investigations into corruption and the murder of a candidate for Boyle's office.

Two weeks before he died, Lewis was called upon by Ralph Nader and other concerned observers to rescue the union from Boyle's heavyhanded policies. But Lewis was too old, and further, there was a conflict of interest inherent in the situation; Boyle was a devoted disciple of Lewis, and held his position partially through Lewis' influence in the union.

Lewis' tenure as a major influence in American labor was rivaled by few men in its length and probably no man in its power. His commitment to his union membership and its needs was single-minded, and for decades he was able to leave political and economic wreckage around the nation's convulsive policies. When he died the miners closed the mines in memoriam to him, as they had done many times in response to his strike call.

ISSUE XI
DID THE NEW DEAL CREATE A NEW PROSPERITY FOR WORKERS?

Unionism Takes Off

The NIRA

We pointed out in the last chapter that one of Roosevelt's avowed purposes for establishing the National Recovery Administration was to prevent cutthroat competition among entrepreneurs and to keep wages up by allowing the formation of collusive arrangements among employees. Roosevelt reasoned that purchasing power would then remain high because workers would be getting higher wages. That would allow them to purchase more goods and services and, hence, total demand would increase. This would start a cumulative process which would eventually pull the economy back on the road to recovery. Section 7a of the National Industrial Recovery Act gave the workers the right to organize, and the National Recovery Administration was supposed to grant "justice to the worker." The NIRA was declared unconstitutional. But that was not the end of the union movement in the United States. As a matter of fact, Section 7a was replaced with an even broader law under the National Labor Relations Act, otherwise known as the Wagner

Act, for its sponsor. The Wagner Act was organized labor's Magna Carta.

Wagner Act Declared Constitutional

The Wagner Act was passed using a slightly different argument than Roosevelt had used for establishing Section 7a of the NIRA. It was argued that the inequality in bargaining power between workers as individuals and large businesses depressed "the purchasing power of wage earners in industry" and prevented "stabilization of competitive wage rates and working conditions." To remedy all this, the Wagner Act guaranteed the workers the right to start labor unions, to engage in collective bargaining, and to be members of any union that was started. This act was declared constitutional by the Supreme Court in 1937, after which the strength of organized labor grew rapidly in our economy. The question remains, then, Was this legislation passed under the New Deal responsible for a new prosperity for the working class? Before we can answer that

question, we have to look a little deeper into the history and workings of collective labor unions.

Union Membership

Of course, it was not in the 1930s that unions first got started. The concept of unions goes back as far as the Middle Ages, when journeymen's associations were formed. We talked about them in Chapter 3.

Craft Unions

The American labor union movement started with what are called local **craft unions.** These were groups of workers in individual trades, such as baking, shoemaking, and printing. In the beginning many of the earlier craft unions were put down by unfavorable court judgments. We see in Figure XI-1 that the percent of the labor force organized into unions was still extremely small in 1930. Then, at the beginning of the Depression, labor union membership fell drastically from 12.1 percent to 7.4 percent of the labor force. However, within a few years after the passage of the NIRA and then the Wagner Act, membership jumped by more than 100 percent. By this time, many national unions had been formed. In fact, as early as 1852 the National Typographic Union—today known as the International Typographical

189

ISSUE XI   DID THE NEW DEAL CREATE A NEW PROSPERITY FOR WORKERS?

Union—got its start as a permanent federation. In 1869 the Knights of Labor was formed and by 1886 they had reached a membership of almost 1 million. That particular federation lost its appeal after the famous Hay Market Riot on May 4, 1886, which, although probably caused by anarchists and police, was blamed on the union.

Industrial Unions

To take the place of the Knights of Labor, the American Federation of Labor under the leadership of Samuel Gompers got started in 1886. By 1900 the AFofL boasted a membership of over 1 million workers. These federations were basically composed of numerous craft unions. **Industrial unions,** on the other hand, seek to organize the workers in an entire industry, regardless of the individual jobs these workers are doing.

In any event, during World War I an increasingly favorable climate of opinion toward unions developed. By 1920 membership had reached 5 million. Then there was a great decline until the New Deal. After the Wagner Act was passed, several other great unions were organized, one being the United Mine Workers Union under the presidency of the famous John L. Lewis. He became head of the Congress of Industrial Organizations, a group of industrial unions. As can be seen in Figure XI–1, the combined efforts of the AFofL and the CIO increased the percentage of workers unionized by leaps and bounds from the Great Depression until the end of World War II.

What Happened to the Working Man?

Did this increase in unionization brought on by a favorable environment and the passage of favorable legislation during the New Deal in fact help out the working man, give him a new prosperity? A cursory look at some of the evidence would indicate that, yes, indeed, this is exactly what happened. Remember that by 1933 wages and salaries were only 57.5 percent of those in 1929. The average working man was indeed down and out. And if we then look at what happened to real wages after the passage of the NIRA, we find that they went up. In other words, nominal or money wages were going up faster than prices at this time. This can be seen in Table XI–1.

However, go back to Figure 11–3, where we show the percent of the labor force unemployed during the Depression. Even though real wages were going up, the number of workers who had jobs did not significantly increase until the latter part of the decade, and even then there were still around 9 million workers who

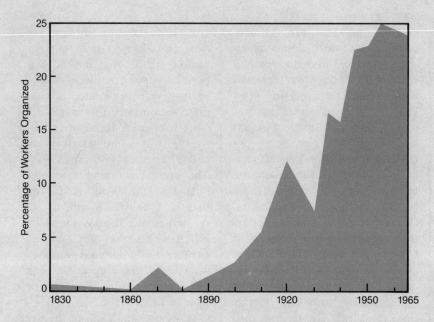

FIGURE XI-1 GROWING UNION MEMBERSHIP, 1830-1965

It wasn't until the twentieth century that union membership exceeded 3 percent of the United States labor force. Membership hit its peak as a percentage of the total labor force in 1954 and has been declining ever since. (*Source:* L. Davis, et al., *American Economic Growth,* New York: Harper & Row, 1972, p. 220, and U.S. Department of Labor, Bureau of Labor Statistics.)

TABLE XI-1

REAL WAGES DURING THE DEPRESSION

YEAR	REAL WAGES (1957 DOLLARS)
1930	0.892
1931	0.935
1932	0.918
1933	0.959
1934	1.110
1935	1.110
1936	1.120
1937	1.240
1938	1.270
1939	1.290
1940	1.350

Even though there was massive unemployment, real wages fell only slightly in 1932 and then started a rise upward. (*Source:* A. Rees, *New Measures of Wage Earner Compensation in Manufacturing, 1914-57,* New York: National Bureau of Economic Research.)

couldn't find jobs. What does this indicate? That those who were lucky enough to have jobs did indeed benefit from the NIRA and the Wagner Act. However, those who did not have jobs of course benefited not at all. When we discuss whether unions helped the working class, we have to make sure we are referring to the total number of workers in the economy, not just those who have union jobs. Therefore, we must be careful to examine the average wages for all workers. When we have 25 percent who are unemployed, they have a wage rate of zero. Averaging that in with all the workers who are employed certainly brings down our figure for the average wage during that period.

Now if we switch and look at real wages in all of manufacturing from 1933 on, depicted in Figure XI-2, it seems that unions must have had an effect on the living standards of the working class. And therefore the New Deal legislation was favorable. But that's a facile conclusion: Real wages did not rise any faster than before the New Deal. We have to compare what actually happened with what *would* have happened in the absence of favorable labor legislation. It is not obvious that all wages would not have risen any more rapidly than they did without the growth of unions.

What About Nonunion Workers?

Remember that when we first started talking about certain principles in economics we established the law of demand. As the price of something goes up, the quantity demanded of it falls. The same law can apply to the demand for

191

ISSUE XI   DID THE NEW DEAL CREATE A NEW PROSPERITY FOR WORKERS?

labor. If the price of it goes up, less of it is demanded by entrepreneurs. Hence, in the absence of other changes in the economy, if a union succeeds in raising a wage rate higher than it would have been without the union, entrepreneurs often respond by reducing the quantity of labor demanded. This means that an effective union will cause unemployment in the unionized sector of the economy. This unemployment, however, will not necessarily last, for those workers unable to get union jobs will move into the nonunion sector. In this manner, many economists contend that the effects of unionization are to increase union wages at the expense of nonunion wages. In fact, some empirical studies have been done to show that what actually happened after the growth of the union movement was a union/nonunion wage differential that averaged around 15 percent. Those workers lucky enough to be employed and in a union could experience a real wage rate 15 percent higher than those who were not so lucky.

This union/nonunion differential has not been constant, however. For example, in the period of recession with inflation during the latter part of the '60s and early '70s, this 15 percent differential disappeared almost completely, for unions were under the rule of longer-term contracts than nonunion members. When inflation took off *without people anticipating it,* nonunion workers were able to change jobs and/or demand higher money wages to account for the rising cost of living. Union members were stuck with their longer-term contracts. They could only make up their lost real wages that had been eaten away by inflation after termination of a three- or five-year agreement with their employers. Hence, the differential got extremely narrow. However, later on it widened and probably is around 15 percent today.

What About the Share of National Income Going to Labor?

Another piece of evidence we might look at is the share of national income going to labor. If in fact unionism has been responsible for getting the working class a larger share of national income, then we might contend that the New Deal brought a new prosperity for the man in the street. Looking at Table XI–2, we don't

FIGURE XI-2   REAL WAGES FROM 1933 TO 1965

Except for a few downturns, real wages in manufacturing have risen constantly since the depths of the Depression. (*Source:* Rees, *op. cit.*)

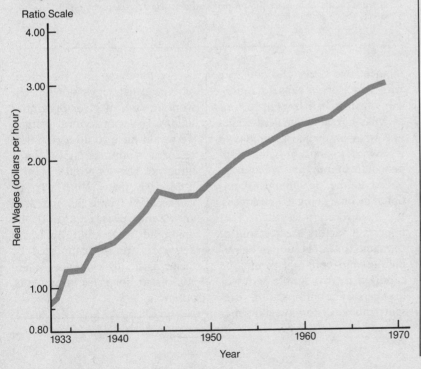

see any significant trend in the percent of national income that goes as compensation for employees. Back in the depths of the Depression it was 73.2 percent, falling by 1940 to 64.2 percent, not changing very much until the latter part of the '60s and early '70s. It still is about the same as it was 40 years ago. In fact, we might contend this evidence shows that unions decreased the percentage of national income going to the working man. After all, in the depths of the Depression he had almost three-fourths of national income. Soon after the passage of favorable NIRA and Wagner Act legislation, this percentage fell to 65. It didn't start rising until the middle 1950s, but this is precisely the time when unionization became less significant in the total labor picture, for in 1953 the height of the union movement was reached when 26 percent of our entire labor force was unionized. During the rest of the '50s only 24 percent of workers were in unions, and by 1961 that had dropped another percentage point. Today the figure lies below 22 percent.

Simple Correlation Not Enough

But it is actually very misleading—as can be easily seen by these numbers—to correlate the movement of two series and come up with some sort of causal relationship. Just as it is unwise to look at what happened to real wages and what happened to unions, it is unwise to look at what happened to unions and what happened to the percentage of national income going to employees. We have to consider what other important factors are working at the same time. These may be numerous and certainly cannot be captured in two simple series of numbers. The information presented above in no way establishes a case for or against the effects of New Deal legislation on the working man, nor for or against unions. To get an accurate picture, we would have to do a complete research study, certainly something not very appropriate for a book like this. What can be learned, however, is that the facile arguments presented both by union advocates and by union detractors can be supported by facile pieces of evidence. When you listen to these arguments, beware.

TABLE XI-2

SHARE OF TOTAL NATIONAL INCOME GOING TO WORKERS

YEAR	PERCENT OF NATIONAL INCOME AS COMPENSATION TO EMPLOYEES
1933	73.2
1935	65.2
1940	64.2
1945	67.8
1947	64.8
1950	64.1
1955	67.8
1960	71.0
1965	69.8
1967	71.5
1968	72.1
1969	73.3
1970	74.9

The percentage of national income paid as compensation to employees has remained between 64 percent and 75 percent since 1933. In less-developed countries this percentage is much smaller, for much of national income is paid in rents, profits, and interest to property owners. (*Source:* Department of Commerce, Office of Business Economics.)

193

ISSUE XI   DID THE NEW DEAL CREATE A NEW PROSPERITY FOR WORKERS?

Definitions of New Terms

CRAFT UNIONS: unions consisting of workers who have one particular skill, such as printers, bakers, or shoemakers.

INDUSTRIAL UNIONS: organizations of workers in an entire industry irrespective of their particular job classification, such as the United Auto Workers.

Questions for Thought and Discussion

1. Do you think it is possible for unions to benefit all workers? Why?
2. Is it possible that the law of demand does not hold for labor services?
3. Do you find it repugnant to apply the law of demand to other than goods?
4. Why do you think it matters whether people do or do not anticipate inflation?

Getting Ourselves Caught in Another World War

12

Tнe decade of the '30s was dismal indeed. Workers and businessmen were concerned with saving their skins, with pulling themselves out of a deep and dark depression. The publication in Germany of an outrageous book called *Mein Kampf* didn't seem to make much difference in the American way of thinking. Even the outbreak of European hostilities in 1939 did not concern many Americans. Little did they know that they were soon to enter into the most devastating war in the history of the world. On the eve of World War II, in September 1939, we had 9.5 million men and women out of work. This accounted for 17 percent of the entire labor force. At that time we were spending 1 percent of GNP on war production.

SITUATION WORSENS

This was indeed a period of isolationism; the rest of the world mattered little to the average American or the Congressmen and Senators who walked the halls of the Capitol Building. Businessmen were hardly in the mood for any kind of military-preparedness program even when fighting broke out. Although Roosevelt succeeded in getting a War Resource Board appointed in August of 1939, it quietly closed its doors a mere five months later. Then things started taking a turn for the worse in Europe. France fell in 1940; the incomplete "invulnerable" Maginot Line didn't hold an effective German air force attack. In May 1940, the Office of Emergency Management was appointed, to be succeeded a few days later by the Council of National Defense.

We started to really get worried. The Selective Service Act was passed in

September 1940 and war production started to increase. We entered into a lend-lease agreement with the Allies, thereby increasing demands even further for war production. In Figure 12–1 we can see the impressive efforts made to help supply our Allies and to supply ourselves with war materials once we got involved in the fighting. From an index of 100 to start with in 1939, it had risen to 5600 by 1943. In 1943 our war production was as great as the combined war production of Italy, Japan, and Germany.

MANAGING FOR WAR PRODUCTION

We were still quite unsure of ourselves in 1941. Nonetheless, an Office of Production Management was established that January. It was to provide for emergency plant facilities in case we entered the war. There was no doubt by the summer of '41 that we were in trouble with respect to our defense capabilities. When the Japanese attacked Pearl Harbor in December we were really unprepared. Nobody had anticipated that the war would

involve us so fast. A War Productions Board was immediately set up to oversee industrial output. Agencies multiplied rapidly; we list a number of them in Table 12–1. Because this rapid multiplication of war agencies cried out for overall management, in May 1943, at the height of hostilities, the Office of War Mobilization was created. But by then it was literally impossible to oversee all of the war activities that the industrial sector of the economy was engaged in. The next year this office had a word tacked on to the end—Reconversion—for by 1944 we were convinced that the war would end and we would have to face the arduous task of reconverting the economy back to peacetime endeavors.

MANPOWER PROBLEMS

We had a problem of providing sufficient manpower not only to fight the war on several fronts but also to run the war production in the factories. A War Manpower Commission was established in April 1942. Its task was to provide an adequate

FIGURE 12–1

THE INCREASED WAR EFFORT

Starting out with the base year of 1939, the index of war production is set at 100. It doubled in one year, and then skyrocketed until it reached 56 times its 1939 level by 1943! (*Source:* Simon Kuznets, in *National Product Since 1869*, New York: National Bureau of Economic Research, 1946, p. 44.)

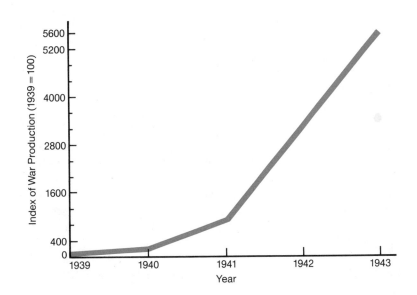

TABLE 12-1

**THE PROLIFERATION OF
GOVERNMENT AGENCIES
DURING WORLD WAR II**

Office of Emergency Management
 Committee of Fair Employment Practice
 Foreign Economic Administration
 National War Labor Board
 Office of Defense Transportation
 Office of Inter-American Affairs
 Office of War Information
 Office of Scientific Research and Development
 War Production Board
 War Shipping Administration
National Housing Agency
 Federal Home Loan Bank Administration
 Federal Housing Administration
Board of War Communications
Office of Censorship
Office of Price Administration
Office of War Mobilization and Reconversion
 Surplus Property Board
 Retraining and Reemployment Administration
President's War Relief Control Board
Selective Service System
Joint Chiefs of Staff
 Office of Strategic Services
Joint War Production Committee—United States
 and Canada
Permanent Joint Board of Defense—United States
 and Canada
Combined Chiefs of Staff—United States,
 United Kingdom, and Canada
Combined Shipping Adjustment Board—United States
 and Great Britain
British-American Joint Patent Interchange Committee
Munitions Assignments Board—United States
 and Great Britain
Joing Mexican-United States Defense Commission
Pacific War Council
United Nations Relief and Rehabilitation Adminis-
 tration
United Nations Information Organization

---

supply of manpower to all sectors of the military and the civilian economy. The draft, of course, solved the military manpower problem. We had 11.5 million men and women in the Armed Services in 1944 and 1945. As can be seen in Figure 12-2, the employed civilian labor force first grew quite rapidly and then leveled off toward the peak of the war. What happened was that members of the economy who were formerly not in the labor force decided to join. These included women, retired people, and teenagers who quit their schooling early. That is, the labor-force **participation rates** of various groups in the economy increased. A participation rate is the percentage of the total number of people in any given subsector of the economy who are actually in the labor force. The participation rate of women over age 14, for example, was about 25 percent at the end of the '30s; by 1944, it had risen to 36.5 percent. Overall, the participation rate in the over-14-year-old population jumped from less than 55 percent before the war to about 62.4 percent in 1944. Many of these changes were permanent, particularly with respect to female participation rates.

Participation rates of various subsectors of the population are generally determined by economic variables. In boom times participation rates go up, and in recessions and depressions they go down. During war periods there is an additional factor which we do not know how to quantify—patriotism.

THE WAR MUST BE PAID FOR

We have pointed out time and again that the government must finance war expenditures somehow. It has only three ways to do so, at least in a democratic society: by taxation, borrowing from the private sector, or money creation. All three were used in the Second World War. Federal expenditures grew by leaps and bounds from 1939 to 1945. So, too, did the deficit—that is, the difference between federal expenditures and

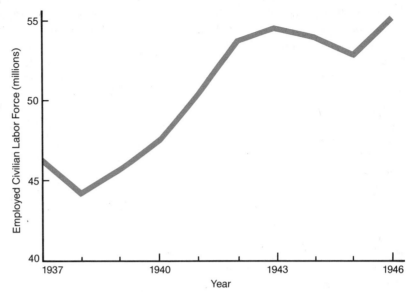

FIGURE 12-2

THE EMPLOYED CIVILIAN LABOR FORCE DURING THE WAR

The number of Americans who were in the civilian labor force and had jobs grew quite rapidly at the beginning of the war, then peaked in 1943. There was a noticeable reduction at the termination of the war and then a further increase. (*Source: Economic Report of the President.*)

federal tax receipts. The deficit reached an astounding $53.9 billion in 1945. This was more than one-half the federal expenditures in that year!

Taxation

Don't get the mistaken impression that the President did not attempt to get more taxes out of individuals and businesses. As early as January 1940 Roosevelt asked for additional taxes to pay for anticipated war expenditures. What did Congress do in June 1940? It merely lowered personal income tax exemptions and added a little bit to the personal income tax surtax rate, in addition to charging a little more to corporations. There were some nominal increases in gift, excise, estate, and other assorted taxes. But receipts quickly fell behind expenditures. In October 1940, when it was obvious that the war was going to get worse, not better, an excess profits tax was passed with rates ranging from 25 percent to 50 percent. The corporate base rate was raised to a maximum of 24 percent. About a year later, the maximum

personal income tax rate went up to 77 percent, and the corporate base rate to 31 percent. The next year taxes were raised again, personal to a maximum of 88 percent and corporate to 40 percent. Additionally, the maximum excess profits rate on corporation income was now 90 percent. When the President asked Congress the following year, 1943, for even more taxes, they refused. However, a year after his request they were amenable to increasing the maximum tax rate on individuals to 94 percent.

None of these measures was enough. Only 61 percent of the entire war effort was financed by taxation.

Selling Bonds

This growing government deficit had to be made up somehow, and one of the most obvious ways was to sell debt to the private sector. Just as there were liberty loans in the First World War, there were liberty loans in the Second World War. In fact, the Treasury conducted seven of them, plus one victory loan. All told, during the period under study loans from the private sector accounted for 28 percent of government expenditures. That left 11 percent to be made up by money creation.

Money Creation

During these years when government expenditures increased beyond increases in taxes, the Treasury found itself in a more and more embarrassing position. It was either unwilling or unable to sell all of the bonds that it had to print to private individuals, businesses, or banks. Consequently, the Federal Reserve System was almost *forced* to help out the Treasury. Its primary objective was to insure the Treasury adequate funds to meet all government expenditures. In March 1942, a special committee in the Federal Reserve System asserted its desire to prevent a rise in the interest rates of government bonds during the war. So from that date until 1951 the Federal Reserve

either "pegged" or supported the interest rate at a very low level: 2.5 percent on long-term bonds, 3/8 of a percent on 90-day Treasury bills. To maintain such a low rate of interest, the Federal Reserve had to buy all the government bonds offered when interest rates started to rise above the support level. (The interest rate is inversely related to the price of a bond.) At that time anybody could get cash in exchange for government bonds. But every time the Federal Reserve bought a bond it increased the base on which the money supply rested. It is not surprising, then, that the money supply grew 12.1 percent a year from 1939 to 1948 as a result of the Federal Reserve's forced bond purchases. The Federal Reserve had essentially abandoned control over the monetary system during this period of bond support. This is clearly seen in Figure 12–3, which shows what happened to the money supply from the latter part of the '30s through 1950.

Even children got into the spirit during World War II by growing and selling vegetables in backyard "victory gardens." (Black Star)

FIGURE 12–3

THE MONEY SUPPLY GROWS TO HELP FINANCE WORLD WAR II

The money supply grew at an average annual rate of over 12 percent from 1940 through the end of the war. (*Source:* Board of Governors of the Federal Reserve System.)

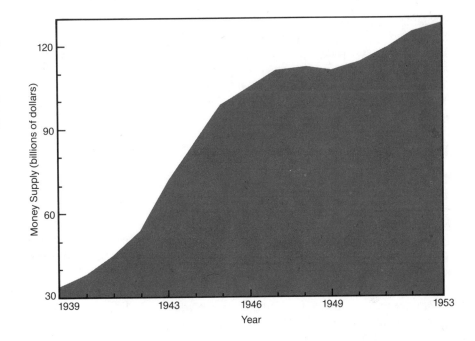

PRICE CONTROLS

Whether it be from an excessive demand by the government for war production—goods and services—or from the increased amount of money that the Federal Reserve was putting in circulation, there was going to be pressure on prices. Everybody knew this was going to happen, but nobody wanted to see it happen. Hence, the Price Control Act of January 1942 established the Office of Price Administration. By mid-1943, fully 95 percent of the nation's foodstuffs were rationed, and maximum prices and rents had been established. The Anti-Inflation Act of October 1942 then established the Office of Economic Stabilization. Its purpose was to limit wages and salaries and to curb prices and rents not yet controlled. At the height of price controls, these two offices, along with the Office of War Mobilization, created in 1943, were aided and abetted by almost 400,000 volunteer "price-watchers" scattered throughout the country.

Through this enormous nationwide effort wholesale prices rose only 14 percent from November 1941 to August 1945. This can be readily seen in Figure 12–4, where we show what happened to prices before, during, and after World War II.

Controls Not New

Price controls were, of course, not new to the American nation. They were first used during the Revolutionary War and they date back quite a bit earlier than that. We know, for example, that in 1800 B.C. the ruler of Babylonia decreed that anyone caught violating his wage-price freeze would be drowned. It seems that Babylonia endured more than 1000 years of such price fixing. Another example has been cited by historians in A.D. 301. The Roman Emperor Diocletian fixed the maximum price on beef, grain, eggs, and clothing, and prescribed the death penalty for violators. He also set wage ceilings for teachers, lawyers, physicians, tailors, and bricklayers. But, according to

Lactantius, writing in 314, "There was . . . much bloodshed upon very slight and trifling accounts; and the people brought provisions no more to market since they could not get a reasonable price for them; and this increased the dearth so much that after many had died by it, the law itself was laid aside."

Repressed Inflation

During World War II we had what is known as **repressed inflation**—that is, inflation that did not actually show up in the price statistics because of the price controls. Some economists argue that during World War II workers and businessmen had quite a bit of extra cash around to spend. They wanted to spend this on things and, hence, there was a situation of excess demand for an amount of resources that was limited since so much was going into war production. Normally when there is an excess demand for goods or services the price rises. But prices were not allowed to rise because of price controls. Queuing and rationing began.

This is one of the stalls in the Reading Terminal market in Philadelphia during the war. The merchant had closed up shop when he had nothing left to sell. (Wide World Photos)

Black Markets

What happened, then, was that in many situations, the so-called black market sprang up. A **black market,** as you may well know, is an illegal market where goods and services are sold at higher than controlled prices. There were also numerous other ways that individuals could obtain goods and services instead of going into a black market. Favors could be done for the supplier of a rationed good or service; special arrangements could be made for under-the-counter payments in addition to the stated price. There is a host of ways in which individuals attempting to get the goods and services they want can circumvent price controls. It's not clear how much of this actually happened during the war, but many accounts indicate that illegal or semilegal wheeling and dealing was quite rampant. Price controls were finally lifted after the end of hostilities, and then stated prices took off like gangbusters, as can be readily seen in Figure 12–4.

This lends further support to the contention that repressed inflation existed during World War II. When prices were allowed to rise, they did, indicating that all along they would have risen in the absence of controls. Note that it took a large amount of manpower to effectively police controls during the war, and this was also a period of active patriotism. Even though inflation was kept down during this war period, it's not at all clear that a similar price control endeavor would work during peacetime, and without a large body of price-watchers.

THE END OF THE WAR WITHOUT A DEPRESSION

Even before the war ended, government officials and concerned economists worried about the possibility of a postwar recession. They remembered what had happened after World War I, and they also were well aware of the new Keynesian model that had become popular in those days, and is still with us. This model, you remember, was presented by Lord Keynes during the depths of the Depression. He pointed out that effective demand must remain high for unemployment to stay low. It appeared that when the war ended there would be a serious drop in effective demand because investment by the government would fall drastically. This would lead to a multiple contraction in the equilibrium level of income, thus leading to high levels of unemployment. Everybody wanted to prevent this but nobody quite knew how. What actually happened was just the opposite: Many individuals had high levels of **liquid assets.** That is, they had large amounts of government bonds and cash on hand when VJ Day came. They wanted to get rid of them now that many restrictions on the production and sale of such consumer durables as automobiles, refrigerators, and washing machines were lifted. This great opportunity to purchase new durable goods whose production had been greatly curtailed for

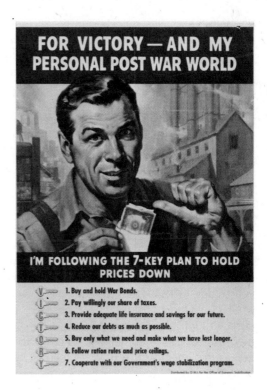

FIGURE 12–4

STEMMING INFLATION DURING THE WAR EFFORT

This index of wholesale prices for all commodities shows that during the war prices held steady, but after termination of hostilities they jumped up drastically. (*Source:* Bureau of Labor Statistics, base period 1947–1949 = 100.)

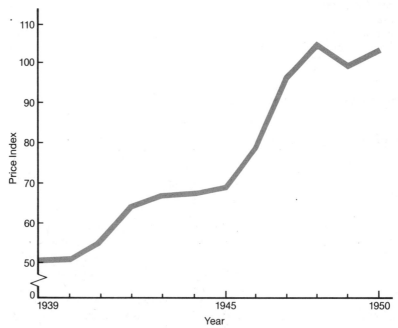

so many years was quickly met by an increased demand. So we found booms in the automobile, refrigerator, and radio industries right after the war.

There was also unprecedented activity in the construction industry. Housing units were being put up right and left. And lastly, government services contracted, but not back to their prewar levels. In fact, we will see in the following issue that government expenditures remained at a high level after the war and have continued upward ever since. While the unemployment rate did jump from about 1.9 percent in 1945 to 3.9 percent in 1946, this latter figure was a more normal peacetime level of unemployment. In fact, it is what is generally called normal or frictional unemployment in a dynamic economy. It wasn't until several years later, in 1949, that we actually experienced what could be considered a recession. Just in case, though, the Congress passed the Employment Act of 1946, sometimes referred to as the Full Employment Act. It read as follows:

The Congress hereby declares that it is the continuing policy and responsibility of the Federal Government to use all practicable means consistent with its needs and obligations and other essential considerations of national policy, with assistance and cooperation of industry, agriculture, labor and State and local governments, to coordinate and utilize all its plans, functions, and resources for the purpose of creating and maintaining, in a manner calculated to foster and promote free competitive enterprise and the general welfare, conditions under which there will be afforded useful employment opportunities, including self-employment, for those able, willing, and seeking to work and to promote maximum employment, production, and purchasing power.

In addition, a Council of Economic Advisors was set up to make a continuing study of the American economy and to assist the president in preparing a report on the state of the nation every year. As you well know, that council still exists today and the government is continuously engaged in smoothing out economic activity in the United States.

World War II was a total war unprecedented for the United States and the rest of the world. During that time government expenditures grew by leaps and bounds and we came out of the most serious depression in our history. However, it is not at all obvious that in fact the war did pull us out of the Great Depression, at least from the point of view of the individuals in society. We will examine this thorny problem in the next issue.

Definitions of New Terms

PARTICIPATION RATE: the proportion of the total population working, or the percentage of the total subpopulation working. We can find participation rates, then, for the entire economy and for various subclasses, such as men, women, married men, married women, etc.

REPRESSED INFLATION: an inflation which is not allowed to manifest itself in rising prices. The symptoms of repressed inflation are shortages, black markets, under-the-counter "deals," and discrimination against certain classes of consumers.

BLACK MARKET: an illegal market where goods and services are exchanged at prices which exceed legally controlled maxima.

LIQUID ASSETS: assets which are easily exchangeable for cash without a change in their value. The most liquid asset is, of course, cash itself. The next most liquid asset might be a savings account, and then a U.S. government short-term bill.

Chapter Summary

1. We had extensive controls during World War II, including a National Housing Agency, an Office of Emergency Management, and an Office of Price Stabilization.
2. Since such a large fraction of adult males went into the war, we had manpower problems. These were countered with entry into the labor force by women, retired people, and teenagers, in addition to others working overtime.
3. As with all wars, the Second World War had to be paid for, and not enough taxes were raised to cover all expenses.
4. The difference was made up by selling bonds and money creation. During this period (1939–1948) the money supply grew at an annual average rate of over 12 percent a year.
5. The great expansionary effects of war spending and money creation would surely have meant excessive inflation. Therefore, a system of strict price controls was instituted in which 80,000 paid employees plus another 300,000 volunteer price-watchers were utilized. However, when price controls were lifted after the war, the repressed inflation became explicit.
6. During the period of price controls, extensive queuing and rationing resulted, as did a system of black and grey markets as individuals attempted to buy goods that were in excess demand at the legally controlled prices.
7. The anticipated depression after the war did not occur. One of the reasons was apparently that people held high levels of liquid assets which they wanted to spend after the cessation of hostilities.

Questions for Thought and Discussion

1. Do you think that the United States could muster as great a war effort as it did during World War II?
2. Female labor-force participation rates rose greatly during World War II and have continued to increase ever since. Do you have any idea why?
3. If the government sells bonds instead of taxing enough to pay for the war, who ends up paying for the deficit? (Hint: Who pays the interest on government bonds?)
4. Price controls seemed to be "successful" during World War II. Was this success bought at a price?
5. Who would lose by a high rate of inflation during the war as opposed to a high rate of inflation after the war, as did actually happen?
6. Could a black market ever exist for a product or service in the United States today?

THE MIRACLE MAN OF WARTIME MERCHANT SHIPBUILDING

Henry J. Kaiser (1882–1967)

An Audacious Industrialist

A WORLD WAR II Liberty Ship was big, very big. Nonetheless, Henry J. Kaiser was able to produce one in eight days flat! In his seven shipyards in Oregon and California he produced over 1500 ships during the war. How did he do it? By introducing prefabrication and assembly-line techniques, along with a new and better welding process. This feat may have seemed a miracle, but should only have been expected from the man who had built up empires in paving and construction before the war. He had done that by submitting lower bids than much larger firms on all the government contracts he could apply for in the 1930s. He went on to help build Bonneville and Grand Coulee dams. Kaiser even had the audacity to bid on providing five million barrels of cement for Shasta Dam even though he didn't have a cement company! He got the bid and founded Permanente Cement Company, which had the largest plant in the entire United States, located in Permanente, California. Between 1931 and 1945 he completed 70 major construction projects.

Kaiser was not a boy to stay in school in his native Sproutbrook, New York. He quit at the age of 13 to become a cash boy, later becoming a salesman for the J. B. Wells Dry Goods Store in Utica. Then he went into the photographic supply business and while still in his teens became a partner in the firm of Brownwell and Kaiser in Lake Placid, New York. Tiring of the photography business, he sold out in 1906 and moved to Spokane, Washington, where he went into the hardware business as a mere employee. Then the paving industry took his fancy, and he soon became a self-employed contractor, handling numerous highway and street projects in Washington, Idaho, and British Columbia. Then he moved his headquarters to Oakland, California. While still a road builder, he constructed 200 miles of highway in Cuba at a cost of over $18 million. One of the biggest innovations Kaiser introduced while in the road-building business was the substitution of diesel engines for gasoline motors in his tractors and steam shovels, thereby greatly reducing operating costs. When he went into the dam construction business, his prowess as an organizer and innovator did not abate: As head of the contractors building the Boulder Dam, he got it completed two years ahead of schedule. Construction of dams led to the building of tunnels, bridges, dry docks, jetties, air bases, troop facilities, and even to the excavation for the third locks in Panama.

Kaiser was perhaps more than any other industrialist of the time convinced that vertical integration was the only way to solve supply problems. For building his ships in California, Oregon, and Washington he needed steel, so he put up an integrated steel plant in Fontana, California. The ships also needed engines, so he and his associates purchased an iron works in Sunnyvale, California, where engines were built for Kaiser and other contractors. He also built a magnesium plant (magnesium wasn't used only for shipbuilding; in one form it was used as the incendiary material known as "goop").

The list goes on, for Kaiser got himself involved in airplane building during the war, also. He designed his plant in Bristol, Pennsylvania, where he not only built parts, subassemblies, and surfaces for flying fortresses, but also put together experimental Army and Navy planes.

After the war Kaiser saw the possibility of profit in the automobile industry. He formed the Kaiser-Frasier Corporation, which was the first major new U.S. independent auto producer after the war. The future of independent auto producers seemed sanguine right after the war, but by the early 1950s it was a downhill road. In an attempt to strengthen his market position Kaiser bought up the assets of the bankrupt Willys Motors in 1953. At the same time Nash and Hudson joined forces under the name of American Motors, and two other car manufacturers merged to form Studebaker-Packard. Finally, though, Kaiser Motors was no more, and its over $90 million in debts were assumed by Henry J. Kaiser's more profitable enterprises.

Kaiser couldn't stop expanding his empire. He went into aluminum right after the war, and within five years Kaiser Aluminum and Chemical Company had sales of $150 million. By 1956 this figure had risen to $330 million, with a net profit of over $40 million. Kaiser has left his mark on American economic and social life. We see Kaiser hospitals, and Kaiser developments such as on Oahu, Hawaii, and there are numerous other less obvious imprints of this audacious industrialist's activities, many of which are based on one man's quest for continued industrial efficiency.

ISSUE XII — DID THE SECOND WORLD WAR PULL US OUT OF THE DEPRESSION?

Were Individuals Really Better Off During the War?

Unemployment Drops

Everyone immediately assumes that World War II pulled us out of the Great Depression. After all, the story goes, we did have lots of unemployment when hostilities broke out in Europe, and that unemployment was eradicated by the stimulus of a war economy. After all, we did have low levels of per capita real income at the end of the thirties, and that changed during the war, too, didn't it? Let's first take a look at what happened to unemployment.

We see in Figure XII-1 that indeed unemployment exceeded 17 percent when hostilities broke out in Europe. This figure was still almost 15 percent in 1940. It then dropped to an incredible 1.2 percent by 1944. Overall, then, it seems clear that the war effort caused a reduction in unemployment. But, let's not stop there. Something else was happening at the same time—conscription. Remember that the Selective Service Act was passed in 1940, and large numbers of men and women joined or were drafted into the Armed Services. These represented a significant fraction of the labor force, as we see in Figure XII-2. Is it fair, then, to say that the war economy reduced unemployment when 17 percent of the labor force was in the Armed Forces at the height of the war? In other words, a significant and increasing fraction of the labor force was conscripted. This, certainly, is one way to eliminate unemployment, but it has little to do with what people usually consider the scenario to be during a war period. Generally, it is assumed that high production rates create increasing demand for more and more workers, thus eliminating any residue of unemployment. This is indeed what most students of World War II believe happened during that period. In fact, however, it appears that conscription had a lot to do with eliminating the unemployment aspect of the Great Depression.

That still leaves us with the fact that the output of the economy expanded rapidly during wartime.

A World War II Liberty Ship, *Samuel Adams*, ready to be launched. (The Bettmann Archive, Inc.)

207

ISSUE XII   DID THE SECOND WORLD WAR PULL US OUT OF THE DEPRESSION?

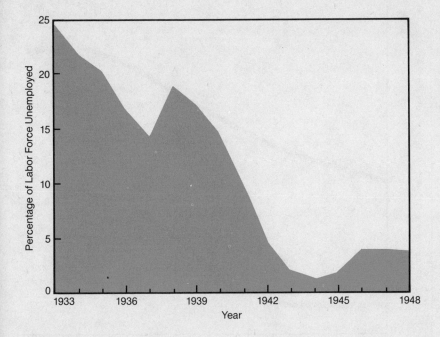

FIGURE XII–1

PERCENTAGE OF LABOR FORCE UNEMPLOYED

Dropping from a high of almost 25 percent in 1933, unemployment fell soon after the start of hostilities in World War II, reaching an incredible 1.2 percent in 1944. (*Source:* Bureau of Labor Statistics.)

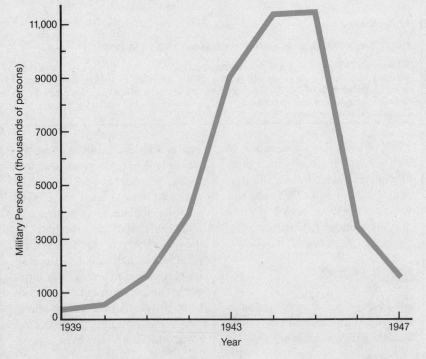

FIGURE XII–2

OUR FIGHTING FORCES DURING WORLD WAR II

Military personnel on active duty grew by leaps and bounds after the beginning of the 1940s, reaching a peak in 1945 of almost 11.5 million men. A large fraction of the unemployed were absorbed by the Armed Forces during this period. (*Source:* Bureau of Labor Statistics.)

Increasing Output

Increases in demand during the war definitely stimulated aggregate demand. The output of the economy increased at a tremendous rate. We see in Figure XII-3 that the total real GNP of the economy grew by leaps and bounds from the beginning of the war to the end. But this doesn't really tell us if individuals were better off during this period. That's what we want to know, isn't it? And that's where the bottom line in Figure XII-3 comes in; it represents the total amount of government purchases of goods and services, and it skyrocketed during the war. Much of the increase in output actually went to the war production effort, not into the personal lives of Americans. If we look, for example, at per capita personal consumption expenditures in Table XII-1 for the period 1940 through 1945, we find a very insignificant trend. In fact, in 1942, '43, and '44, per capita personal consumption expenditures were less than in 1941. This doesn't even tell the true story because those figures include people in the Armed Services, a full 5.5 percent of the population. They obviously were not sharing in the increased production of the nation in any meaningful fashion. In short, the private sector of the economy was not necessarily better off at the end of the war than at the beginning. The Depression

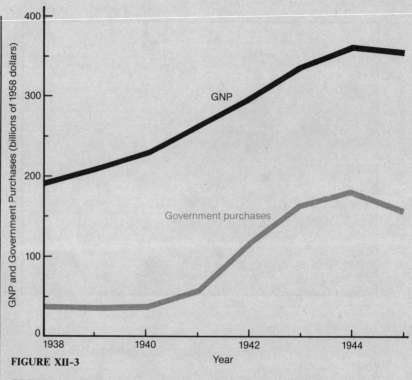

FIGURE XII-3

GROWTH OF REAL GNP AND GOVERNMENT EXPENDITURES

While real GNP grew by leaps and bounds during World War II, so, too, did the government purchases of goods and services (both expressed in 1958 dollars). How much of this growth of GNP, then, actually represented a benefit to the economy since the government was spending most of its income on war materials? (*Source:* Department of Commerce.)

was over, but people were not as well off as previously imagined. Of course, if we consider the psychological benefits of fighting and winning the war, social welfare may have indeed increased.

What Is Income?

All of this discussion brings us to the crucial question of what does income really represent? Does it matter what we produce? Can we treat a tank as yielding satisfaction to the general public? Probably not. In fact, we must treat it as an intermediate good and not a final good. It is intermediate in the sense that it is used to produce what we call national defense. But we certainly don't value the tank per se (unless we are in the Armed Forces). As Adam Smith once said, consumption is the objective of production. However, since

209

ISSUE XII   DID THE SECOND WORLD WAR PULL US OUT OF THE DEPRESSION?

TABLE XII-1

PERSONAL CONSUMPTION DURING THE WAR

YEAR	TOTAL PERSONAL CONSUMPTION EXPENDITURES IN BILLIONS (1958 DOLLARS)	PER CAPITA PERSONAL CONSUMPTION EXPENDITURES IN BILLIONS (1958 DOLLARS)
1940	$155.7	$1,178
1941	165.4	1,240
1942	161.4	1,197
1943	165.8	1,213
1944	171.4	1,238
1945	183.0	1,308

Here we give total personal consumption expenditures in billions of 1958 dollars. There was hardly any trend at all during this period. This is brought out even more clearly if we look at per capita personal consumption expenditures in 1958 dollars in column 3. In 1942, 1943, and 1944, per capita personal consumption was less than in 1941. (*Source:* Department of Commerce.)

World War II modern politicians seem to be saying that tanks and airplanes are objectives also. Who is right? That depends on one's value judgments. Economics cannot answer such a question, but individual reflection will certainly lead most to their own obvious conclusions.

Questions for Thought and Discussion

1. Do you think people were subjectively better off or worse off during the war? Consider that personal income did not increase very much because so much of the output was going to the war effort, at the same time realizing the positive externalities from fighting and winning a war.
2. What is the end of economic activity in your opinion?
3. What differences do you see between the situation before the Second World War and the situation at the start of the War in Indochina?

Three More Decades of Development

THE END OF World War II saw the formation of the United Nations and a desire to prevent future conflicts which could endanger the peace and happiness of the world citizenry. The awesome destructive power of the atomic bomb had been amply demonstrated at Hiroshima and Nagasaki. The possibility of worldwide destruction and the end of the human species now truly existed as never before. But despite the UN and the constant fear of destructive atomic warfare, the three decades that followed were ones of alternating hot and cold hostile actions. Only half a decade was to transpire before American men and machines were again engaged in a conflict—the Korean War.* After the truce in Korea it was again barely one and a half more decades before the American war machine was involved in another costly and, *ex post facto,* senseless engagement in Indochina. But all during this time the economy was growing; the per capita income was increasing. This can be seen in Figure 13–1, which shows the rise in per capita real GNP in the United States from the end of World War II until the mid-1970s. Underlying this long-run trend of increasing prosperity, however, are numerous problems of unemployment and inflation, to which we now turn.

POSTWAR INFLATION AND UNEMPLOYMENT

Remember that very strict price controls were in effect during World War II. These were lifted almost immediately after the end of hostilities, and consequently the repressed inflation that had built up pressure for three or four years was now

*This is euphemistically called the Korean Conflict, in which American forces were merely engaged in a United Nations peace-keeping mission.

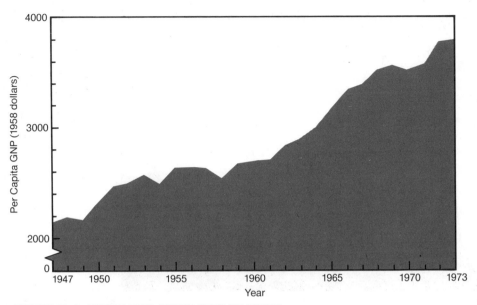

FIGURE 13-1 **RISING REAL STANDARDS OF LIVING**

Since the end of World War I until present, real per capita GNP has been growing, albeit with some unsteadiness. These figures are expressed in 1958 dollars. (*Source:* Department of Commerce.)

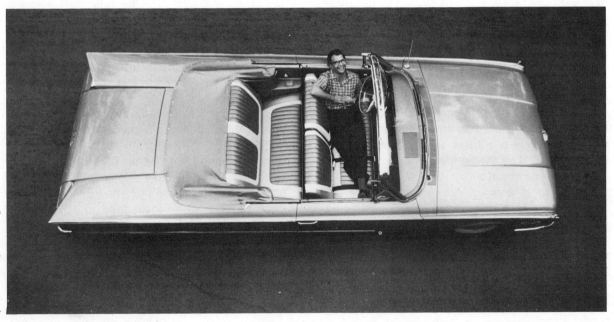

(Bob Henriques, Magnum Photos)

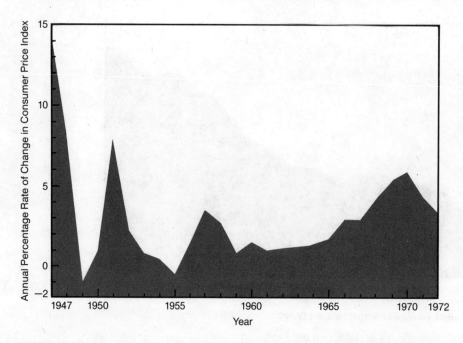

FIGURE 13–2

THE RATE OF INFLATION

Here we see plotted the rate of price rises in every year since World War II. It increased dramatically right after the war and then came back down to very low levels until recently. (*Source:* Bureau of Labor Statistics.)

allowed to vent itself. And it did just that. Looking at Figure 13–2, we see that the rate of inflation increased dramatically after World War II. Then prices slowed down for a while as we had a relatively minor recession at the end of the 1940s. Once the Korean War broke out, however, prices again shot up at a very rapid rate.

This can be easily explained. Neither government spending nor the money supply were increasing at very rapid rates during this period. However, people still had fresh in their minds the effects of price controls and scarcity during World War II. They feared the same thing would happen during the Korean War. At the start of the fifties there was an extraordinary spate of buying—a buying spree, you might say—particularly of consumer durables and automobiles. The American public was not again going to be stuck without those goods and services it wanted to have just because we were going to fight another war. The war turned out to be not so short-lived, although our participation in it was relatively

minor: 5.7 million men were engaged during a three-year, one-month period. There were 157,500 casualties, and the total cost was estimated to be in the neighborhood of $60 billion. The country experimented with a moderate amount of price controls during the war period, but it could be said in retrospect that the effort was not very sincere and the effects were to be expected.

After the war, prices were rising at very low annual rates—between 1 percent and 2 percent —until things started getting hot in Indochina. Starting around 1964, the rate of increase of prices was rising. Not only did this inflation continue, but it got worse, all the way into the next decade. Price controls were again tried in 1971 and a modified form of them continued for a number of years afterward. The evidence of their effectiveness, however, is not very impressive, as can be seen in Figure 13–2. Price controls will not usually work for long if the underlying forces— generally government monetary and fiscal policies—are expansionary, and this is exactly what happened during World War II, during the Korean War, and during the latest period of government price fixing. Although since 1971 there have been some periods of monetary and fiscal restraint, the general direction has been expansionary. In such a situation, it is difficult to imagine that arbitrary actions by government will be effective in controlling prices.

UPS AND DOWNS

During these three decades we not only had times of inflation, but we also had times of inflation simultaneous with high unemployment, a situation hitherto almost completely unknown in the history of the United States. We can see the level of unemployment in Figure 13–3 that occurred since the end of hostilities in 1945. There was an immediate but short-lived jump in unemployment after World War II, as could be expected with large numbers

of servicemen being mustered out. There was again a period of exceptionally high unemployment at the end of the decade, when we suffered a slight recession. We again suffered a recession some ten years later, when the unemployment rate in 1958 jumped up to almost 7 percent. Things got better for a few years, but by 1961 another recession was encountered. Then the longest period of peacetime prosperity in the history of the United States occurred, lasting almost a full decade.

But before that prolonged prosperity could happen, numerous attempts on the part of government officials, and particularly the Council of Economic Advisors, to enlist legislative help from the Congress were necessary. During the presidential campaign of 1960, Richard Nixon was pitted against John F. Kennedy. An advisor to Nixon at that time, Arthur F. Burns, now Chairman of the Board of Governors of the Federal Reserve System, exposed the Vice President to some monetary theory. He contended that if Nixon couldn't

FIGURE 13–3

RECENT UNEMPLOYMENT

Unemployment has jumped around since the end of World War II. However, an unusual phenomenon occurred in 1970 and thereafter —high unemployment and high rates of inflation, or an inflationary recession. (*Source:* Bureau of Labor Statistics.)

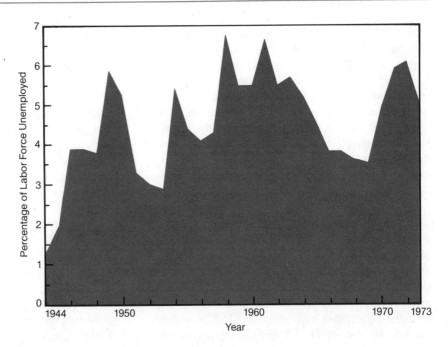

get the administration to force the Federal Reserve System to expand the money supply more rapidly, there would be a recession and Nixon would lose the election. The election was lost, at least in part, over this issue. Kennedy became the thirty-fifth President of the United States. He immediately got an aggressive Council of Economic Advisors, headed by Walter Heller of the University of Minnesota. Kennedy, Heller, and other advisors indicated that the only way to pull us out of the recession was to use expansionary fiscal policy by a tax cut. Their model was Keynesian, referred to in our chapter on the Depression.

Rationale behind Tax Cut

Basically, a tax cut would give individuals more spendable income. When they spent this additional income, those who received it would also have more to spend, and this process would continue so that the tax cut would yield a more than proportionate increase in aggregate demand and spending and, consequently, a decrease in unemployment, as unemployed workers were hired to produce the additional demanded output. If we look at what happened to unemployment, we see in Figure 13–3 that later in that decade it did fall. The tax cut, however, did not actually occur until 1964, when Johnson was President, after Kennedy's assassination. The results of the '64 Johnson-Kennedy tax cut seemed impressive. However, when the reverse tactic was used a few years later to quell an overheated economy, the same could not be said.

The Tax Surcharge

Just about the time we started getting into Vietnam in a very direct fashion, 1965, federal expenditures started creeping ahead of federal tax revenues. In other words, we were having increasingly large deficits. At the same time the money supply was increasing at a rapid rate, except for a slight pause in 1966. Whereas it had increased at 3.3 percent per annum from 1961 to 1965, during the period

1967 to 1969 it increased at 7 percent. In any event, the Council of Economic Advisors told President Johnson that one way to stop the inflation that was occurring by leaps and bounds was to increase taxes. A reverse Keynesian reasoning would hold: Take more income away from consumers and they will be able to spend less, thus causing a contraction in aggregate demand in the economy. Prices would stop rising as fast because people would not be demanding as many goods and services as before. So the small tax surcharge of 1968 was instituted. But it had little effect on prices and they continued to rise into the next decade. They are still rising. The next administration tried another tack, and much to its chagrin and embarrassment, a phenomenon occurred that has been called an inflationary recession.

THE INFLATIONARY RECESSION

Price increases didn't slow down, but employment demands did. The unemployment rate rose steadily during the last year of the '60s and the first year of the '70s. How can we explain this simultaneous increase in prices and unemployment? In general, our notions about inflation equate that unhappy phenomenon with excess demands—that is, people try to buy more goods and services than actually exist, thus bidding the prices up. But when we see lots of unemployment around, we know that there is no such thing as general excess demand, for unemployed workers imply the opposite. There are basically three popular explanations for what happened during this period of inflationary recession.

Monopoly Power Arguments

The first explanation has to do with the power of unions. Presumably unions have become so powerful that they can raise wages high enough to cause unemployment. At the same time, entrepreneurs are forced to raise prices to pay for these higher union labor costs. Thus we should see increasing unemployment and increasing prices. The second explanation is that businessmen have acquired large discretionary powers over setting prices, contrary to what we would predict in a competitive model. During this period they desired to increase prices even more in order to increase profits, but consumers balked. Since the law of demand indicates higher prices lead to lower quantity demanded, entrepreneurs who raised prices found that they didn't sell as much as they used to, and hence, they laid off workers.

These two theories may make some sense, but they are not really very useful, for we have no idea when to predict this type of **cost-push inflation.** In what year will we expect unions to assert their monopoly power? In what year will we expect businessmen to assert theirs? The theories tell us nothing.

Changing Expectations

An alternative, and perhaps more useful, theory concerns the lag in the expectations of both workers and businessmen. **Expectations** or **anticipations** have to do with what people think is going to happen. A worker will anticipate that the demand for his labor services will yield him a certain wage rate, depending on what he was used to in the past and what he sees his friends and colleagues receiving. Businessmen will have anticipations about what prices they can set on their products in order to maximize profits. In periods of rapidly increasing aggregate demand, such as started in 1965, each year workers and businessmen were temporarily fooled. The businessmen found that they could raise prices and still sell all the goods and services they had anticipated selling. In fact, at the end of the year they found lower levels of inventories than they had anticipated. This told them that they could have raised prices even more and made even more profits.

Workers, on the other hand, were demanding higher wages and getting them, or were switching jobs to obtain them. Some of them were finding that they could get jobs at higher wages faster

than they had anticipated. In other words, the demand for their labor services was going up faster in money terms than they were used to. During the Vietnam expansionary period, both businessmen and workers were continually faced with an ever-expanding economy which implied rising prices and rising wages in this particular episode.

A CHANGE IN TACTICS

In 1969 and 1970 the government's monetary and fiscal policy was suddenly very contractionary: The growth rate of the money supply decreased and federal government purchases fell. This led to a lower rate of growth in aggregate demand. But businessmen, who had no idea that this was anything more than a random occurrence, continued to raise prices because they based their predictions of what they could sell on what had happened in the past. However, at the same time consumers were not getting higher incomes. They reacted to these higher prices by demanding less than anticipated by businessmen. Inventories started piling up and layoffs occurred.

On the other side of the picture, workers started demanding ever-higher wages, for in the past several years they had been fooled into accepting nominal wage increases which did not fully take account of increases in the cost of living—inflation. Many union contracts were renegotiated during this period. The union leaders wanted not only to make up for the lost real income of the last three or four years, but also to anticipate future erosions of their paychecks by inflation. Hence, they made extraordinary wage demands. At first businessmen gave in to them, fully anticipating that they could pass these higher labor costs on to the consumer while still maintaining their previous sales records. Such was not the case. So both laborers and businessmen were fooled because they did not realize that the growth rate of aggregate demand had slowed down. Hence, we had a period of rising prices and rising unemployment.

Eventually, though, people started learning, so we saw a decrease in the rate at which inflation was growing until mid-1970. In fact, it appeared that the rate of inflation was abating when President Nixon instituted his New Economic Policy on August 15, 1971. The slowup in price rises was soon to be reversed as the government's expansionary monetary and fiscal policies, instituted to pull us out of the recession, reinjected purchasing power into the economy and started us off on another inflationary rampage.

All during the '60s and early '70s, the problems of inflation and unemployment were expressed in terms of a trade-off.

THE TRADE-OFF BETWEEN INFLATION AND UNEMPLOYMENT

Back in the early '50s, a British economist named Phillips discovered an empirical relationship between rates of inflation and rates of unemployment in the United Kingdom. He found that the higher the rate of inflation, the lower the rate of unemployment. This seemed to indicate that there could be a trade-off. If one wished to have lower unemployment, all he needed to do was to raise the rate of inflation. In other words, we could buy less unemployment by paying in the form of a higher rate of inflation. This so-called Phillips curve relationship is given in Figure 13–4. It seemed quite neat and amenable to policy decisions.

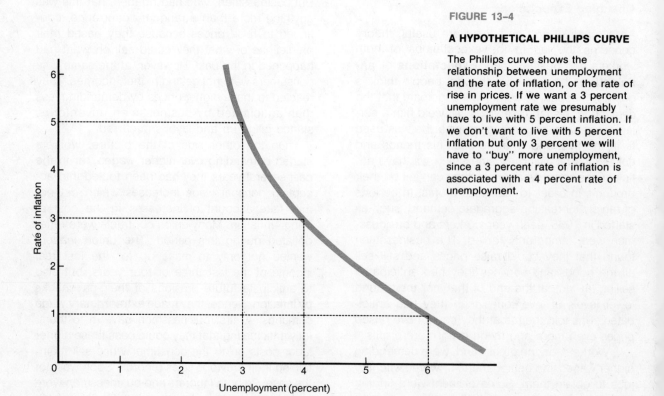

FIGURE 13–4

A HYPOTHETICAL PHILLIPS CURVE

The Phillips curve shows the relationship between unemployment and the rate of inflation, or the rate of rise in prices. If we want a 3 percent unemployment rate we presumably have to live with 5 percent inflation. If we don't want to live with 5 percent inflation but only 3 percent we will have to "buy" more unemployment, since a 3 percent rate of inflation is associated with a 4 percent rate of unemployment.

Unions have invaded the public sector. New Yorkers found out what could happen. (Joe Covello, Black Star)

However, policy makers soon found out that the relationship was not stable: The Phillips curve was shifting all the time as people adjusted to new rates of inflation. Ultimately, a debate occurred among economists: Did the Phillips curve exist, or was it all a temporary phenomenon which cannot be used for policy makers? While we cannot answer this complicated question here, we can indicate that a Phillips curve arrangement seems to rest on a pretty shaky assumption about how workers react to increases in the price level.

When inflation occurs *unexpectedly* entrepreneurs seem to be the first ones to take advantage of it. They raise prices and obtain higher profits. Wages don't go up immediately, if for no other reason than that many workers are under long-term contracts. In this initial period, as the price of what workers make goes up but their wages don't go up as rapidly, the real wage rate falls. This is the price the entrepreneurs pay for labor—the law of demand holds. As the real wage

rate falls, the quantity of labor demanded rises, and hence unemployment is reduced. However, after this initial period of adjustment, workers probably soon figure out what is happening. They demand wage increases that take account of the expected inflation.* If this were the case, then there could be no long-run trade-off between a stable rate of inflation and the level of unemployment. It seems that only when workers can be fooled could such a trade-off exist. It's hard to imagine that workers could be fooled forever.

Since we're talking about the labor force, we can examine some of its developments since World War I.

FORMS OF UNEMPLOYMENT

During the '50s and '60s, there was much talk about different kinds of unemployment. The first kind of unemployment that we're all familiar with is the so-called friction that occurs in any dynamic economy. People change jobs in order to get higher wages or better working conditions. Workers are laid off and have to seek other jobs. At any moment tremendous numbers of workers are quitting or changing jobs. They don't find another job immediately and hence there is friction in the labor market. The level of **frictional unemployment,** as it is called, is also sometimes referred to as the normal rate of unemployment. It is probably some number like 3 to 5 percent of the labor force. The only way it can be reduced is by improving information flows in the labor market itself, or alternatively, by passing a law which states that no worker can be fired or quit unless he has another job already lined up.

To some people, a much more perplexing form of unemployment is what is known as **structural unemployment.** Structural unemployment occurs when the structure of the economy

---

*Even if they didn't, employers would eventually bid up money wages so that the readjustment would still occur.

changes. A prime example would be that when the automobile replaced the horse as a means of transportation the horseshoe industry was wiped out. All those people who had learned to make horseshoes would be structurally unemployed; they would have to retrain themselves in order to get employment. Sometimes structural unemployment is mixed up with the so-called **hard-core unemployment.** Generally, hard-core unemployment refers to those subsectors of the unemployed labor force who are discriminated against or have few or no skills—blacks, teenagers, out-of-work Appalachian coal miners, etc. There are also those who remain unemployed because the benefits from not working, such as unemployment compensation or welfare payments—exceed their expected wages from working.

We note that it is extremely difficult to ferret out the different types of unemployment from one overall unemployment figure. It is also interesting to note that the number of magazine and journal articles concerned with structural unemployment is positively correlated with the level of unemployment. In other words, when unemployment is low, we no longer hear that "something has to be done about structural unemployment."

LABOR LEGISLATION

We noted that the passage of New Deal legislation fostered the growth of American union activity. However, there was a certain amount of antilabor sentiment after World War II. John L. Lewis' United Mine Workers defied a court order to go back to work after a long and violent strike. The union and its leader were fined for contempt of court, and the miners finally did go back to work. However, legislation against unions was already in the wind, and the Labor-Management Relations Act of 1947 was passed. It is sometimes called the Taft-Hartley Act—and other times called the Slave Labor Act by union people. It allowed individual

states to pass their own **right-to-work laws**. A right-to-work law makes it illegal for union membership to be a prerequisite for employment in any individual establishment. In general, the Taft-Hartley Act outlawed unfair labor practices of unions such as "make-work" rules and the forcing of unwilling workers to join a particular union before being hired. But the most famous aspect of this act is its provision that the President can obtain a court injunction that could last for 80 days for any strike that is believed to imperil the national safety or health. President Nixon applied this 80-day injunction to striking longshoremen in 1971. President Eisenhower had done the same thing to striking steel workers in 1959. On the other hand, during this postwar period some favorable legislation was passed. Some of it involved increases in the minimum wage, which we have yet to treat in this book.

MINIMUM-WAGE LEGISLATION

Minimum-wage legislation essentially puts a floor on what employers can pay certain employees. Minimum wages have been around for at least three quarters of a century. This type of legislation grew out of the general movement against "the exploitation of the poor working girl" and the low pay for those toiling under bad working conditions. But until 1912 the movement for a minimum wage produced very few results. In that year, however, Massachusetts passed a "moral suasion" law to compel employers to pay standard wage rates which were to be set by a state Wage Board. Any employer who did not comply would have his name published and would therefore be subject to ostracism from the community. A year later, eight more states passed minimum-wage laws, seven of them making the rate compulsory. The laws, however, applied only to women and minors. The bulk of workers was unaffected.

Roosevelt's New Deal and the National Industrial Recovery Act in 1933 set up the first federal minimum wage. It started at a rate between 30 and 40 cents an hour. When the NIRA was declared unconstitutional, the Fair Labor Standards Act was passed in 1937, establishing a minimum wage rate of 25 cents for all industries that were involved in interstate commerce. This act has remained the basis for the current federal minimum wage. The national minimum wage went to 30 cents in 1939. By 1950 it was 75 cents. Then it increased in steps up to $1.60 per hour by the start of the 1970s.

Unions in Favor

Now why could we say that this was favorable legislation for the unions? It's quite simple. Union workers are already making considerably more than minimum wage rates. Union labor services are obviously to some extent substitutable by nonunion labor services. If nonunion workers must be paid a higher wage rate than they would be paid otherwise, the demand for union workers will, in fact, be greater. In other words, the high union wage rate will no longer be *relatively* as high if other workers must be paid more than they would receive under competitive conditions.

Some people are definitely hurt by minimum wages. Growing evidence from reports by the Secretary of Labor, by Dr. Arthur Burns, and comments by such respected economists as Paul Samuelson and Milton Friedman indicate that teenagers and blacks are hurt the most by the minimum wage. In fact, Paul Samuelson once said, "What good does it do a black youth to know that an employer must pay him $1.60 an hour if the fact that he must be paid that amount is what keeps him from getting a job." Milton Friedman called the minimum wage law "the most anti-Negro law on our statute books—in its effect, not its intent." How is this so, you might be asking. Doesn't a minimum wage merely mean that employers have to pay workers higher wages? Yes, it does, but it doesn't require them to hire the same number of workers.

Demand for Labor

The demand for labor is derived from the demand for the final ouput that the laborer makes. In the aggregate, employers hire workers up to the point where the value of the additional output made possible by the new workers just equals the increases in the employers' wage bill. If the wage rate is arbitrarily increased by government edict, some marginal workers may become unprofitable to employ. Marginal workers are those whose value, measured by the addition to output, is just equal to what they are paid. If they have to be paid more they will be fired. In this case, the market value of their contribution to total output is less than the minimum wage rate. Producers cannot simply raise prices to finance the increased wages of all those marginal workers because at higher prices less output will be purchased by consumers. This would make part of the labor force redundant when sales fell off. What happens is that those marginal workers who lose their jobs do not receive the minimum wage; they receive nothing. They have to find work in sectors of the economy which are not covered by minimum-wage legislation. And in those sectors of the economy the additional supply of workers will cause wage rates to fall. By eliminating marginal job opportunities, the minimum wage rate actually hurts the very people it was intended to help.

This argument may not seem compelling, for how can a few cents increase in required wages cause employers to lay off any of their employees? To be sure, small changes in the minimum wage will not in fact be translated into any very noticeable change in employment. On the other hand, given a sufficiently large change in the minimum wage, some increased unemployment will surely ensue unless aggregate demand is simultaneously increased. Let's take the year 1956.

Some Facts

In that year, the minimum wage was increased from 75 cents to $1.00 an hour. That's a one-third jump, which is quite substantial. Three years later, the Secretary of Labor concluded in a report that "there were significant declines in employment in most of the low wage industries studied," after the increase in minimum wage in 1956. Looking at some more evidence, we find that teenagers are going to be predominantly in the low-wage groups if for no other reason than that they have less experience in working and therefore are less productive than older people. We would expect that they would be most affected by the minimum wage, and in fact they were. If we look at white teenage unemployment from 1950 to 1956, it ranged between 6.5 percent and 11 percent. When the minimum wage was raised in 1956 to $1, white teenage unemployment shot up from 7 percent to almost 14 percent. Ever since then, it has remained in excess of 12 percent. Even more startling is what happened to black teenagers. In 1956, unemployment in that category jumped from 13 percent to 24 percent. A 1965 study by Dr. Arthur F. Burns concluded that "the ratio of the unemployment rate of teenagers to that of male adults was invariably higher during the six months following an increase in the minimum wage than it was in the preceding half year."

LOSING ALL OUR GOLD

The postwar era saw numerous ups and downs in the international monetary situation. It was a period of an unprecedented loss in our gold stock. But to understand what happened we must first examine the creation of an international monetary system which started in Bretton Woods, New Hampshire, July 1944. The war was quickly coming to a close and leaders of the Western world decided to create a new international payments system to replace the old gold standard.

Gold Standard

In the old gold standard, a country's money supply was directly tied to a gold base. In fact, in a pure

gold standard, gold also circulated as part of the money supply. Individual countries' currencies were pegged to the price of gold because currency units were defined as equivalent to a certain weight of gold, and hence they were pegged to each other in a fixed manner. Whenever one country would buy more goods (and financial securities) at the fixed exchange rate than other countries would purchase from them—that is, whenever the total value of imports exceeded the total value of exports—the deficit country would have to ship gold out. If this continued, it would eventually run out of gold. But in the meantime there were forces that would correct the situation. What actually happened in a gold standard was that since gold was part of the money supply, shipments of gold to other countries would reduce the amount of money in circulation in the deficit country. This would lead to a general rise in prices in the nation receiving the gold. That would also mean that in the deficit country, domestic prices fell; the relative price of foreign goods would rise, while exports would rise, so there would be less incentive to import. In the surplus countries, as domestic prices rose, the relative price of foreign goods would fall, exports would fall, and there would be more incentive to import. The trade imbalance would correct itself automatically, albeit after a certain period of time.

The IMF

This kind of system was no longer desired after the war and in fact it hadn't really existed for many years. What was to take its place was the **International Monetary Fund.** Upon becoming a member of the fund, each country was assigned a reserve quota. This quota was set according to a formula that took into account the economic importance of the country, its trade volume, and so on. The quota was paid to the IMF in a country's own domestic currency and in gold. The IMF was then able to loan foreign currency to any country that needed it in order to maintain a stable exchange rate. The U.S. dollar was convertible to foreigners into 1/35th of an ounce of gold. All other major currencies were convertible into dollars at fixed exchange rates which IMF member nations agreed to enforce and support.

Remember that at this time Europe was devastated by a total war. It required numerous imports of capital equipment. There would have been no way for Europe to obtain all this capital equipment in as short a time as it did without the **Marshall Plan.** Under this plan we voluntarily lent large quantities of dollars to Europe. These loans enabled European countries to finance their imports from the United States. The situation eventually changed. The balance of payments in the United States fell into deficit in the 1950s and has continued so ever since, as we can see in Figure 13–5.

Even though we were on a modified gold standard, we still ended up shipping large quantities of gold out of the country, as can be seen in Figure 13–6. Our gold stock fell from over $20 billion just after the war, down to $10 billion at the start of the 1970s. What did this mean? Simply that at the fixed exchange rate between the dollar and gold and other currencies, we were spending more in the rest of the world than the rest was spending in the U.S.A. We were paying for this in various ways, one being by shipments of gold. Foreign central banks were holding increasing amounts of dollars in their coffers. The dollars are relatively useless, of course, until they are spent. They don't earn any interest and, in fact, during this period they lost some of their value as inflation continued unabated in the United States.

FIGURE 13–5 **POSTWAR U.S. BALANCE OF PAYMENTS HISTORY**

In the 1950s the United States fell into an almost perpetual balance of payments deficit. That is, the value of our "out-payments" has continually exceeded the value of our *in*-payments. (*Source:* Council of Economic Advisors.)

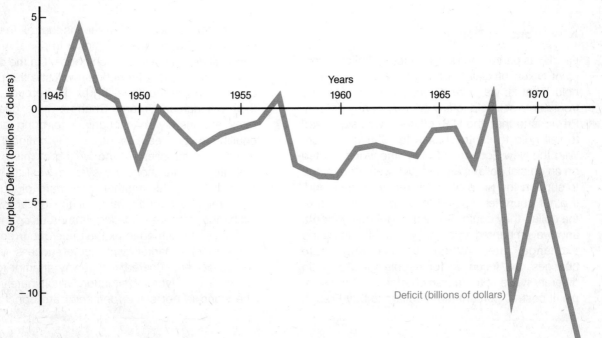

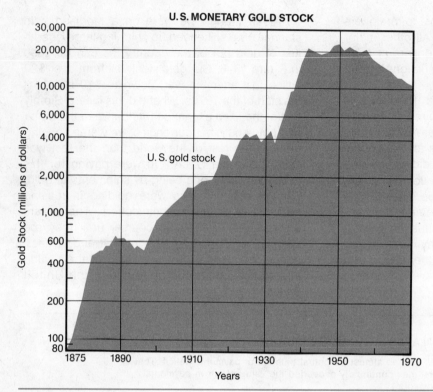

U.S. MONETARY GOLD STOCK

Gold Stock (millions of dollars)

U.S. gold stock

Years

FIGURE 13–6

U.S. MONETARY GOLD STOCK

By the middle of World War II, we had amassed more than $20 billion worth of gold at the official price of $35 an ounce. By 1970, we had a little more than $10 billion worth of gold. Our chronic balance of payments deficit was responsible for this drain. (*Source: Federal Reserve Bulletin.*)

New Economic Policy

Finally, as part of the New Economic Policy, President Nixon officially untied the U.S. dollar from gold. That is, we were committed neither to buy from nor to sell gold to any country or any person. Previous to that, the U.S. officially was supposed to sell gold to central banks for $35 an ounce. With the New Economic Policy, the world started on an official dollar standard. We were committed to support the price of no currency in the world. If other countries wanted to support the price of the dollar, they could. Some did. But many didn't, and we embarked upon a period of fluctuating exchange rates. When the exchange rate changes, the incentive for people to engage in different types of trade also changes. If, for example, it cost 10 percent more dollars to buy French

francs than it used to, that means that all French products will be 10 percent higher in price. Americans will demand less French goods. On the other side of the Atlantic, Frenchmen will see the price of American products falling by 10 percent, and they will demand more. Changes in exchange rates are merely a mechanism to bring about equilibrium between countries' international demands and supplies. At the writing of this book, the international monetary system was still in a state of flux. After another downward plunge in the foreign exchange value of the dollar, while exchange rates were floating, numerous countries and regions still tried to fix the price of currencies in the money markets with some success. What should be remembered is that any attempt to fix any price in a dynamic situation will ultimately fail. The world is not static; demands are constantly

changing; and the comparative advantages of individual countries change all the time. Even after several official **devaluations,** where the value of the dollar in terms of gold and other currencies fell, the United States continued to have a deficit in its balance of payments. What did that mean? Simply that exchange rates were still out of line with reality. Have no fear, though, for in the *very* long run the balance of payments must balance, by definition.

GOING ON TO THE COLD WAR

All throughout this postwar time, there was a rise in government expenditures on military manpower and equipment. In fact, after World War II, U.S. expenditures for defense were a higher percentage of national income than in any other peacetime period. Did all this defense spending foster a military-industrial complex? Let's see, in the following issue.

Definitions of New Terms

COST-PUSH INFLATION: a theory of inflation which states that costs are pushed up either by strong unions or by monopolistic businessmen, thus causing prices to rise.

EXPECTATIONS AND ANTICIPATIONS: formulations in people's minds about what will happen in the future. Individuals have expectations about future rates of inflation, future rates of change in wages, and so on.

FRICTIONAL UNEMPLOYMENT: unemployment caused by friction in the economy. In other words, frictional unemployment results from the imperfect information that exists in the labor market. Workers must take time to find alternative employment because they do not have perfect information. Frictional unemployment is sometimes called "normal" unemployment.

STRUCTURAL UNEMPLOYMENT: a type of unemployment caused by a shift in the structure of the economy; more specifically, unemployment caused by a permanent shift in the demand for different products.

HARD-CORE UNEMPLOYMENT: unemployment specifically associated with overt minority groups, such as blacks, Puerto Ricans, and Chicanos. Hard-core unemployment usually involves people with little schooling and few skills.

RIGHT-TO-WORK LAW: a law deeming it illegal for union membership to be a prerequisite for employment in an individual shop.

INTERNATIONAL MONETARY FUND: an international organization set up in 1944 to control the rates of exchange of currencies throughout the world.

MARSHALL PLAN: a plan of aid whereby the United States sent billions of dollars to devastated European countries after World War II.

DEVALUATION: an official reduction in the rate of exchange of a currency. The devaluation of the dollar involves reducing the price that the dollar will fetch in the foreign exchange market in terms of other currencies.

Chapter Summary

1. The rate of inflation increased dramatically after World War II, but then slowed down until the Korean War. During the bulk of the '50s and early '60s this nation experienced much lower rates of inflation than today.
2. The three postwar decades under study suffered from large ups and downs in the business cycle, even though the average rate of growth was fairly impressive.
3. The Johnson-Kennedy tax cut of 1964 was designed to keep the country from going into a recession. It seemed to work, but the opposite tack, the Johnson surcharge of 1968, was not successful in stemming inflationary pressures.
4. We ended up with a situation called an inflationary recession starting in 1969—prices were rising while unemployment was increasing.
5. There are several cost-push theories of inflation, resting on arguments concerning the monopoly power of unions and businessmen.
6. There is also an anticipations or expectations theory that has been used to explain the phenomenon of an inflationary recession. Even though the growth in total economic demand slowed in 1969–70, workers and businessmen anticipated that it would grow as it had in the past. They were therefore fooled and were willing to have prices and wages rise as in the past, but the results were unsold goods and unemployment.
7. There is supposedly a trade-off between inflation and unemployment that was observed by the economist A. Phillips. The relationship is now called the Phillips curve of the trade-off between unemployment and inflation. However, this trade-off seems to have worsened in the last few years, thus putting into doubt the long-run validity of the argument.
8. There are several forms of unemployment: frictional, structural, and perhaps hard-core. It is difficult to identify each particular type in many situations.
9. Minimum wages require that employers in covered occupations pay a specified federal minimum to all workers. The consensus among economists is that the minimum wage has caused higher rates of unemployment among blacks and teenagers than there would be otherwise. Remember, the demand for labor is a derived demand, derived from the demand for the final product. A minimum wage law does not require an employer to keep a specified number of workers. Therefore, if the minimum wage exceeds the value of a worker to an employer, he will lay off that worker.
10. Since the Korean War, this nation's balance of payments has been an almost continuous deficit. In 1971 we officially went off the vestiges of the gold standard.

Questions for Thought and Discussion

1. Why would workers remain unemployed rather than take severe wage cuts?
2. Do you think you can identify periods when cost-push inflation is at work?
3. Why do you think the tax surcharge in 1968 did not stop inflationary pressures?
4. Would you rather be employed at below the minimum wage or unemployed at the minimum wage?
5. Why are teenagers paid less than adults on average? Does this constitute discrimination?
6. Why is the dollar still worth something if it is not backed up by gold?

WIDE WORLD

THE CONSUMMATE AMERICAN BUSINESSMAN

Henry Ford II (1917–   )
Industrialist

Henry Ford II is a businessman who can do exactly as he pleases because, as he says, "my name is over the door." And he has done just that—from giving $50,000 to a Detroit ghetto recreation center to promoting change in his company, his city, and the country's business community. He had the privilege of being descended from one of America's wealthiest industrial families, but he also had to face the task of turning a money-losing organization into a major industrial power.

Between 1929 and 1941, the Ford Motor Company was on the brink of financial collapse. Edsel Ford, Henry Ford II's father and titular president of the company, was only a figurehead and the senile Henry Ford was actually steering the sinking ship. The company was foundering because of mismanagement, poor cost control, and antiquated production methods. In 1945, Henry Ford agreed to make his grandson president of the company. Although the younger Ford had little formal training, he knew the advantages of strong, trustworthy counsel. He brought in the "Whiz Kids," a group of sharp, ambitious men who were willing to apply modern technological and managerial techniques to the problems of the company. "I knew it could be turned around; it never occurred to me I couldn't do the job," said Ford at the time. He fired hundreds of top management personnel and brought in former General Motors men who decentralized and reorganized the company along the lines GM had perfected over the preceding decade.

One of Ford's major problems has been with the United Auto Workers (UAW). He has generally succeeded in his determined efforts to improve relations with Walter Reuther's men, but the Ford Motor Company remains a particularly tempting target for UAW strike action. Nonetheless, Ford has actively defended his company's interests in labor negotiations. He charged that the 1964 UAW job-security demands amounted to featherbedding and an undermining of the efficiency of the industry.

During his first eight years in the presidency, Ford made capital investments totaling an extraordinary $1 billion. The company acquired Philco Corporation in 1961, which turned out to be a profitable move toward electronics and defense contracting. Ford's high and low points have been associated with auto models. The Edsel, introduced in 1957, became one of the major disasters in the history of the industry, selling only 110,000 units in three years and incurring a loss of $250 million for the company. The Maverick and Mustang, though, have had substantial success on the market.

Because of his interest in urban renewal of the depressed sections of Detroit, his backing of the Ford Foundation, and his position (by default) as the most "concerned" of America's big automakers, Ford is considered a model of enlightened corporate management. According to Ford,

we are in "the worst domestic crisis since the Civil War," and we must "make some basic changes in our schools, our housing, our welfare system. We also need to make basic changes in our employment practices—in whom we hire, how we hire, and what we do with people and for people after they are hired." As early as the 1940s, Ford ordered his managers to hire blacks and members of other minorities. After the Detroit riots of 1967, Ford opened two hiring centers in the ghetto, recruiting the hard-core unemployed—those who had never worked and who were often illiterate and ex-cons. Ford gave them bus fare and lunch money until they received their first paycheck. Most started at $3.25–$3.80 per hour as sweepers, stockboys, assemblers, or press operators. Now about half of the work force at the River Rouge plant are blacks.

But many have discovered the limits of this image. Ford refuses to read Ralph Nader's *Unsafe at Any Speed,* a book that strongly attacks the design failings of auto manufacturers. In response to the proposed "safety cars," Ford said, "If you want to ride around in a tank, you won't get hurt. You won't be able to afford one though. . . ." He also balks at safety legislation, maintaining that "if you start by law to fool around with model changes, to tell the industry it must do this, that or the other thing within a period of time in which it cannot be done . . . you upset the whole cycle of this industry."

Areas such as safety and antipollution programs have, however, become more important in Ford's budget. In 1972 there were 6600 people employed in these endeavors. From 1967 to 1972 over one-half of a billion dollars went to safety and pollution research and engineering. In spite of these outlays, the company has remained profitable.

ISSUE XIII
DID THE COLD WAR FOSTER A MILITARY-INDUSTRIAL COMPLEX?

How We Live with the Generals

The Start of War

The uneasy truce between the Allies at the close of World War II quickly disintegrated into what we have long known as the Cold War. The United States pitted itself against the communist countries in general and Russia in particular. We were not going to let the Russians "bury us" in economic output, as former Premier Nikita Khrushchev once said to the American people. We were not going to let communist aggression engulf ever-increasing parts of the world. Whether or not the Cold War political philosophy of this nation was indeed correct or valid is beyond the scope of this book. However, we can determine to some extent whether the era of Cold War diplomacy brought about the rise of an unmanageable military-industrial complex. The question is not new.

FDR Strikes Out

Back in the '30s President Roosevelt himself raised the specter of a mammoth improper military influence in the domestic economy. On the eve of a Senate investigation of the munitions industry, for example, he said very plainly that the arms race was a "grave menace ... due in no small measure to the uncontrolled activities of the manufacturers and merchants of the engines of destruction and it must be met by the concerted actions of the people of all nations." FDR even had a campaign pledge in 1932 to "take profits out of war."

Eisenhower Bids Farewell to the Nation

During his eight years in office, the former five-star general of the Second World War experienced firsthand what kind of duress could be brought against him and the other policy makers by the munitions manufacturers. This was the time when Ike's Secretary of the Defense said, "What is good for General Motors is good for the country." Eisenhower decided to

Charles E. Wilson, Ike's Secretary of Defense (Hank Walker, Time-LIFE Picture Agency)

(Peter Curlis)

give the country a solemn and, as he saw it, necessary warning of what could happen if things weren't stopped. On January 17, 1961, he said:

This conjunction of an immense military establishment and a large arms industry is new in the American experience. The total influence— economic, political, even spiritual —is felt in every city, every State house, every office of the Federal government. We recognize the imperative need for this development. Yet we must not fail to comprehend its grave implications. Our toil, resources and livelihood are all involved; so is the very structure of our society.

In the councils of government, we must guard against the acquisition of unwarranted influence, whether sought or unsought, by the military industrial complex. The potential for

the disastrous rise of misplaced power exists and will persist. . . . Only an alert and knowledgeable citizenry can compel the proper meshing of the huge industrial and military machinery of defense with our peaceful methods and goal, so that security and liberty may prosper together.

Military Expenditures

There is no doubt that at the time Eisenhower was speaking expenditures for defense (and offense) were increasing. This can be easily seen in Figure XIII-1. The big jumps were during the Korean War and the War in Indochina. However, unlike what happened after the Revolutionary War, the War of 1812, the Civil War, and World War I, we did not reduce our military expendi-

tures to prewar levels immediately at the end of World War II. Today, although the estimates vary, we have a military budget in the United States that may account for 10 percent of total output. The Pentagon, center of all government defense activities, is in itself a small country. In fact, it has been called the largest planned economy outside the Soviet Union. Almost 10 percent of all assets in the United States belong to the Pentagon. It owns, for example, around 40 million acres of land, and it employs, directly or indirectly, over 4 million workers. Its budget is only 25 percent less than the entire gross national product of Great Britain! The Defense Department is, in fact, richer than just about any small nation in the world.

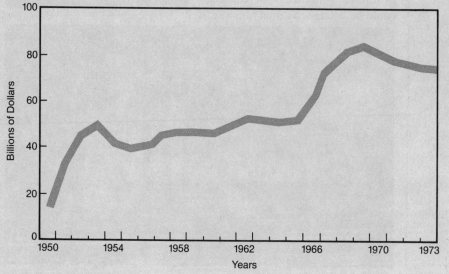

FIGURE XIII-1

NATIONAL DEFENSE SPENDING IN THE UNITED STATES

National defense spending in the United States peaked out in 1967 and fell slowly but steadily from then until 1973. (*Source:* Office of Management and Budget.)

229

ISSUE XIII   DID THE COLD WAR FOSTER A MILITARY-INDUSTRIAL COMPLEX?

The Military and Economic Activity

Although it is not clear that military spending is necessary for full employment, the military is involved in numerous aspects of economic activity in the United States. In fact, at the height of the war in Indochina in 1968, almost 10 percent of our entire labor force was employed in defense-related work. The spending of the military machine is, furthermore, highly concentrated. In 1967 a Defense Department study found that 72 employment areas depended on war output for about 12 percent of their employment; 80 percent of these employment areas were small communities with labor forces numbering less than 50,000. The impact of any cutback on military spending to these selected communities can obviously be very detrimental. It is not surprising, then, that Congressmen whose constituents will be affected lobby vigorously against any cutback in specific spending by the armed services.

When we look at defense employment, it is obvious that it is concentrated among a very specially skilled set of people who are defense oriented, just like the companies they work for. Scientists in specialized companies often have an extremely hard time finding alternative employment if and when the military decides to cut back on spending. Just look

(Black Star)

at what happened to the aerospace industry when the government started cutting back in 1969. Lockheed almost went under, and Boeing's Seattle employment fell from over 100,000 to less than 30,000 in less than two years.

Military business is big business. The existence of a military-industrial complex seems almost obvious. In fact, if one looks at the workings of a military-industrial firm, the abuses to which the taxpayer is subjected are indeed disconcerting.

The Military-Industrial Firm

One of the most outspoken students of Pentagon capitalism, Dr. Seymour Melman, has presented several propositions concerning military-industrial firms:

Proposition One: The military-industrial firm is not autonomous.

Proposition Two: The military-industrial firm is controlled by the state management.

Proposition Three: The military-industrial firm does not minimize costs.

Proposition Four: The military-industrial firm is not a profit-maximizing entity.

Proposition Five: The military-industrial firms as a group lack flexibility for conversion to civilian work.

Professor Melman's stinging indictment of business practices in defense industries seems to be borne out somewhat by many of the scandals that have so afflicted defense contractors in recent years. We can't say that we weren't warned. President Eisenhower cautioned the nation to beware of the military-industrial complex in his famous farewell address to the nation. In 1961 Eisenhower was thinking of a fairly informal group of high military officers, defense-oriented firms, and Congressmen who would be bound together by an ideology of continual expansion of the military machine. If one looks at the way prime government contracting firms have been able to operate in past years, some argument might be made in support of the idea of a "complex."

Approximately 22,000 firms are deemed prime contractors with the Department of Defense. These firms in turn subcontract much of their work to smaller enterprises. When all the contractors and subcontractors are added up, there are perhaps 100,000 firms directly or indirectly engaged in supplying the Department of Defense with whatever it wants. There are, however, a few very large firms which supply most of the manufactured goods to the Pentagon. The hundred largest prime contractors supply almost 70 percent of manufactured goods to the Department of Defense. Many of these firms actually employ government-owned capital, such as land, buildings, furniture, office machines, and material.

Military Procurement

Though there has been much recent criticism of the way defense contractors manage their firms, we might want to look at some of the incentives they have for *not* managing these firms correctly.

Headed by Senator William Proxmire of Wisconsin, the Joint Economic Committee of the Congress of the United States looked into the economics of military procurement and made a public report in May of 1969. Essentially, the report was a stinging criticism of the problem of "uncontrolled costs." It was attributed to an unmanaged, unshapen military procurement policy. The Joint Economic Committee stated that a set of practices and circumstances exist in the Department of Defense which leads to: (a) economic inefficiency and waste, (b) a subsidy to contractors, and (c) an inflated defense budget.

The circumstances in the Department of Defense which led to these three undesirable results had to do with the following practices:

1. Low competition and high concentration among prime defense contractors.
2. Allowing contractors to use government-owned property.
3. Using progress payments to reimburse contractors for up to 90 percent of incurred costs on a pay-as-you-go basis, even if these costs are greatly in excess of original estimates.
4. No uniform accounting standards.
5. Voluminous change orders and contractors' claims.
6. The absence of on-going reports to Congress.
7. No incentive contracting.

(Roger LeRoy Miller, Inc.)

231

ISSUE XIII   DID THE COLD WAR FOSTER A MILITARY-INDUSTRIAL COMPLEX?

Some of the results of careless military procurement have indeed been incredible. The original cost estimates of the F-111 jet fighter turned out to be one-third of the actual cost per plane. The cost overruns on the infamous Lockheed C5A jet transport are on the order of $2 billion.

A Symbiotic Relationship

The relationship between prime defense contractors and the Pentagon is indeed close and seems to be getting closer all the time. Congress finally has taken heed of certain practices within industries that lead to some dubious actions by Pentagon officials. Not only does the Pentagon support a large sector of our economy through defense contracts, it supplies a large number of key executives to large defense-contracting firms. Senator William Proxmire has criticized the "incestuous hiring" that industry engages in among retired Army officers and high Pentagon officials.

In 1959 a survey was made by Congress. It brought to light that almost 800 retired officers of the rank of colonel, Navy captain, and higher were employed by the largest 100 defense contractors. In 1969 the Defense Department made a similar survey which showed that the number of former top military men working in defense industry firms was over 2000. In 1969 Lockheed Aircraft had

210; the Boeing Company 169; McDonald-Douglas Corporation 141; General Dynamics Corporation 113; and North American Rockwell Corporation 104. You can imagine that something less than hard-nosed business rules would be used in dealings among retired generals and current generals running the Defense Department. Moreover, you can expect that officers looking forward to a cushy retirement job might act differently toward prospective employers than if there were no chance of getting such a job after retirement.

The military establishment also has a powerful political arm. The Department of Defense employs almost 350 lobbyists on Capitol Hill; it maintains some 2850 public relations men in the United States and foreign countries.

The close relationship between the Pentagon and defense contractors has led one staunch critic, Professor John Kenneth Galbraith, to hypothesize the following:

Where a corporation does all or nearly all of its business with the Department of Defense; uses much plant owned by the government; gets its working capital in the form of progress payments from the government; does not need to worry about competitors for it is the sole source of supply; accepts extensive guidance from the Pentagon on its management; is subject to detailed rules as to its accounting; and is extensively staffed by former service personnel, only the remarkable flexibility of the English language allows us to call it private enterprise. Yet this is not an exceptional case, but a common one. We have an amiable arrangement by which the defense firms, through part of the public bureaucracy, are largely exempt from its political and other constraints.*

The Trends

That there is a large defense establishment is not really subject to debate. All one need do is look at how many tax dollars go to the Pentagon. However, the trend seems to be, if not downward, at least not upward. In other words, the percentage of the U.S. federal budget going to defense has actually declined slightly in the last few years. Whether or not we can establish this as a long-term trend is another matter. Moreover, in no way could we answer the question in this issue of whether a military-industrial complex actually has prevented us from achieving an enduring world peace.

One can note that by using economic theory we would predict that if unusually large profits could be obtained by those supplying Defense Department needs, then there would be an

*John Kenneth Galbraith, *The Military Budget and National Economic Priorities*, Part 1. Washington, D.C.: U.S. Government Printing Office, 1969, pp. 5–6.

economic incentive for these firms to foster an atmosphere in which hot and cold wars were continuously fought, so that the demand for their products would stabilize or increase. And if they could make higher profits doing defense work than other work, they would be better off.

However, as in all competitive systems, there would be countervailing forces, for those dollars which are spent on defense cannot be spent on improved health conditions, alleviation of poverty, improvement in the environment, increases in higher education spending, and so on. All of those who would benefit by the expenditure of defense dollars elsewhere in the economy would have an incentive to counter the influence that the military-industrial complex has on our foreign policy. At this point, a prediction of which countervailing force will prevail would seem premature.

Questions for Thought and Discussion

1. Do you think that in this issue we have proven that a military-industrial complex exists? Why or why not?
2. Do you think the Defense Department is run like a business?
3. John Kenneth Galbraith has suggested the nationalization of defense firms which do a large percentage of their business with the government. Do you think this would cause an improvement in their efficiency? Why or why not?
4. Look at a current *Economic Report of the President*. Has the percentage in the total federal budget going to military endeavors increased or decreased in the last two years?

Other Ways of Running an Economy

14

THE ECONOMIC SYSTEM with which you and I are most familiar is a modified form of capitalism. Capitalism can be defined as an economic system in which individuals privately own productive resources and possess the right to use these resources in whatever manner they choose, subject to certain legal restriction. Now, capitalism has nothing to do with capital in the way we have used the word throughout the book. We have referred to money capital and to physical capital such as machines, land, and natural resources. Capitalism is definitely not only an economic system in which there is physical capital, or in which machines are used to produce goods, because obviously *every* economic system, regardless of its label, has some sort of capital, if only the ground on which individuals work.

The United States has always been a capitalist economy, even though the trend since the Great Depression has been toward more government control. There are, to be sure, other systems than the one we are familiar with in the United States. For example, in the third chapter we studied another economic system called feudalism. And among current alternative systems, under the broad heading of **socialism,** to be explained below, there is state socialism, guild socialism, fabian socialism, and utopian socialism. There is also fascism and communism, anarchism, and a host of variants on these systems.

LOOKING AT THE SPECTRUM OF SYSTEMS

One possible way of comparing alternative economic systems is to look at them according to how decentralized their economic decision-making processes are. We can see in Figure 14–1 that on the extreme right-hand side is pure free

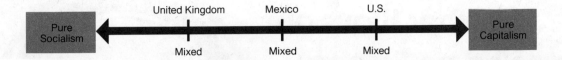

FIGURE 14-1   SCALE OF DECENTRALIZATION

On the extreme right-hand side of the diagram we find pure capitalism, which no country
follows. On the extreme left-hand side is pure socialism, which again no country follows. In the
middle are all of the mixed economies in the world. The United Kingdom, Mexico, and the
United States are shown, with the United States being closer to capitalism, of course, than any
of the others.

enterprise capitalism, where all economic decisions are made by individuals without government intervention. On the extreme left-hand side of the scale we will put pure command socialism, where most economic decisions are made by some central authority. Somewhere in between would be the mixed economic systems such as we have in the United States and in the United Kingdom. The closer we go to a pure capitalist system, the less political centralization there is, and vice versa. Some economists like to distinguish economies according to whether or not they are planned; that is, whether or not the economy is a (political) *command* economy or a decentralized economy.

We've been talking about economic systems without really defining them, and actually without finding out what an economic system is all about.

WHAT IS AN ECONOMIC SYSTEM?

We might want to define an economic system as the institutions which have evolved and are accepted as the means of utilizing national resources and satisfying human wants. Thus, an economic system will consist of all the ways a particular nation uses its resources to provide whatever its citizens desire. The institutions referred to here are principally the laws of a nation, but they may also include the habits, ethics, and customs of the citizens of that nation.

It should be obvious that all economic systems are man-made; none of them is god-given or brought from the stars. All economic institutions

are just what human beings have made them. There are, for example, continual modifications of laws and the other institutions that make up the economic system. All of these modifications are man-made; the judges, workers, government officials, consumers, and legislators are the ones who change, destroy, create, renovate, and resuscitate economic institutions. All of the institutions that make up our system or, for that matter, any other system are quite flexible. They may be modified by one group of people or another and, in fact, this is constantly happening. After all, in the Middle Ages we had a feudal system. In the sixteenth and seventeenth centuries mercantilism was the dominant system. After mercantilism came laissez faire or capitalism. Institutional change may take time, but it is occurring all of the time. The proof is in our history of constant change.

Now that we know what an economic system is, let's go into the origins of the principal alternative system to the one we have in the United States; that is, socialism.

THE ORIGIN OF SOCIALISM

Now, of course, socialist ideas have been around for a long time, but Karl Marx, perhaps more than anyone else in the history of economic thought, is responsible for the proliferation and importance of socialism as we know it today. In a socialist system, the government owns the major productive resources, such as land and capital goods. Individuals can generally own consumer goods and consumer durables, like cars and radios, but they are not allowed to own factories, machines, and other things that are used to produce what society wants. There are other aspects of socialism which we will get into after examining Marx's economic theories.

MARXIAN ECONOMICS

One of the key analyses offered by Marx in his economic works was his theory of the exploitation of laborers by capitalists. Marx came up with the notion of surplus value. In his theory, he pointed out that workers spend part of every working day covering the costs of maintaining themselves and their families. These are, in fact, their wages. The rest of the day it appears that they work without payment, creating for the capitalist some sort of surplus value, a source of wealth and profit for the capitalist class. In other words, in Marx's world the value of any good or service is directly proportional to the amount of labor used to make it. That means that the worker will work all day to make, say, $50 worth of shoes, but he will only be paid, say, $30. The difference is surplus value, and accrues to the capitalist. It is this small group of lucky capitalists—that is, those who happen to own capital—who are able to garner this surplus. The reason the workers will not get more is because they supposedly only "require" wages which allow them to subsist. And the reason this is possible is because of an ever-increasing **reserve army of unemployed.** So long as a subsistence-level wage is paid them they will reproduce and capitalists will continue to exploit them.

Economic Crises

In Marx's world, capitalists strive continually to accumulate capital, and this creates many of the contradictions capitalism develops. As more and more things were produced and economic development continued, however, the reserve army of the unemployed would become depleted. Wage

rates would have to rise. But capitalists would seek to increase their profits by introducing more sophisticated production equipment and techniques. Eventually, however, capitalists would no longer be able to sell their increased output. Unemployment would result, thus reducing purchasing power. This would lead to a recession and depression. Marx saw continuous cycles of recessions and depressions in the capitalist economy, but these were different from the ones we've talked about in this book.

Business Cycles

Marx's theory of the business cycle is one of explosion and collapse of capitalism where there is an eventual revolution of the workers' class. He predicted that the long-run tendency would be for the rate of profit to fall. Industrial power would become increasingly concentrated in fewer and fewer monopolistic firms. Wealth also would become concentrated in the hands of fewer and fewer capitalists. Laborers would become more and more exploited as production became more and more capital intensive. Eventually, the workers of the world would unite and revolt. The whole system would be overthrown, and a more rational socialist economy would prevail:

The revolt of a working class, a class always increasing in numbers and discipline, united, organized by the very mechanism of the process of capitalist production itself. Centralization of the means of production and socialization of labor at last reach a point where they become incompatible with their capitalist integument. This integument is burst asunder. The knell of capitalist private property sounds. The expropriators are expropriated.*

Marx envisioned the fall of capitalism leading to the rise of socialism and eventually to the world of ideal communism. In the worlds of socialism and communism, Marx foresaw a final state where

*Das Kapital, Volume 1, p. 763, Moscow: Foreign Language Publishing House, 1961.

the relations of production and distribution would be "from each according to his ability, to each according to his needs." In fact, in the ideal communist world that Marx predicted would eventually emerge, there would be little or no need for government. Everything would take care of itself, for man's basic human nature would have been changed because the relations of production and distribution would no longer create class conflict and alienation would not occur. We will find out in the next issue what one economist has to say about human nature actually being changed in Mainland China today. But more on that subject later.

LENIN TAKES HOLD OF THE TORCH

The most influential disciple of Marx's thought has to be Nikolai Lenin, who was able to lead the Russian Revolution in the name of Marxism. Lenin spent much of his time analyzing imperialism, which he called the highest stage of capitalism. In this stage capitalist economies were completely dominated by monopolies. This, after all, was what Marx had predicted. Lenin considered monopolies as any industries which were dominated by cartels, trusts, or a very few firms. Lenin used the experience of Germany as his example of what could happen with monopoly capitalism.

According to Lenin, as all the different capitalist countries in the world became more and more monopolized, their various governments would fight to gain access to protected markets within each other's boundaries. They would try to partition the world markets through international cartels, but competition would always rear its ugly head. National conflicts and wars would be the inevitable result. Lenin stated that

the epic of the newest capitalism shows us that certain relations are being established between capitalist combines, based on the economic division of the world:

while parallel with this and in connection with it, certain relations are being established between political alliances, between states, on the basis of the territorial division of the world, of the struggle for colonies, of the "struggle for economic territory."*

Lenin was apparently as good a politician as he was a writer, for with the help of Leon Trotsky Lenin's Bolsheviks obtained power in 1917 from the moderate regime that had recently overthrown the monarchy. What followed has been called "ten days that shook the world." Trotsky trained and organized an army and the revolutionary forces took over town after town. A civil war ensued between the White and Red armies. In the end, you know who won.

The world expected a collapse of the new revolutionary government, but communism was here to stay and is still with us. Lenin didn't immediately get rid of all capitalist institutions in Russia. He set up his New Economic Policy in the twenties. After his death **five year plans** were started for increasing manufacturing and collectivizing the agricultural sector. When Lenin died, Stalin won the struggle for succession and the age of Stalinism was upon the Russian landscape; decades later came Khrushchev and an era of more freedom, both economic and political. The Soviet economy of today can be called socialistic, although each socialist country in the world has its own brand; they all have as their foundation Marx's doctrines. But Marx spent much of his time writing about the faults of capitalism rather than laying out a blueprint for what a socialist economy should look like.

RUSSIA TODAY

In the Soviet Union the state owns almost all the factors of production. Workers are paid wages and they do have a considerable choice in what they

*Lenin, *Imperialism: The Highest Stage of Capitalism*, London; Lawrence and Wishart, 1939, p. 69.

In Uzbekistan, USSR, workmen shove raw cotton from a "cotton pyramid" into pipes which suck it away to the barns. (Paolo Koch, Rapho Guillumette)

spend their lives doing. However, citizens do not have as unlimited a choice in movement around the country as we do in the United States. In other words, a citizen has to ask permission to obtain a job in another region or in another industry. However, he usually can move to a place where he thinks he could make higher wages: The current system now tries to attract workers to different locations by wages.

In the past, physical quotas were set for factories, but this caused too many problems: Factories would put out numerous items, all of poor quality, just to meet the physical quota. The typical Soviet factory is now generally evaluated according to some overall concept of profitability. It is not yet to the stage where profitability is measured in the same way a factory in the United States measures it, but it may be getting there. Within the factory itself, the managers obtain special benefits that workers are not allowed to have, such as travel expenses, perhaps a car, and other privileges in addition to a much better than average paycheck. There is a continuous hierarchy within an individual firm and within economic life itself. For this is a centralized system, although there seems to be a change toward more and more decentralization. Right now there are regional economic councils, above them a council of ministers, and, additionally, planners who decide what industries should do what.

Resource Allocation

The decision as to how many of the economic resources available should be used in producing what consumers want as opposed to producing what we'll call **capital equipment**—machines and the like—is a decision generally made by the planners. After the Russian Revolution there was a distinct drop in the percentage of production going to satisfy consumer wants. That is one of the reasons Russia grew so rapidly: It spent a large

amount of its resources in capital formation so that it would have a higher level of living in the future. Remember that in the United States, resources flow to where their relative rates of return are highest. If the highest rate of return is in making consumer durables, then resources will flow into making consumer durables. The decision as to how much should be saved and invested is made more or less by individuals. That is, the amount of saving that the economy actually engages in is determined basically by how much each individual decides he wants to put away and not consume today. Such is not the case in the Soviet Union.

And until recently very little market information was used to determine which consumer goods should be produced. The obvious resulted: Lots of things were in short supply and lots of other things were never bought at all. Today, however, central planners realize that when consumer goods are not bought production should be slowed down. And when goods are bought rapidly production should be increased. Russian planners are even starting to engage in marketing surveys to see what consumers really want.

Other Variations

While Russia may represent the largest testing ground for the socialist-communist type of economics, there are variations which seem to have worked just as well. Without going into them, we can mention the Yugoslavian experiment in decentralized socialism. It is sometimes called Titoism after the party leader, Josip Brozovitch Tito. For a while Czechoslovakia tried its own experiment in decentralization but, as we all know, Soviet intervention prevented the completion of that experiment. Poland and Hungary have their own forms of socialism which are not too different from that of the Soviet Union. While one does not get a full panoply of economic systems within communist Eastern Bloc countries, there are still variations to be studied.

MILDER FORMS OF SOCIALISM

There are certainly much milder forms of socialism than that of the Soviet Union. Britain has its own type of socialism, which seems, however, to vacillate between trends toward increased government ownership of the means of production and increased private ownership. For example, the steel mills have been nationalized and denationalized several times. Whenever the Labour Party

Red Square, Moscow. (R. J. Fleming, Black Star)

gets into power it tries to extend the welfare services of the state and redistribute income and wealth by progressive taxation. When the Labour Party came into power after World War II it did an effective job of nationalizing the railroads plus the coal and power industry. Today, however, there is considerable debate within the Labour Party itself as to the advisability of increasing socialist economic institutions within England. The same kinds of debates are raging in other countries which have experimented widely with socialism. These include Australia, Norway, Sweden,

Denmark, and New Zealand. One might say that as the more socialist countries tend toward capitalism, the more capitalist countries tend toward socialism. The result is what we will call a **mixed economy:** neither socialism nor capitalism but a mixture of both.

The one country that seems firmly embedded in a very particular socialist mode of economic control is China. Marx predicted that by the final stage of socialism, man's basic nature would change. Is there, then, a new man on the mainland? Let's see if we can find out.

Definitions of New Terms

SOCIALISM: an economic system in which the chief means of production are owned by the state.

RESERVE ARMY OF THE UNEMPLOYED: in Marxian terminology, the mass of unemployed workers, the size of which will grow as workers become more and more exploited by the capitalist classes.

FIVE YEAR PLANS: economic plans set up by the central government in various countries. The first five year plan was devised in Russia after Lenin's death.

CAPITAL EQUIPMENT: machines and equipment that businessmen use to produce goods and services for consumption. To be contrasted with consumer durables, which consumers use over a period of time, such as TV sets and stereos.

MIXED ECONOMY: an economy in which some of the tenets of socialism and some of the tenets of capitalism coexist. In other words, a situation in which there is both free enterprise and government intervention in the marketplace.

Chapter Summary

1. Capitalism is an economic system in which individuals privately own productive resources and possess the right to use them in whatever manner they choose.
2. Socialism is broadly defined as a system under which the government owns at least the major means of production. There is more political command of economic decisions in a socialist system than in a capitalist system.
3. An economic system is man-made and consists of all the economic institutions in it. These institutions may change and are not immutable.
4. Karl Marx is considered the father of communism and socialism. However, much of his writing was a critique of capitalism rather than a blueprint for a socialist society.

5. Marx felt that there would be an ever-increasing reserve army of unemployed which would lead, among other things, to economic crises and a revolt of the proletarian class against the bourgeoisie.

6. Lenin spent much of his time analyzing imperialism, which he called the highest stage of capitalism. He instituted a New Economic Policy in the 1920s. After his death five year plans were initiated.

7. In Russia today, however, a number of market incentive systems are in use, although political decision making for economic activity is still highly centralized.

8. Many of the economies of the world today are often called mixed because they involve various mixtures of free enterprise and government intervention.

Questions for Thought and Discussion

1. Which economic system do you think is more conducive to economic growth?

2. If you could change the current American economic arrangement, what would you do? How would you solve the problem of allocation and distribution of output?

3. Why did Marx's prediction that there would be an ever-increasing reserve army of unemployed not come true?

4. Some observers maintain that Russian economic policies are not Marxian. Why would this be true or not true?

THE BETTMANN ARCHIVE, INC.

THE PROPHET OF CAPITALIST DOOM

Karl Heinrich Marx (1818–1883)
Philosophical Economist and Social Critic

"WORKERS OF the world, unite!" So ended the *Communist Manifesto* written in December 1847 by a man who must rank as one of the most important individuals who has ever lived. Why? Simply because his thoughts and ideas have helped shape the policies of numerous nations, affecting the lives of millions upon millions of people. From Marx we have Marxism, as well as a panoply of encyclopedic works, ranging over philosophy, economics, politics, and sociology.

The prolific social critic started his existence on May 5, 1818, the son of Jewish parents in Trèves, Prussia. When he was barely six years old, his father, a new convert to Christianity, baptized his entire family as Protestants. An intellectual childhood awaited him. He studied at the Universities of Bonn and Berlin, where he was greatly influenced by the philosophical ideas of Georg W. F. Hegel. The Hegelian notion of *dialectic* was to permeate much of Marx's later writing. Dialectical reasoning basically involves analyzing phenomena in a "black and white manner." That is to say, everything can be broken down into thesis and antithesis, with an eventual merging called a synthesis. History presumably would record the progress from lower to higher manifestations of this dialectic principle. Marx's philosophy of history finally became known as dialectical materialism: All change in history is a result of conflicting forces, these forces being basically economic or materialistic.

As a student he was brilliant. His doctorate was awarded him in 1841 at the University of Vienna before he had even reached his twenty-fourth birthday. The subject of his dissertation: Atomistic Philosophy of Democritus and Epicurus.

Marx wanted to become a teacher, but finding an academic position proved impossible. He therefore turned to his second choice, journalism. He became editor of *Rheinische Zeitung,* a paper that soon ran into censorship problems with the reactionary Prussian regime. He moved to Paris with his new wife, née Jenevonne Westphalen. There he became acquainted with his lifelong colleague and benefactor, Friedrich Engels. It was with Engels that he wrote the *Communist Manifesto,* which was prepared for the Communist League Convention that was to take place in London. In the *Manifesto* Marx spread out very clearly his theory of the process of social change: "The history of all society that has existed hitherto is the history of class struggles." He meant, of course, economic classes, whose functions were determined by their relationship to the mode of production. At that time he spoke of two broad classes fighting against each other, the bourgeoisie (property owners) and the proletariat (propertyless workers). Marx attempted to show in all of his analyses of capitalism that the class struggle reflected the contradictory nature of the productive system itself. He saw "the state [as] nothing but the organized collective power of the possessing classes." Hence, it was an agency controlled by the bourgeoisie to advance that class's own interest. The state was for Marx an agency of oppression for the masses comprising the proletariat.

Marx never seemed able to make a living for himself. Fortunately Engels' father was a rich businessman who owned factories in England and Germany. It was to London that Marx moved in 1849 after being harassed by police and expelled from three countries. His survival in London was certainly not sumptuous. Marx was paid $5 to $10 for each article accepted by the *New York Tribune* plus benevolent handouts from Engels. In London Marx formulated the finishing touches on his economic thinking to go into the monumental *Das Kapital.* This was the period of the Industrial Revolution. Marx could see while it had increased the average income of the population, it had also caused unacceptable amounts of misery—crowded slums, unemployment, and the instability of the business cycle. Marx came to the conclusion in *Das Kapital* that no reforms could save a system which could create such horrendous problems for society. The working class, disciplined by the routines of industry, would become well organized and would expropriate the expropriators in the name of the people. Hence, it was inevitable that the workers of the world would unite in the last phase of a dialectical struggle between two opposing economic classes.

Marx died on March 14, 1883, fifteen months after the death of his wife. He died, by the way, before the completion of volumes II and III of *Das Kapital.* His long-time benefactor, Friedrich Engels, finished the last two volumes.

During his lifetime Marx was never a great leader of any movement. His own followers were only a minority among the members of the one important direct political undertaking—leadership of the International Working Men's Association, the First International. Marx never made much contact with the British labor movement; in France and Germany he was overshadowed by Proudhon and Lassalle, respectively. Only many years later was the political and economic heritage left by Marx fully appreciated by the rest of the world. Even many non-Marxist economists have been forced to turn their attention to such critical economic and social issues as entrenched economic power, vested interests, and the possibility of underspending and, hence, permanent unemployment.

ISSUE XIV

IS THERE A NEW MAN ON THE MAINLAND?

China Today

The System under Mao

One of the economic systems in the world that is most different from ours in the United States is in Mainland China. Since Mao took power, the country has become a model of collectivist economic planning and operation. The differences between that system and ours are so significant that it is worthwhile to describe them in some detail.

Maoist Economics

The main features of the Chinese economy include public ownership of all industries, agricultural cooperatives, communes, and massive central planning. The state makes all the decisions regarding investment versus consumption, how labor should be supplied to different sectors of the economy, and the prices of various goods and services. In the Chinese economy, there is always full employment. Although in theory workers have complete freedom to change jobs, there are internal police regulations and particular quota systems which prevent complete job mobility. For example, university students are generally assigned their future positions while still in school.

The Planning Operation

After taking power in 1949, the communists under Mao Tse-tung set out to devise plans which would help their devastated country back onto the road to economic well-being. The first Five Year Plan was instituted in 1952. It stressed investment in heavy industry, retention of small-scale and handicraft industries, and a land reform in which land was taken from wealthy Chinese and given to poor peasants. Farms were also collectively organized. In 1958 the second plan was put into effect. It started out with the so-called "Great Leap Forward," of which everybody in the world was aware at that time.

Involved in that plan was the desire by Chinese economic policy makers to increase individual output by over 25 percent per year. Heavy industry was to develop even more rapidly than it had in the last five years. More

Behind these women at the embroidery research center at Soochow is a drawing of the item they are embroidering. The drawing represents Chinese farmgirls during the liberation wars before 1948. (Paolo Koch, Rapho Guillumette)

Farmers cleaning string beans at a commune outside Shanghai. Behind them is a quotation of Chairman Mao to stimulate their work. (Paolo Koch, Rapho Guillumette)

labor would be used in order to reduce underemployment of the labor force. Instead of directing all heavy industrial plants from the central government, there was to be some decentralization in the sense that local managers would have more control over what their plants bought and sold and what production methods would be used.

From the very beginning, there were unexpected and tragic consequences of the Great Leap Forward. The program was, in a word, too ambitious. Many goods were being produced that were not really wanted in the economy, and many large-scale irrigation

projects that were undertaken were poorly planned and managed. The result was often complete fiasco. Steel was being made by many unskilled workers in unsafe, often quite primitive production environments. Many times steel produced was so poor in quality that it could not be used.

A food shortage began to develop. Many workers had been transferred from agriculture to the city to help in the great industrial expansion program. The consequence was too little production of food. Finally, the much needed New Economic Policy was instituted.

The New Policy

The leaders of China finally realized that agriculture had to be built up before rapid industrialization could be attempted. Remember, we pointed out in Chapter 9 that the only way that urbanization can occur is for productivity in the agricultural sector to rise fast enough to allow those who stay in agriculture to feed those who go to the city. The Chinese leaders finally realized this. Agriculture then became the foundation of the entire economy.

One of the most interesting aspects of the agricultural program in China is a system of communal farming. Here work teams are essentially self-governing with the workers being paid work points which can provide a daily income comparable to less than $1 today in American purchasing power. In a communal system, the workers live together on the same site where they work. However, not all the communes worked out well, and we found fewer and fewer communes being started even after the Great Leap Forward. Today the vast majority of farms are merely collective rather than communal.

Growth in the Chinese Economy

The most recent estimates we have for real economic growth in the Chinese economy are indeed surprising. They show that Mainland China has grown much faster than we originally thought. For example, the average annual growth rate from 1952 to 1957 was a whopping 19.2 percent per year. If we look at Figure XIV-1 we see that the index of gross output value of Chinese industrial production started at 100 in 1952 and ended up at almost 1000 in 1971. The annual growth rate for this period is about 12 percent per annum.* Some economists who have visited Mainland China contend that the reason this tremendous rate of economic growth was possible was that there is a "new man" on the Mainland, who is different from the worker in the United States. In the following section we discuss the attributes of this new man as outlined by Professor John W. Gurley.**

The New Man

It appears that Maoists believe that the principal aim of a nation should be not only to raise the level of material welfare of the population, but also to develop the full human being. That is, each person in the economy

*Thomas G. Rawski, "Chinese Industrial Production, 1952 to 1971," *The Review of Economics and Statistics,* Vol. LV, No. 2, May 1973, p. 169.

**John W. Gurley, "The New Man in the New China," *The Center Magazine,* Vol. 3, No. 3, May 1970, pp. 25–33.

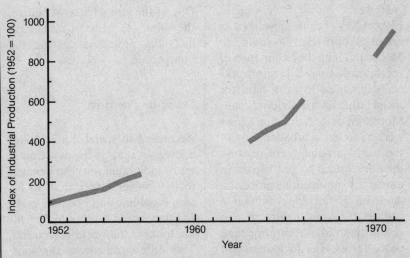

FIGURE XIV-1   CHINESE INDUSTRIAL PRODUCTION

Starting off with an index of 100 for the year 1952, Chinese industrial production has grown at an average annual rate of about 12 percent a year. (Data for certain years were not available.) (*Source:* T. G. Rawski, "Chinese Industrial Production, 1952–1971," *The Review of Economics and Statistics,* Vol. LV, No. 2, May 1973, p. 169, Table 1.)

should develop his myriad creative powers, and all this should be done on an egalitarian basis. Presumably, Maoists believe that rapid economic development will not occur unless everyone rises up.

We have often referred to investment in human capital and, in fact, this notion also exists in Maoist China, but with a little different emphasis. Instead of merely investing in human capital as a necessary means of raising productivity, the investment in China involves the making of the communist man—that is, a transformation of his ideas. In other words, ideology is a large part of his educational process. This may, in fact, be true in the United States, but certainly it is not so

obvious to an outsider or to a person obtaining the investment in his own human capital.

There is a tendency toward nonspecialization in Maoist China which is just the opposite of what has happened in the United States. Remember that Adam Smith said specialization was determined by the extent of the market. In China, even though the market is huge, there is a tendency to *de*specialize workers so that there is no upper echelon of leaders, experts, authorities, and technicians. It appears, then, that Maoists are willing to pursue the goal of transforming workers into the communist man even if it means some slowdown in short-run economic growth.

However, as we have seen in Figure XIV-1, the slowdown is not at all apparent. According to Maoist thought, the elimination of specialization will increase workers' willingness to work hard for social rather than individual goals. Moreover, despecialization allows workers to get a broader view of the world around them because they are forced to participate in numerous production processes. And this is not done without a cost to the worker himself, for according to Mao, "Unprincipled peace [gives rise] to a decadent philistine attitude. . . ." Progress, then, must be made by struggling with the world around oneself.

One of the struggles is, of course, the same old Marxist class conflict: the proletariat versus the bourgeoisie.

Serving the Proletariat

According to social thinkers and decision makers in the new China, every individual must be devoted to the masses rather than to his own economic and personal ends. In other words, he should be willing to serve the world proletariat. This differs little from the standard Communist Party "workers of the world, unite." The worker will work hard for the community or the nation rather than for his own selfish goals. To this end, Maoists deemphasize all material incentives because they are the very manifestation of the decadent bourgeois capitalist society which Maoists do not want in the new China. Hence, workers must be disciplined and they must become selfless. There must be unity. This is the aim of all of the doctrinaire teachings which are so evident throughout Mainland China.

Going to the Countryside

In keeping with the view that man should not specialize, Maoists

Mass demonstrations of students in Tien An Men square. Although they come in large numbers, it seems that these demonstrations are organized so often that there is visible lack of enthusiasm. (Paolo Koch, Rapho Guillumette)

have tried to eliminate the distinction between the city and the country. Consequently, most people who work in the city have to spend time out in the country engaged in agriculture. Each person thus becomes an all-around communist man or woman, not allowed to specialize in some specific type of career. And to avoid creating a hierarchy of bureaucrats and experts, much decision making is done by "the masses." This involves establishing new industries in rural areas even though the economic environment may not be most favorable in those areas. The growth of cities as cultural and industrial centers has been discouraged for some time now. This, of course, costs the new China in real output. But "So what," say the Maoists. "We are after the development of the communist man. And whatever development we have will be equitable, even if it is relatively inefficient."

What the New Man Has Done

We already noted the tremendous economic development in communist China in Figure XIV–1. More impressive than that, however, is the conclusion Professor Gurley made:

The basic overriding economic fact about China is that for 20 years she has fed, clothed, and housed everyone, has kept them healthy, and has educated most. Millions have not starved; sidewalks and streets have not been covered with multitudes of sleeping, begging, hungry, and illiterate human beings; millions are not disease ridden. To find such deplorable conditions one does not look to China these days but, rather, to India, Pakistan, and almost anywhere else in the underdeveloped world. These facts are so basic, so fundamentally important, that they completely dominate China's economic picture, even if one grants all of the erratic and irrational policies alleged by her numerous critics.*

*Gurley, *ibid.*, p. 31.

What is important, according to Gurley, is that communist China is engaged in a social and economic experiment in which there is an attempt to develop industrially without dehumanization. The Marxist-Leninist goal is that eventually a communist man will emerge in a classless society where every person works according to his ability and consumes according to his needs.

Is there a new man in communist China? According to Professor Gurley, yes. One expert's account on the subject is hardly enough to answer the question, but it does give us a beginning. The Maoists claim that within each man, numerous powers exist which can be released by proper ideological and economic planning. According to Gurley, "If [the Maoists] are right, the implications for economic development are so important that it would take blind men on this side of the Pacific to ignore them."

Time will tell.

Questions for Thought and Discussion

1. After reading this Issue, do you think there is a new man in China?
2. Is it possible to separate the social from the economic experiment in communist China?
3. Why do you think China isolated herself for so many years? Could this have been important for allowing the formation of the new man?

The Development of the Less Developed

TODAY THERE ARE almost four billion people in the world. Tonight half of these may go to bed either hungry or undernourished.

Today the U.S. population accounts for barely 6 percent of the world's total, yet Americans produce and spend almost one-third of the entire world income.

Today the problems of less-developed countries are as serious as ever before. The inequality in income among nations throughout the world is not narrowing. If anything, it is getting worse. The rich are getting richer and the poor are getting poorer relative to the rich. This is not to say that the less-developed countries in the world have experienced no economic growth. In fact, if we look at Table 15-1, we see that many countries have had growth rates which are greater than those in the United States and other fully developed countries. How, then, is it— you might be asking—that underdeveloped countries with relatively high growth rates are not getting developed? The answer will be discussed in the following issue when we revisit our old friend, the Reverend Malthus. In a sentence: In many of these countries, increases in output are being eaten up by increases in population.

THE PROBLEMS OF THE INFORMATION EXPLOSION

The less-developed countries of today are not as content with their economic lot as they have been in the past. One of the reasons is because information about how the inhabitants of rich countries live is now known in the remotest villages of the most backward nation. Everybody knows about the comforts of modern Western living. The relative poverty of the world's masses is not as accepted as it used to be, for they know that a better life exists elsewhere. That is the life that these people are striving for. What do they want? They want all the good things in life, such as better health conditions, better housing, and a more equal distribution of the wealth, perhaps starting with land reform.

And to be sure, citizens in underdeveloped countries are demanding that their governments do something about all of this. The governments in turn must rely on political and economic theories to determine which policies are most appropriate to obtain the desired ends. But before a useful theory can be obtained, the reasons why living standards differ throughout the world must be explained. That leads us to the different theories of growth: Why do some nations develop and others not?

SIMPLE GROWTH THEORIES

One of the earliest and most simplistic of the theories of growth concerns geographical location. This might also be called the north/south theory of economic development. Nations which are in the colder climates will be more developed than nations in the warmer climates. If one were

to pick a theory which had some predictive power today, the north/south theory works in some places. In the United States, the North is more developed than the South. (However, we have seen that this was not the case before the Civil War and might not be the case had the institution of slavery been *gradually* abolished.) If we look at Italy, the north is more developed than the south; if we look at France, the same is also true. This appears to be the case in many countries. It also appears *not* to be the case in England, Sweden, Norway, and Australia.

Moreover, if this theory had any relevance or validity, it should apply to the past also. It doesn't. Some of the first civilizations were in southern, hot regions of the world. Look at the Mayas in Central America and all of the great civilizations in the Mediterranean and the Near East. The Germans and the Saxons were way behind the development of the Greeks even though the Greeks endured a more torrid climate.

As an offshoot of this north/south theory, some economists have hypothesized that the geographical distribution of natural resources is important: Where the oil and ore deposits are, where the best soil is, where the most useful rainfall is, and so on. However, while this may have had some validity in the past when trade

TABLE 15–1

PER CAPITA GROWTH RATES AND INCOME

Here we show the per capita income in 1969 for selected countries and the average annual rate of growth of GNP per capita from 1960 to 1968. Notice that there is no correlation between income per capita and the growth rate. *(Source: Statistical Office of the United Nations.)*

COUNTRY	INCOME PER CAPITA (1965)	AVERAGE ANNUAL RATE OF GROWTH OF INCOME PER CAPITA (1960–1968)
U.S.	4664	3.7
Argentina	828	1.6
Brazil	337	1.1
Canada	2997	3.5
Dominican Republic	290	−0.6
France	2783	4.4
Greece	858	6.3
Iran	295	4.7
Italy	1548	4.3
Korea (South)	227	6.2
Uruguay	650	−0.9

Lagos, Nigeria. (Ken Heyman)

population in raising its standard of living is the most obvious. Moreover, the first great developers of the Egyptian, Greek, and Indian cultures, as well as of ancient China, were not very white, to say the least. Ethiopia developed to a relatively high degree without the help of many white faces. Race per se does not seem to be a very useful device for explaining why or predicting where prosperity will occur in the world economy.

MORE MODERN THEORIES

As can be expected, there are more modern and more sophisticated theories of development presented by today's economists. One of the most widely discussed concerns the need for balanced growth.

Balancing Industry with Agriculture

One of the characteristics of most developed countries is their high degree of industrialization. In general, nations with relatively high standards of living are more industrialized than countries with low standards of living. Some economists have taken this to mean that industrialization can be equated with economic development. The policy prescription is then obvious: So-called backward nations in which a large percentage of total resources are devoted to agricultural pursuits should attempt to obtain a more balanced growth; they should industrialize.

While the theory is fairly acceptable at first glance, it leads to some absurd results. We find that in many underdeveloped countries with steel factories and automobile plants the people are actually worse off because of this attempt at industrialization. The reason is not hard to find. Most underdeveloped countries currently do not have a comparative advantage in producing steel or automobiles. They can engage in such industrial activities only by a heavy subsidization of the industry itself and by massive restrictions on

was not as widespread as it is today, Japan, Denmark, and Israel demonstrate successful counterexamples of this theory.

THE RACE THEORY OF DEVELOPMENT

Even more simplistic and certainly less easily defended is the race theory of development. Prosperity, according to this theory, is a matter of race: The whiter the race, the more productive the economy. There are so many counterexamples to this theory that they cannot all be mentioned here. The incredible success of the Japanese competitive imports from other countries. For example, in India a steel mill may produce steel at two or three times the resource cost that would be required if the steel were imported. It seems quite apparent that the country is worse off, not better off, because of the steel mill. It may have the national prestige of owning a large, smoke-producing factory, but its citizens get less economic value out of their given resources than they would otherwise. This circumstance occurs throughout the entire underdeveloped world. Import restrictions abound, preventing the purchase of foreign, mostly cheaper, substitutes for the industrial products that the country itself produces in a usually subsidized environment. Sometimes the subsidization is not grossly obvious, but it usually exists in one form or another. In general, when an industry must be subsidized in order to exist the subsidy leads to a misallocation of resources and a lower economic welfare for the country as a whole. The owners in the subsidized industry and the workers with skills specific to that industry are obviously better off. But the consumer ends up paying a higher *total* cost for the domestically made goods he receives, and the total output of the nation remains less than it could be were the resources reallocated.

The Stages of Development

If we look at the development of modern nations, we find that they do go through three stages. First there is the agricultural stage when most of the population is involved in that endeavor. Then there is the manufacturing stage when much of the population becomes involved in the industrialized sector of the economy. And finally there is a shift toward services. That is exactly what is happening in the United States: The so-called tertiary or service sector of the economy is growing by leaps and bounds, whereas the manufacturing sector, in its percentage employment, is declining.

However, it is important to understand the need for early specialization in one's comparative

advantage. We have continuously referred to the doctrine of comparative advantage, and it is even more appropriate for the developing countries of the world. If trading is allowed among nations, a nation is best off if it produces what it has a comparative advantage at producing and imports the rest. This means that many underdeveloped countries should continue to specialize in agricultural production.

Agriculture Subsidized

There is a problem here, to be sure, and that involves the fact that the modern Western coun-

Brasília, Brazil. (Georg Gerster, Rapho Guillumette)

tries have continually subsidized their own agricultural sectors so as to partially eliminate the comparative advantage that underdeveloped countries might have in agricultural pursuits. If we lived in a world of no subsidization, we would probably see much less food being produced in the highly developed Western world and much more being produced in the underdeveloped nations of the rest of the world. They would swap food for manufactured goods and we would do the converse. It would appear, then, that one of the most detrimental effects of our entire economic policy on the Third World has been the continued subsidization of the American farmer. America, of course, is not alone; Germany, France, and England do exactly the same thing.

Nonetheless, even within the current institutional situation, it still can be said that a policy of balanced growth, or increased industrialization, may lead to more harm than good in the less developed countries of the world. Industrialization is generally only beneficial if it comes about naturally. That is, when the economic market conditions are such that the countries' entrepreneurs freely decide to build factories instead of increasing farm output, then industrialization will add to the prosperity of a nation.

PEOPLE AS RESOURCES

It is quite obvious that large amounts of natural resources are not by themselves sufficient to guarantee economic growth. Many Latin American countries, for example, are fantastically rich in natural resources, but they have not been overly successful in exploiting those resources through efficient economic activity. Natural resources must be converted to useful forms. Look at the United States. Before the colonists came over, the Indians had tremendous amounts of natural resources available to them. They were, however, not increasing their standard of living or experiencing any form of economic growth.

In order for natural resources to really have an effect on economic growth we have to include among them people. People must devise the methods by which other resources can be converted into usable forms. This is where the United States has been more fortunate than most other countries, particularly than those with similar natural resources. The founding fathers of our nation were a biased sample of the people on the earth at that time. Many of the "criminals" who were transported to the colonies were guilty of such crimes as religious heresy, going into debt, being poor, evading economic laws made by the government, and disagreement with government itself. Thus, we see that many of the people who came to the United States were those who either wanted to or were forced to escape regimentation in the Old World by a more structured society. These are just the types of people who would attempt to devise new methods to utilize the natural resources in America—and that they did.

We have also examined in this book another feature of the American people: their desire for investment in human capital—that is, for improving the productivity of the people themselves. This has been done by formal and informal schooling and training. Increases in human capital come about not only by going to college, as you are doing, but also by obtaining on-the-job training. In formal education alone, we can see from Figure 15–1 that the median years of education completed has been increasing since before the turn of the century.

It is not unusual, then, that many development economists have suggested that perhaps one road to economic prosperity lies in increased expenditures on education in underdeveloped nations. But this may not be enough if the expenditures are not wisely carried out. In fact, it is not uncommon for a large percentage of lucky young people in underdeveloped nations to study such things as political science and diplomacy in high schools and colleges while using government resources.

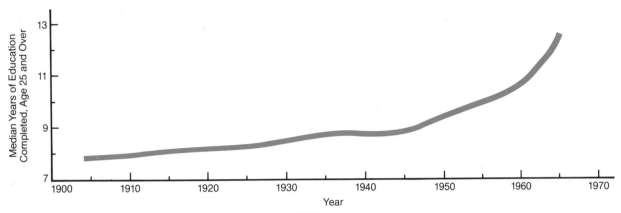

FIGURE 15–1 **MEDIAN YEARS OF EDUCATION COMPLETED**

In the United States at age 25 the median years of education completed in the population has risen from under eight years at the turn of the century to almost 12 years by the middle of 1965. (*Source:* Department of Commerce, Bureau of the Census, "Long-Term Economic Growth," p. 43.)

But certainly these nations could better use trained technicians, engineers, nutritionists, and the like, instead of a surfeit of would-be diplomats. As always, care must be taken when the government decides to adopt a program designed to expand a certain sector of an economy.

THE NEED FOR CAPITAL

Another theory of economic development concerns the needs of poorer countries for capital—machines, factories, raw inputs, and so on. If we look at more-developed countries, we find that indeed the capital stock per capita is much higher. And, as we shall see below, in most situations the larger the capital stock the higher the possible level of output. This country, as well as other developed ones, has, in fact, given away massive amounts of capital to those countries seeking economic development. In fact, if we include the Marshall Plan, we have given away more than $100 billion to the rest of the world. But lack of capital cannot be the only reason for underdevelopment in most of the world. After all, since

World War II immense sums have been made available to developing areas. To some extent, these funds have been well applied and have produced sound results. In other cases, though, this foreign aid has been applied to uneconomic purposes, or to good projects that have been poorly planned and executed. The results are not positive but negative. To efficiently spend large amounts of money capital and to wisely use large amounts of physical capital require organization and experience and a competence that is often lacking in administrators in other nations. If this is taken into account, it appears that large injections of capital into developing nations may cause more harm than good.

WHY IS CAPITAL SO IMPORTANT?

Capital is extremely important for growth not only in underdeveloped nations but in all nations. For capital accumulation is the only way to grow. This is true by the definition of capital. We define it as additions to our wealth which permit greater future production and consumption. The only way, then, to have an increased capital stock without outside help is to not consume today. That is, if we consume all of our income today, we add nothing to our wealth. We eat it all up. That means that in the future, our incomes cannot grow. What we find is that there is a trade-off between goods today and goods tomorrow—or, otherwise stated, between present consumption and future consumption. By decreasing the amount of present goods, we increase the amount of future goods. We have to sacrifice present consumption in order to have *more* future consumption. There is no way out of this, even for the richest nation on earth.

Now, each individual, of course, is faced with this very decision. He must make it with respect to how much he wants to save. After all, there are only two things you can do with your income: Spend it or save it. If an individual wants to have a lot of future consumption, he has to cut back on what he spends today. He therefore ends up saving more. If he puts this saving into, say, the stock market, the bond market, or a savings and loan association, later on he will be able to consume more than otherwise because in the interim he will have earned interest, the income on this type of personal investment.* For the economy as a whole, to decide whether there should be more present consumption or more future consumption is to decide whether there should be more movies and food consumed or more buildings and machines constructed. When you decide not to consume but to save part of your income, you will perhaps put it in a savings and loan association. That money will then be available to borrowers for housing. You might also invest your savings in a new company or in expansion of an old one. In this way, the money that you save ends up providing the money capital for businessmen so that they can construct or purchase physical capital—machines and equipment.

*A personal investment is merely a means of using savings. Investment in the economic sense of the term refers only to building new plants, etc., or generally increasing the capital stock.

SAVING DECISIONS

Saving decisions are based on lots of things. However, one key determinant is what we call a person's **personal discount rate.** If you just can't wait to consume all of the income you make, you have a relatively high discount rate. If you are not so impatient and can wait longer, you have a relatively low discount rate. The lower your discount rate, the more you'll be willing to save at any given yield on those savings. Whenever your personal discount rate exceeds the yield you can get on savings, you will not save; you have to be offered a yield which is higher than your discount rate. Otherwise you'll be better off by consuming today. The saving behavior of economies taken as a whole therefore depends on the collective discount rate of the population and the average rate of return on saving. Note here that we are talking about the rate of saving—that is, how much of current income people want to put away for a rainy day.

Saving and the Poor

It is often stated that poor people in underdeveloped countries cannot save because they are barely subsisting. This is not actually true. Many anthropological studies—of villages in India, for example—have revealed that saving is in fact going on, but it takes peculiar forms that we don't recognize in our money economy. In some places saving, or capital accumulation, may involve storing dried onions. In any event, saving does take place even in the most poverty-stricken areas.

The Hard Facts

Look at it this way: Even if you are very, very poor and just barely making a living, you know that sometime in the future you will no longer be able to work. You will either reach mandatory retirement or you will become so debilitated and unproductive that nobody will be willing to hire you. Your income stream will be cut off. Unless there is some benevolent government around or some charitable people (perhaps your family) who will take care of you, you will starve. There is a way out: You can have accumulated savings, the income and principal of which you can live on. Therefore, today you must make the decision on how much of your current, albeit meager, income you want to set aside for those retirement years, or for those years when you are sick or debilitated and cannot work. Unless it is literally true that you will starve if you reduce your current level of consumption by very small amounts, you probably will attempt to save a little bit out of your meager income. That's because most people would rather reduce current consumption by a small amount so as to be able to at least exist after they no longer can work. If this is not done, they will face certain starvation as soon as their income stream falls to zero.

Basically, then, saving is a method by which individuals can realize an optimal consumption stream throughout their expected lifetimes. Be careful. The word optimal here does not mean adequate or necessary or decent. It means most desirable from the *individual's* point of view. Even if the individual faces the constraint of a very low income all of his life, he will still want to provide some savings to live off when he can no longer work.

IMPROVING TECHNOLOGY

When people save, there has to be a profitable outlet for those savings so that in fact the capital stock will grow and future incomes will be higher. Otherwise, saving will not lead to higher economic growth. One of the main ways that underdeveloped countries have been able to increase their capital stock and productivity in general is by adapting foreign techniques to their own situation. The most obvious and helpful technological advances which underdeveloped countries have

Savings in poor countries can take the form of storing dried vegetables. (Ken Heyman)

been able to borrow from the developed world involve those in agriculture—improved pesticides, hybrid seeds, improved irrigation techniques. One of the most striking examples of technological breakthroughs which have aided underdeveloped countries concerns the cultivation of "miracle" rice.

When we see the importance of technological progress in the growth of an underdeveloped country (or a developed country), we might come to a tentative conclusion that technological progress, along with the *associated* accumulation of human and material capital, is *the* crucial aspect of successful development.

SO WHAT CAN BE DONE FOR THE THIRD WORLD?

We have just outlined numerous theories of economic growth and talked about the possibility of increasing investment in human capital and how important it is that capital be accumulated in order to ensure higher rates of growth in the future.

But we certainly didn't come up with any clear-cut, guaranteed model of economic growth. This does not mean there is no hope for the future of the Third World. Perhaps economists will become better attuned to the actual determinants of growth in different situations so that more specific rather than general models can be made and applied. The economics of development and growth is perhaps one of the less well-defined disciplines in the entire study of economics. That, of course, does not mean that there is a paucity of development literature. On the contrary, the number of books written on this subject could fill a room. A few of the more interesting ones are listed at the end of this book. You should be warned, however, that in no case is there a generally accepted theory of economic development. While most economists will agree with most of the economic principles used in analyzing the development of the American people in the world economy, the same cannot be said of almost all of the literature that has been written on economic growth. Many disagreements still exist. Be warned.

Definitions of New Terms

PERSONAL DISCOUNT RATE: the rate at which you as an individual discount future pleasure or future consumption. If you have a high personal discount rate, then you will want to consume a lot today because you don't want to wait until tomorrow. If you have a low personal discount rate, you will be willing to wait in order to have more consumption in the future; you will be willing to save more.

Chapter Summary

1. There are numerous theories of why nations grow. Some of the most simple involve the north/south theory, the race theory, the natural resources theory, and so on.
2. One of the modern theories is that of balanced growth, in which agriculture and industry should grow in a balanced manner in order for the whole nation to develop. However,

often this would involve heavy subsidization of industrial projects against the dictates of comparative advantage, thus leading to reduced total output of the nation.

3. Modern Western nations have continuously subsidized their own agricultural sectors, thus putting a crimp in the apparent comparative advantage that underdeveloped countries might have in agricultural pursuits.

4. We should never forget that people are resources, too, and that the investment in human capital may be as or more important than the investment in capital equipment.

5. The larger the capital stock, the higher the possible level of output. Therefore, less-developed countries often seek help in building up their capital stock.

6. The decision to save is based, among other things, on one's personal discount rate. Saving is a decision based on a person's desire to optimize his consumption stream throughout his lifetime. Therefore, even the very poor end up saving in one form or another, so that when their income stream falls, their consumption stream will not fall by as much, no matter how low it may be to start with.

Questions for Thought and Discussion

1. It is often said that the rich are getting richer and the poor poorer. Do you agree?

2. Why do you think there is so much disagreement about what less-developed countries should do in order to grow faster?

3. Do you think that the prestige value of industrial development is so important as to negate certain economic arguments against that development?

4. Some people have stated that since we have given underdeveloped countries death control, we have a moral obligation to help them out today. Do you agree?

5. After reviewing the section on saving decisions, do you still think that poor people cannot ''afford'' to save? Why or why not?

ISSUE XV

MALTHUS REVISITED

The Population Explosion

U.S. in Good Shape

A Bureau of the Census report in 1973 indicated that for every 1000 females, 2085 infants were born. What does this mean? Simply that the United States is already well on its way to zero population growth. Why, then, talk about Malthus revisited? The answer is not far away, for the United States may indeed be experiencing a leveling off of its population, as may Japan, France, and a few other developed countries. But just the opposite is happening in the Third World. However, before we can talk about the Malthusian specter, we have to do a little bit of population growth arithmetic.

The Arithmetic of Population Growth

Demographers like to look at the difference between birth rates and death rates. They calculate for a given country and a given year what is called the **crude birth rate**—the number of babies born per 1000 people in the population. Then they look at the **crude death rate,** which is the number of deaths per 1000 people in the population. When you subtract

the crude death rate from the crude birth rate, you come up with the increase in population in that year, assuming no international net migration. If we divide that by 10, we'll get the result as a percentage, and we'll have the rate of increase of the population. Let's look at a few examples. In

Table XV-1 we have listed the crude death rate and the crude birth rate for several countries. The difference is divided by 10, and we find that the rate of population increase of the countries listed varies from 3.69 percent per year in Venezuela to as low as -0.03 percent per year in East Germany.

Since the rate of population growth is not just a function of the birth rate but also of the death rate, we would expect that any reduction in mortality would lead

TABLE XV-1 BIRTH AND DEATH RATES AND RATE OF INCREASE OF POPULATION FOR SELECTED COUNTRIES

COUNTRY	CRUDE BIRTH RATE	CRUDE DEATH RATE	RATE OF INCREASE
U.S.	17.7	9.5	0.82
Australia	20.0	9.1	1.09
Canada	17.6	7.3	1.03
Costa Rica	36.2	6.5	2.97
Denmark	14.6	9.8	0.48
France	16.7	11.3	0.54
Germany—East	14.0	14.3	-0.03
Iceland	20.7	7.2	1.35
Israel	26.1	7.0	1.91
Mexico	41.6	9.4	3.22
Pakistan	49.0	18.0	3.10
Poland	16.3	8.1	0.82
So. Africa			
White	23.6	8.8	1.48
Other	40.0	14.4	2.56
Sweden	13.5	10.4	0.31
USSR	17.0	8.1	0.89
Venezuela	43.6	6.7	3.69
Vietnam	27.7	6.4	1.13

In column 2 we show the crude birth rate per 1000 people in each of these countries. In column 3 we show the crude death rate. Column 4 is the difference between the crude birth rate and the crude death rate, divided by 10. It represents the percentage rate of increase per year of the population. (*Source:* Statistical Office of the United Nations.)

to an increase in population growth. In fact, if death control proceeded at a faster pace than birth control, we could still have a rapidly growing population even though birth control methods were being used.

Doubling Time

Population experts like to translate rates of population growth per annum into what is called the **doubling time.** In other words, if

TABLE XV-2 THE DOUBLING TIME FOR POPULATIONS OF SELECTED COUNTRIES

COUNTRY	DOUBLING TIME
U.S.	93
Albania	26
Australia	62
Canada	70
Costa Rica	23
Denmark	150
France	133
Iceland	47
Israel	35
Luxembourg	175
Mexico	21
Pakistan	22
Poland	82
So. Africa	
White	46
Other	28
Sweden	232
USSR	72
Venezuela	19
Vietnam	62

Here we show how many years it takes for each country's population to double. The range is immense, from Venezuela's 19 years to Sweden's 232 years. (*Source:* Statistical Office of the United Nations.)

the population of Luxembourg is growing at 0.4 percent a year, how many years will it take for the population to double? For Luxembourg, it would take almost 175 years!

In Table XV–2 we see the doubling time for the population of the world and for selected countries. A good rule to use to figure out the doubling time is "the rule of 72." If you divide 72 by the percentage rate of increase in population, you come up with an approximate doubling time. In our example of Luxembourg, the growth rate of population is 0.4 percent a year. Thus, 72 divided by 0.4 equals 180 years, just about the figure we came up with before.

Doubling times are fascinating numbers because if we extend them indefinitely into the future and assume static present conditions, we find that the population of very small Latin American countries will increase until there are so many people there will no longer be any place to walk. The countries will literally be covered with people. Even if the doubling time is 175 years as in Luxembourg, if you extend that rate of growth far enough into the future the result is one horrendously large number. That's one of the reasons Zero Population Growth people are so adamant about how the number of births must be limited not only in countries where the populations are unbelievably

dense, as in Hong Kong, but also in countries where population is much less dense.

Net Reproduction Rate

Demographers also like to talk in terms of **net reproduction rates.** These rates are calculated on the basis of the total number of female children born to every 1000 potential mothers. If every mother has exactly one daughter in her lifetime, then the net reproduction rate will exactly equal 1. What do you think will happen to the population? It will remain stable, neither decreasing nor increasing (assuming life expectancy doesn't change). If mothers tend to have more than one daughter throughout their child-bearing years, then the net reproduction rate will be in excess of 1 and the population will grow.

The net reproduction rate is probably the most important statistic to look at when you want to find out what the future holds for the population of a particular country. Japan is a good example. There the crude birth rate is about 17 per 1000, and the crude death rate is about 6.5 per 1000. The rate of growth in population is therefore in excess of 1 percent per annum. Even a 1 percent annual growth rate in population leads to a doubling every 72 years. But Japan really isn't worried about that. In fact, Japan's worries are in the opposite direction. The

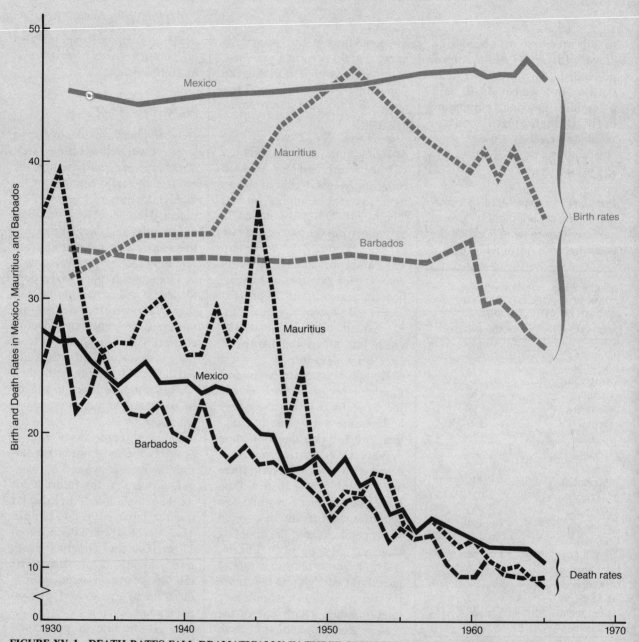

FIGURE XV-1 DEATH RATES FALL DRAMATICALLY IN THREE SELECTED UNDERDEVELOPED COUNTRIES

Although the birth rates in Mexico, Mauritius, and Barbados have remained constant or fallen slightly, the dramatic change has been in death rates, which have fallen since the 1930s in all of these countries. This has caused a widening gap between birth and death rates and, hence, higher rates of growth in population. (*Source:* Statistical Office of the United Nations).

net reproduction rate is now less than 1 in Japan. The Japanese have legalized abortion and also promoted widespread birth control. With a net reproduction rate of less than 1, after a few more years of growth the Japanese population will begin a long, steady decline. In fact, by extending the present net reproduction rate long enough into the future, you will see the population of Japan eventually disappear. Some time ago, Japanese businessmen were publicized as complaining that their profits were going to fall in the future because of a diminishing labor supply. They would have to start paying higher wages in order to have a sufficient number of workers.

Malthus Again

Now that we know a little bit about the arithmetic of population growth, let's see the reason why underdeveloped nations are facing Malthusian crises.

"Passion Between the Sexes" Not the Answer

Remember that Malthus maintained that passion between the sexes produced population growth at a geometric rate whereas food production would only grow at an arithmetic rate. This isn't what has really happened in underdeveloped countries. In fact, the de-

veloping nations may be more at fault for the rapid population rise in these countries than the countries themselves. For example, in Figure XV-1 look at the birth rate in three selected underdeveloped countries in the world: Mexico, Mauritius, and Barbados.

The birth rate in Mexico has been steady; the one in Mauritius has already started to fall, as it has in Barbados. However, the big change has been in the death rate. It has fallen dramatically and persistently since the 1930s. Obviously, if the birth rate remains fairly constant and the death rate falls, the rate of population growth is going to rise dramatically, just as it has done. Population increases of 1 percent a year were fairly high in years past, but today in countries like Costa Rica, Mexico, Pakistan, and Venezuela, growth rates of 3 and 4 percent a year are not unknown. All of it has to do with the improved chances of people to live a longer and healthier life. Crude death rates in many developing countries are lower than in European countries. And in a number of these developing countries, life expectancies have risen by a year or more per annum for a decade. In Taiwan, for example, the life expectancy is well over 60 years for men and women. In Puerto Rico, it is over 70 for women, and not much less for men! Mortality and morbidity have decreased so rapidly because public health

knowledge has been imported into the Third World to eradicate disease and pestilence. Also, developing countries have exported their knowledge of nutrition and living standards most amenable to healthy lives.

Death Control a Mixed Blessing

In other words, the developed countries have been extremely

(Jason Lauré, Rapho Guillumette)

humanitarian in helping the underdeveloped countries improve their health science and gain more healthful living conditions. The result is a population boom in these countries, a mixed blessing at best. There are, of course, other reasons why the mortality rate has fallen in developing countries, not the least of which have been better education, a rising income level, and so on. All of these contribute to a lower death rate.

What Has to Be Done to Break Out of the Malthusian Cycle?

There is no question of what has to be done for developing countries if they ever want to raise the per capita standard of living at a faster rate than they are now doing. (For in fact, in some of them, population is growing just as fast as output, so the economy is essentially standing still.) We can hardly suggest that crude death rates be allowed to rise again. There is only one variable left to change, and that is the birth rate. Fertility among underdeveloped populations must fall if there is ever to be any hope of contradicting Malthus in these countries. We are all aware of how this can be accomplished: later marriages, more widespread use of birth control techniques, subsidizing legalized abortion—in short, whatever available birth reduction techniques a country is willing to use. The results of such techniques are indeed amazing. In Hong Kong and Singapore, crude birth rates per 1000 fell from 36 and 38.7, respectively, in 1960 to 24.9 and 29.9 in 1966. That is an amazing reduction, probably unprecedented in the history of modern man. Another country which has been successful in reducing its birth rate is Japan, as we've seen. At the moment, the net reproduction rate in Japan is less than unity. In other words, eventually, if nothing changes, its population will contract.

The conclusion is obvious: To reduce birth rates and, hence, reduce the population growth rate is indeed possible right now for many, if not all, developing nations. The implementation of the necessary policies is now in their hands.

Definitions of New Terms

CRUDE BIRTH RATE: the number of births per 1000 people in the population.

CRUDE DEATH RATE: the number of deaths per 1000 people in the population.

DOUBLING TIME: the number of years it takes the population in a specific country to double, assuming static conditions.

NET REPRODUCTION RATE: the number of daughters born to every mother. When the net reproduction rate is 1, the population will remain stable.

Questions for Thought and Discussion

1. Do you think that Malthus will finally be vindicated?
2. Does the United States suffer from a population explosion?
3. Do you think that reducing the individual income tax exemption for dependents will reduce the birth rate in the United States? (If not, why do children not fit into the law of demand?)

The Mid-Seventies Economy

16

W E'VE COME A long way. In the mid-70s the average American citizen enjoys the highest standard of living in the world and the highest ever known to mankind. The prospects for the future look good. Although other countries may eventually surpass us in living standards, we will never be less than one of the richest countries in the world. If we wanted to list all of the great things that are happening in the American economy, we could go on forever. But in doing so, we would be ignoring the very problems that some observers believe could ultimately destroy our economic system as we know it: Discrimination in the labor force and in social life still exists. Poverty has not been eradicated, even in the midst of plenty. The environment is being despoiled at an alarming rate. The cost of living is rising monthly (so noticeably, in fact, that we have come to expect it to happen). We have not yet solved the problem of unemployment and the business cycle.

There is increasing dissatisfaction with how the government has handled things. This dissatisfaction extends to government-provided welfare, educational, and medical care services, plus a host of other public endeavors which don't seem to result in the kind of changes that Americans want to see. All of these problems are real, for even the incomplete examination that we can provide here demonstrates the magnitude of the problems facing the United States in the middle of the 1970s.

POVERTY IN THE MIDST OF PLENTY

Here we are, the richest nation on earth. Does that mean we have all rich members of the society and no poor ones? Not on your life. We have a problem of poverty, one that has persisted for many, many years. If we were to examine the incomes and resultant life styles of the lowest one-fifth of the population, we would indeed be appalled. The estimated median income per family in the mid-1970s is $12,300 per year. However, 17 percent of families will have incomes of less than $6000—less than 50 percent of the median. Poverty and income inequality exist in this country, and there is no way to believe otherwise.

Income Distribution

If we look at the distribution of income by fifths in the population, we see in Table 16–1 that the lowest fifth of households obtained about 5 percent of national income right after World War II and about 5 percent at the beginning of this decade. The second fifth showed a slight improvement, the third fifth almost none, and the fourth fifth almost none. The only other difference was that the highest fifth lost out slightly during this period. What does that mean? Simply that the poor are not getting any better off relative to the rich. There has been some improvement since before the Depression, but income inequality is still a fact of life, in spite of a highly progressive individual income tax system—which is supposed to "soak the rich," presumably to redistribute income to the poor; in spite of a massive system of agencies to help the poor; and in spite of an incredibly complex welfare network.

Poverty seems more prevalent now than in the past because today we are an urban society with fully 74 percent of the population living in cities. When poor people lived on the farm, they could (usually) eke out an existence no matter how bad off they were. They were not all concentrated in a well-defined area where the less poor could see them. Poverty may have been more of a problem in the good old days, but it was not as obvious.

Is Poverty Absolute?

If we took a specific poverty line, as it is called, we would find an amazing trend. Back in 1959, the poverty line was set at $3000 for a family of four. If you take that as the standard, back in 1935 about one-third of all Americans were poor. By 1955, 1 in 5 were poor, and today, less than 10 percent are poor. If this trend were to continue, there would be almost no poor by the end of the decade. But you know very well that this is not what will happen. The poverty line does not stay put. *Poverty is a relative concept.* Today's poverty would have been considered opulence 200 years ago. Moreover, the poverty line in the United States is greater than the average income level in most other countries in the world.

But even in 1980, when we will have supposedly eliminated poverty in this country, most people will still think that there are a large number of poor members of the society. This will certainly

PERCENTAGE OF HOUSEHOLDS	PERCENTAGE OF NATIONAL INCOME	
	1947	1971
Lowest 5th	5.0	5.4
Second 5th	11.8	12.3
Third 5th	17.0	17.8
Fourth 5th	23.1	23.8
Highest 5th	43.1	40.7
	100.0	100.0

TABLE 16–1

THE DISTRIBUTION OF INCOME, 1947–1971

Here we cut up the total number of households into fifths and show the lowest fifth to the highest fifth. The distribution of income has not changed very much since just after World War II. (*Source:* Department of Commerce.)

(Roger LeRoy Miller, Inc.)

Strictly speaking, people make small incomes because their economic value to society is small. But this might not always be true, and the most obvious reason why some people might be making incomes lower than they "deserve" is discrimination.

DISCRIMINATION

Discrimination in the marketplace exists. Of that there is no doubt. If we look at the median income of blacks as compared to whites, we will find that on average they earn only about 60 percent of what their white cohort does. If we look at the median income of women, we find that they earn only about 60 percent of the median income of men. These large differences in income have been attributed to discrimination, pure and simple. Another way of describing this phenomenon in economic jargon is to say that employers have tastes for discrimination and are willing to pay for them. How do they pay for them? Easily. By paying nondiscriminated workers more than discriminated workers. This raises their labor cost and then lowers their profits. But we should be careful not to ascribe all differences in wages to tastes for discrimination. There are also differences in the productivity of different types of workers, whether they be male, female, black, white, or whatever. These differences in productivity can be traced to the length of schooling, the quality of schooling, the amount of experience, age, health, and so on.

In fact, if one corrects black/white wage differentials for these variables, the difference in earnings possibly attributable to discrimination falls drastically, although it is not completely reduced, to be sure. The same holds true when data specific to women as compared to men are analyzed. For black/white differentials, one thing that could be done is quite obvious: More and better schooling could be offered to minority members in our society.

be true if the distribution of income stays the same. The reason is simple: Whenever some people are worse off than others, there will be the less rich and the more rich, and there will be a cry to eliminate poverty. It seems quite apparent that no matter what we do, if we are always going to define poverty in this relative manner, we will never eliminate it. But that doesn't mean we shouldn't keep trying. In fact, in the next issue we suggest how poverty might be eliminated in a better manner than is actually being used in our current welfare mess.

THE ECOLOGICAL MESS

Fresh air used to be a free good. We could get all we wanted without taking it away from somebody else; it wasn't scarce. Clean water used to be a free good. We could go to a nearby stream and fish and swim in that water to our hearts' content. Today things are different. Air quality in major cities has deteriorated. Water is polluted in so many places that we can't begin to enumerate them. The Cuyahoga River became so polluted that it was declared a fire hazard!* Ecological problems are not, however, new to Americans or foreigners. In fact, London has had smog problems for centuries due to the burning of soft coal. Only recently did it decide to ban the burning of that pollution-causing heating source. (And the air cleared up remarkably fast.) There were killer fogs in London many years ago and awesome smog attacks in New York as far back as the

*It even caught fire, and caused bridge damage estimated at $70,000.

1950s. But today the problem seems worse than ever, probably because we are more aware of it and because we demand more social amenities.

Clean Environment Costs

Remember that a clean environment is a good; it doesn't come free of charge. But today people are willing to pay more for a cleaner environment because their real incomes have risen. We might say that the income elasticity of demand for a better environment is quite high. As we become richer, we are willing to pay more to have environmental amenities around us. Whether or not we are willing to pay the price that would be necessary for obtaining a much purer environment is another question. In any event, Congress has passed numerous pieces of legislation aimed at controlling the degree of pollution-causing activities of producers and consumers alike. The Clean Water Act specifies that all rivers and lakes should be swimmable by the year 1985. The Clean Air Act specifies maximum limits of how much pollution is to be allowed in every city, of how much pollution will be allowed from cars, and so on. Individual cities and states have passed their own environmental legislation. The results in some cases are impressive. In others, only the magnitude of the costs seems worthy of mention. From the very beginning, for example, automobile producers have complained about the tremendous costs involved in cleaning up automobile engines. Soon after the passage of the Clean Water Act, lobbyists started their efforts to reduce its requirements. And, in fact, they had a fairly good argument.

It may be uneconomic to clean up *all* the waterways and all the lakes in the United States. After all, who wants to swim in the Houston Ship Canal or the Calumet River? These places are too dangerous for anything except ships. Why bother wasting resources to clean them up?

We also have to realize when discussing ecological problems that every clean-up effort involves a cost. And the closer we try to come to purity, the higher the costs get. Look at Figure 16–1. Here we show the estimated cost of reducing pollution from automobiles. In the beginning, the curve doesn't slope up very fast. To obtain a 50 percent reduction in pollution requires not too much money. But as we get closer and closer to 100 percent purity, the costs become astronomical. At the far right-hand part of the scale, a 1 percent reduction in the pollution from an engine may cost as much as a car itself.

Reduce Pollution to What Level?

We obviously have to make a choice, and the best choice to an economist is obvious. *Reduce pollution up to the point where the additional cost of pollution abatement is just equal to the additional benefit, then stop.* But this means that the level of pollution desired is not zero. That's exactly right. The world would indeed be a dismal place if the optimal level of pollution were in fact zero. Then we'd be able to do nothing, not even exist. We have to make a choice, and the choice should be governed by costs and benefits. Don't do anything that costs more than it's worth. That's a pretty simple behavioral dictum, but often ignored by policy makers.

Nationwide standards for automobiles, smokestacks, and factories may be the best we can come up with to control pollution, but they do cause inefficiencies in our system. After all, we shouldn't really be concerned with the physical quantities of pollution, but rather with how harmful they are in any given situation. Sulfur oxides are emitted in much smaller quantities than are numerous other pollutants. But they are much more injurious to our health. It would be absurd to set

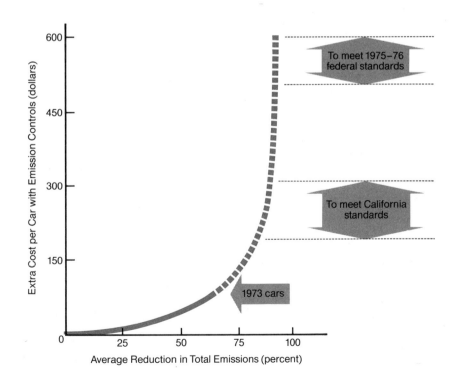

FIGURE 16–1

ESTIMATED COST OF CLEANING UP CARS

As we go to higher and higher levels of emission clean-up, the extra cost per car rises steeply. In other words, the cost of clean-up rises at an increasing rate. (*Source:* Mobil Oil Company.)

the same physical standard for sulfur oxide emissions as for, say, particulate emissions. What we have to examine is the actual economic costs of different types of pollution in different types of situations. The billowing, belching smokestacks of New York's Con-Edison electric utility coal-fed steam generators certainly cause much more damage than the same amount of pollution would cause in the middle of the Mohave Desert.

If we are going to be economically efficient in our pollution abating system, pollution must be hampered more in the heavier populated areas of our nation than in the less populated areas. National standards do not in fact take account of different degrees of population density and, hence, the different degrees of economic damage sustained per unit of physical pollution. That leads up to another seemingly serious problem in the United States—concentration and urbanization.

THE CONGESTED CITY

We are living in an age of urbanization. By 1980 it is estimated that 79 percent of the population will be living in urban areas. Cities have become so crowded that one can barely walk the streets or drive through them in a car. In fact, congestion due to automobile traffic is overwhelming in New York, Los Angeles, Chicago, Atlanta, and numerous other big cities. The crowded environment in the cities seems also to be correlated with poverty and ghetto life, deteriorating housing conditions, and deteriorating air. But the urban environment is the one sought by Americans. After all, they continue moving out of the country into the city in spite of the high costs that are involved in city life. They do this partly because income earning opportunities are highest in urban areas. But they also do it because the urban environment allows for more diversity in life styles and entertainment. After all, specialization—as we have said many times before—is a function of the size of the market. You don't hear of many symphony

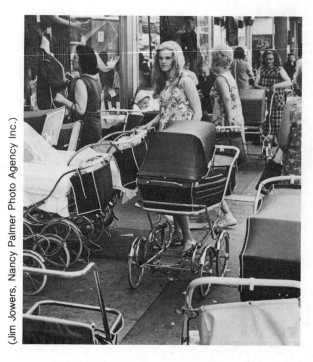

(Jim Jowers, Nancy Palmer Photo Agency Inc.)

orchestras in towns of 5000 people. You don't have many movies to go to there, either. The list of what you don't have in such towns is long indeed.

The problems of the cities seem at times insurmountable, and to top this all off city governments clamor for more money from the federal government to help solve their problems. Cities contend that they are facing a fiscal crisis as their needs rise faster than their revenues. We will examine the validity of these pleas for continued assistance in the issue that follows.

AND LASTLY, THE GOVERNMENT

If we look at a graph of total government spending as a percentage of GNP, such as depicted in Figure 16–2, we see an unmistakable trend upward. Until the Great Depression and World War

II, government expenditures never exceeded 10 percent of GNP (except for World War I), and in general were much less. On the eve of the Great Depression they were only 8.2 percent. At the beginning of the twentieth century they were closer to 6 percent. No theories have succeeded in explaining why there has been a continued rise in the percentage of total expenditures accounted for by government—local, state, and federal—in the United States. It has nothing to do with our level of GNP, for if we look at other countries we find no correlation between high levels of government spending and high levels of per capita income. We can't just say that people *need* more government expenditures because that's no theory at all.

What we have noticed in the last few years, however, is a growing dissatisfaction with the results of increased government expenditures. Johnson's Great Society and Nixon's New Prosperity have done little to alleviate the problems they were designed to cure. In fact, it is common knowledge now that much of the money spent on the War on Poverty simply filled the pockets of government bureaucrats who were well paid and had sinecures. Government aid and support of education is under increasing fire. The taxpayer is just not content with what he is getting. He doesn't think that he's getting much value for his educational tax dollar. Many students will agree.

But the growing dissatisfaction with government doesn't seem to be due to recent fiascos

---

FIGURE 16–2 **RISING GOVERNMENT ACTIVITY**

Here we show government spending at all levels—federal, state, and local—on goods and services as a percentage of total gross national product. The big jump occurred during World War I and there has been a continued upward trend ever since. (*Source:* Department of Commerce.)

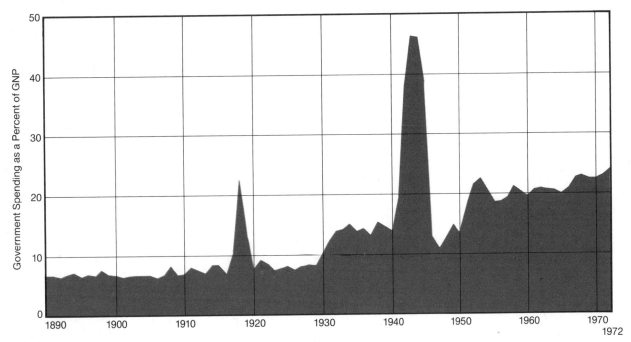

within the government, either. After all, many of the programs set up by the New Deal were immediately recognized as boondoggles. The agricultural program could only end up helping the rich farmer. The National Recovery Administration could only end up fostering business monopolies which would keep consumer prices high. But that didn't stop the public from allowing an extension of government powers throughout the economy from then on. We are at a loss to explain why government spending has increased and, further, if the current dissatisfaction with government will actually lead to a reduction in this trend. Perhaps such a reduction will become more of a possibility if we ever manage to live in a period void of crises. But that seems to be an impossible dream, for every period seems to be one of crisis. Today is no different.

Chapter Summary

1. The distribution of income in the United States does not seem to have changed in the last two decades; the lowest fifth of households still receive only around 5 percent of national income.
2. We still have poverty in the midst of plenty, but because poverty is a relative concept, we will never eliminate it. In other words, we always define poverty as relative to average income. Only if income were distributed with absolute equality would poverty under this definition be eliminated.
3. Discrimination can exist in the marketplace for workers. However, we must also look at differences in productivity of different types of workers before we attribute all differences in wages to discrimination.
4. We are faced with an ecological crisis today that is being met with increased government legislation. However, Americans would probably be unwilling to eliminate *all* pollution because the cost would be too high. From an economic point of view pollution continues to be reduced up to the point where the additional cost of pollution abatement is just equal to the additional benefit to society.
5. Government expenditures as a fraction of GNP have been increasing since the Great Depression. As yet we have no universally applicable theory to successfully explain this growth.

Questions for Thought and Discussion

1. What do you consider to be the most important crisis facing the nation today?
2. Do you think all pollution should be stopped?
3. How do you think we could eliminate congestion in city centers?
4. Are you for or against the increase in government expenditures? Why or why not?
5. Do you think poverty should be a relative or an absolute concept?

ISSUE XVI

ARE WE FACING A CRISIS?

Have We Ever Not?

Politicians Speak

Politicians will tell you that today is a period of crisis, one in which the United States is testing its inner strengths. But are we really facing a crisis? We see the word so often that it seems we're in one continual crisis. There's a poverty crisis, an energy crisis, a pollution crisis, a congestion crisis, a discrimination crisis—you name it and we have it. But some of the problems that we discussed in the previous chapter do have readily identifiable solutions. And hence, they cannot properly be called crises without hope. The first one we talked about was poverty.

Poverty Can Be Reduced

Poverty indeed exists. We are attempting to alleviate it by massive amounts of interrelated and conflicting welfare programs. And we are probably transferring upwards of $60 or $70 billion a year in one form or another to poor (and not so poor) people. But we haven't done very much good. It hasn't been all bad, but a much more effective system is in the wind and, in fact, may become a reality

soon. It all centers upon an extension of our income tax system.

One thing we could do is scrap our entire welfare mess—welfare payments, food stamps, payments in kind, plus all the additional subsidy programs to help specific groups, like the farmers—in favor of one comprehensive overall income redistribution system that has been called a negative income tax. It would work very simply: If a family or individual made less than a certain poverty income, or standard income as it could be called, once he fills out his income tax form it would turn out that instead of having to pay taxes, he would receive a negative tax—that is, a transfer payment. Another such alternative is a guaranteed income. In either case, we go directly to the heart of the problem: People are poor because they have low incomes; the way we make them unpoor is by giving them higher incomes. In the process, we might eliminate all of the present inefficiencies and inequities in our welfare system.

Poverty will never be eliminated because it is always a relative concept, but we can certainly do a better job than we have done in the past.

The True Urban Perspective

Today we face what is called an urban crisis. We mentioned some of the problems in the last chapter: increased congestion, increased slums, increased pollution, and so on. But to get a true perspective of what is actually happening and the trends that can be readily seen in urbanization, we have to be careful to compare the real world with the real world. We can't look at what has happened in a few major cities and say things are getting worse. The urban problem must be put in proper perspective. Moreover, many of the problems that plague urban environments also exist in the countryside. Go to any town of 10,000. You will find welfare mothers, substandard housing, functional illiteracy, hard-core unemployment, drug abuse, venereal disease, vandalism, and violence, perhaps not in the same proportions as in big cities, but there nonetheless.

Now the Census Department tells us that by the year 2000, 85 percent of all Americans will live in metropolitan areas. This is a misleading statistic, however; nobody really knows what a metropolitan area is. It can be a bunching of suburbs which have a total population of 50,000, or New York with millions of people. Actually, though, the percentage of the population living in cities of 100,000 or more already peaked, way back at the start of the Great Depression. It has actually dropped over time since then. Moreover, it should be realized that most people who live in standard metropolitan statistical areas, or SMSAs as they are called by the Census Bureau and other government agencies, do not live in the center of the city. Most live in contiguous suburban environments. This is not the same thing as being in a congested area. In fact, many suburbanites also work in suburbia and hardly bother to go into the center of the city they are near. Further, it appears that small, relatively isolated towns are becoming increasingly important for manufacturing employment. One study in Pennsylvania

showed that between the beginning and the middle of the '60s manufacturing employment grew faster in cities of less than 25,000.

But even if we look at the core areas of large cities, they are not becoming more congested, but less.* In the past decade, over half the central cities of every size lost population. If we look at density as expressed by persons per square mile, standard metropolitan areas have shown a downward trend, as expressed in Figure XVI-1.

Also, certain things within central cities are getting better, not worse. The 1950 Census indicated

*In fact, now some cities fathers are worried about the abandonment of the central city.

that well over 15 percent of housing units in cities were occupied by more than one person per room. By 1970 the figure dropped to less than 7 percent. Paradoxically, it appears that attempts at urban renewal have caused almost as much harm as good. In 1972 part of a huge public housing project in St. Louis was torn down. The "proper" environment in a public housing project turned out to be unlivable. Similar results have been found elsewhere in the United States. Without any help at all from public housing projects, the poor and the black have been able to improve their own housing environments. Between 1960 and 1968 housing occupied by blacks which the Census Bureau called "not meeting specified conditions" fell from 25 percent to less than 9 percent.

FIGURE XVI-1   FALLING POPULATION DENSITIES

There has been a continuing decline in the densities in standard metropolitan statistical areas in the last two decades. In 1950 in these areas, the density was 5408 persons per square mile, but at the start of the 1970s it had fallen to 3376. (*Source:* Department of Commerce, Bureau of the Census.)

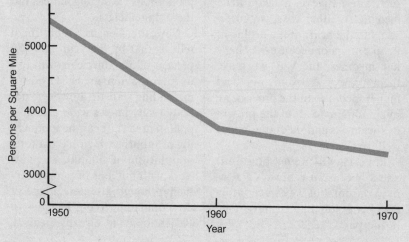

Racism

While racism still abounds in the United States, blacks as a class have improved their lot remarkably in the last few decades. It appears that the attitudes and behavior of whites toward blacks have changed since World War II. This has shown up in a number of public opinion polls, particularly those sponsored by the National Opinion Research Center. An article in *Scientific American* in 1971 concluded that "the trend has been distinctly toward in-

(Ray Ellis, Rapho Guillumette)

due to the flight to the suburbs, they have made up for in federal and state grants. In fiscal 1973 almost $45 billion was given to local governments. In any event, it is estimated that by 1975 all cities taken together will come within a mere $5 billion of meeting their revenue needs. A fiscal crisis is certainly not in the wind.

Improvements in the Environment

While the general tenor of the environmental cause has considerably calmed down in the last few years, many people are still convinced that we face a crisis in the ecology. The evidence is not in favor of this view, however. Recent studies have shown that the quality of air in major cities is improving, albeit slightly, as compared with a few years ago. Certain cities in the world have experienced dramatic improvement in their air quality. Witness London after the ban on the burning of soft Newcastle coal.

We are licking the problem of automobile exhaust pollution and in fact may come up with even cleaner-burning engines in the future. Numerous cities are installing sufficient treatment facilities to prevent nearby lakes and streams from being polluted by raw sewage that used to find its way into the recreation spots of

creasing approval of integration."* As evidence that blacks are sharing in the general mainstream of economic growth, we find that the black suburban population grew by 42 percent over the previous decade. And in the 1970s this trend is continuing. This doesn't mean that discrimination will be eliminated, but the situation may not be as bad as previously thought.

*Andrew M. Greely and Paul B. Sheatsley, "Attitudes toward Racial Integration," *Scientific American,* Vol. 225, No. 6, December 1971, p. 13.

Are Cities Worse Off?

We continually read about fiscal crises in the cities. Their problems are growing by leaps and bounds, but their revenues from taxes are not. Much of this is presumably related to the flight from the cities to the suburbs. This has reduced the tax base for the core of the cities. But this can't be true, for today the credit ratings of the large city governments are as high as or higher than they were 20 or 30 or even 40 years ago. In fact, what cities have lost in tax base

America. Industry* in general is being forced to pay an ever-increasing environmental cost in order to produce without destroying the ecology. We still have a long way to go, but the world is not coming to an end, in spite of several recent studies that propose the contrary. In fact, most studies which show the world coming to an end due to overpollution ignore the possibility that technology might help solve the problems at least as fast as they are created.

Problems—Past, Present, and Future

Yes, we may be facing "crises," but as we saw throughout this book, we have faced "crises" from the very beginnings of this country, and we will face them in the future. We have had numerous problems in the past and

*But ultimately the consumer.

we have solved them. We have numerous problems in the present and a more sanguine view of the future indicates that we will solve them, too. Most problems lend themselves to eventual solutions. If we analyze things in an economic manner, we can predict what these solutions will be from an economic point of view. If we face an energy crisis today we would predict that the price of energy sources would rise so that substitute sources would be found in the future. At the same time consumers would cut back on their consumption of energy. If we face a problem of continuing inflation, we can learn to live with it and adjust all our contracts so that cost of living clauses are included. Or else we can somehow force the government to maintain stable monetary and fiscal policies so that the specter of inflation will fade.

If we face a continuing ecological crisis, we can start charging people for their misuse of the environment. We can also start making people treat goods held in common—like water and air—as if they were owned by somebody. State and local governments can take on the ownership responsibilities of these so-called common property resources. Payments would then be required for the use of these scarce resources. If we face an automobile congestion problem, we can start charging automobile drivers for the true costs of using their four-wheeled beasts. These true costs include noise and air pollution and the congestion which forces people to spend more time on the road.

Economic answers to grave problems sometimes seem simple—indeed, too simple—but they at least offer a rational and predictable start for ameliorating the problem-laden environment in which we work and play.

Questions for Thought and Discussion

1. Do you think racism has been reduced in the United States?
2. Would you prefer to live today or to have lived 100 years ago?
3. Do you think that environmental destruction has gone past the point of no return?
4. Will we ever live in an age without crises?

SELECTED REFERENCES

General Economics and Economic Theory

Maher, John E. *What Is Economics?* New York: John Wiley & Sons, 1969.
Miller, Roger LeRoy. *Economics Today.* San Francisco: Canfield Press, 1973.
Snider, Delbert. *Economic Essentials.* Pacific Palisades: Goodyear, 1972.
Weiss, Roger. *The Economic System.* New York: Random House, 1969.

Economic History and Development

Hacker, Louis. *The Course of American Economic Growth and Development.* New York: John Wiley & Sons, 1970.
Hession, Charles H., and Sardy, Hyman. *Ascent to Affluence.* Boston: Allyn & Bacon, 1969.
Nash, Gerald. *Issues in American Economic History.* 2nd ed. Boston: Heath, 1972.
Robertson, Ross M. *History of the American Economy.* 3rd ed. New York: Harcourt Brace Jovanovich, 1973.

European and Medieval History and Development

Cipolla, C. *The Economic History of World Population.* New York: Penguin, 1962.
Clough, S. B. *European Economic History: The Economic Development of Western Civilization.* 2nd ed. New York: McGraw-Hill, 1968.
Hohenberg, Paul M. *Primer on the Economic History of Europe.* New York: Random House, 1968.
Huizinga, J. *The Waning of the Middle Ages.* London: E. Arnold, 1955.
Pirenne, Henri. *Economic and Social History of Medieval Europe.* New York: Harcourt Brace Jovanovich, 1937.

Other Selected Topics

Bogue, Allan G. *From Prairie to Corn Belt: Farming on the Illinois and Iowa Prairies in the Nineteenth Century.* Chicago: University of Chicago Press, 1963.
Chandler, Lester V. *America's Great Depression.* New York: Harper & Row, 1970.
Fishlow, Albert. *Railroads and the Transportation of the Antebellum Economy.* Cambridge: Harvard University Press, 1965.
Galbraith, John Kenneth. *The Great Crash.* Boston: Houghton Mifflin, 1954.
Goodrich, Carter, et al. *Canals and American Economic Growth.* New York: Columbia University Press, 1960.
Higgs, Robert. *The Transformation of the American Economy, 1865–1914: An Essay in Interpretation.* New York: John Wiley & Sons, 1971.
North, Douglass C., and Thomas, R. P., Eds. *The Growth of American Economy to 1860.* New York: Harper & Row, 1968.
Parker, William N., Ed. *Trends in the American Economy in the Nineteenth Century.* Princeton: Princeton University Press, 1960.

Rayback, Joseph G. *A History of American Labor.* New York: Macmillan, 1959.

Rosenberg, Nathan. *Technology and American Economic Growth.* New York: Harper & Row, 1972.

Temin, Peter. *Iron and Steel in Nineteenth Century America: An Economic Inquiry.* Cambridge: M.I.T. Press, 1964.

Population, Development, Alternative Systems

Brunner, John. *Stand on Zanzibar.* New York: Valentine, 1968.

Ehrlich, Paul, and Ehrlich, Ann. *Population, Resources and Environment.* San Francisco: W. H. Freeman, 1970.

Grossman, Gregory. *Economic Systems.* Englewood Cliffs, N.J.: Prentice-Hall, 1967.

Hardin, Garrett. *Population, Evolution and Birth Control.* 2nd ed. San Francisco: W. H. Freeman, 1969.

Higgins, Benjamin. *Economic Development.* New York: W. W. Norton, 1968.

Rostow, W. W. *The Stages of Economic Growth.* New York: Cambridge University Press, 1960.

Schumpeter, Joseph A. *Capitalism, Socialism and Democracy.* New York: Harper & Row, 1950.

Wheelwright, E. L., and McFarland, Bruce. *The Chinese Road to Socialism.* New York: Monthly Review Press, 1970.

More Current Economic Problems

Bach, G. L. *The New Inflation.* Englewood Cliffs, N.J.: Prentice-Hall, 1973.

Barkley, Paul W., and Seckler, David W. *Economic Growth and Environmental Decay.* New York: Harcourt Brace Jovanovich, 1972.

Clayton, James L., Ed. *The Economic Impact of the Cold War.* New York: Harcourt Brace Jovanovich, 1970.

Economic Report of the President. Washington, D.C.: U.S. Government Printing Office, each year.

Fusfeld, Daniel R. *The Basic Economics of the Urban Racial Crisis.* New York: Holt, Rinehart and Winston, 1973.

Gallaway, Lowell E. *Poverty in America.* Columbus, Ohio: Grid, 1973.

Melman, Seymour. *Pentagon Capitalism.* New York: McGraw-Hill, 1970.

Schiller, Bradley R. *The Economics of Poverty and Discrimination.* Englewood Cliffs, N.J.: Prentice-Hall, 1973.

Silk, Leonard. *Nixonomics.* 2nd ed. New York: Praeger, 1973.

INDEX

*Numbers in **boldface** type indicate pages where terms are defined.*